Scenes from a Provincial Life:
Memoirs of a Biblical Scholar

SCENES FROM A PROVINCIAL LIFE:
MEMOIRS OF A BIBLICAL SCHOLAR

David J.A. Clines

SHEFFIELD PHOENIX PRESS

2025

Copyright © 2025 Sheffield Phoenix Press

Published by Sheffield Phoenix Press
Sheffield Centre for Interdisciplinary Biblical Studies (SCIBS),
University of Sheffield, S10 2TN

www.sheffieldphoenix.com

All rights reserved.
No part of this publication may be reproduced or transmitted in any form or by any means, electronic or mechanical, including photocopying, recording or any information storage or retrieval system, without the publishers' permission in writing.

A CIP catalogue record for this book
is available from the British Library

ISBN 978-1-914490-63-7

Contents

Preface	ix
Chapter 1	
EARLY YEARS	1
Provincial Oatley	3
The Beginnings of Oatley	4
Chapter 2	
FIRST SCHOOLS (1943–1950)	5
Peter	6
Opportunity Class	6
Chapter 3	
MY PARENTS AND MY CHURCH	9
My father	9
My mother	11
My grandparents	12
My church	13
The church and the world	15
Bible readings	17
Church activities	18
Conferences	18
Conscientious objection	19
Exclusive Brethren	20
The Open Brethren	20
Open Brethren and biblical scholarship	20
Chapter 4	
SYDNEY BOYS' HIGH (1951–1955)	22
Teachers	23
The Curriculum	24
Galleys	25
Sports days	25
Lunches	26

Knife game	26
Saturday work	26
Bookshops	27
Shopping in Oatley	28
Chickens	29
House extension	29
Politics	29
Radio and Politics	30
Sydney Heat	30
Affording University	31

Chapter 5
SYDNEY UNIVERSITY (1956–1961) 32
Latin	33
Greek	33
Hebrew	35
Ancient History	37
Emmaus Bible School	38
Christian Youth Camps (CYC)	40
Classical productions	40
Travel to Cambridge	42

Chapter 6
CAMBRIDGE (1961–1964) 43
Sailing to Europe	43
Setting foot in Britain	44
Living in Cambridge	46
Hebrew in Cambridge	47
Teachers	48
D. Winton Thomas	48
J.L. Teicher	50
David Diringer	50
E.I.J. Rosenthal	50
Sebastian Bullough	51
Aramaic/Syriac	51
Tyndale House	53
Examinations	54
Beginning research	55
My Marriage to Dawn Joseph	56
Cycling	56
A publication	57
Appointment to Sheffield	57

Chapter 7
SHEFFIELD UNIVERSITY I (1964–1975) 59
  Sheffield 62
  Innovation in Sheffield 63
  Quality 64
  Green Sheffield 64
  Living in Sheffield: Houses 64
  Provincial Sheffield 65
  Sheffield Arts Tower 66
  Paternoster 67
  Writing, 1964–1975 68
  New colleagues 70
    David Gunn 70
  A new house 71
  A Californian interlude 72
  Philip R. Davies 72
  Anthony C. Thiselton 73
  The Clines family in Los Angeles 74
  The car 75
  Fuller Theological Seminary 75
  Churches 77
    The Collection 78
  My first earthquake 78
  A vegetarian holiday 78
  Pledging allegiance 78
  Leaving for home 79
  My New Zealand tour 79
  Home in Sheffield 80

Chapter 8
SHEFFIELD UNIVERSITY II (1976–1989) 82
  The beginnings of *JSOT* 82
  My books 1976–1989 85
    I, He, We and They 85
    The Theme of the Pentateuch 86
    Midian, Moab and Edom 88
    Ezra, Nehemiah, Esther 88
    Art and Meaning 90
  Other literary papers 90
  Job 91
  Writing a commentary on Job 92

The Pleasures of Commentary	95
A Defined Task	95
Avoiding Blank Page Syndrome	96
In the Presence of a Great Mind	96
An Educational Premium	96
Companionship	97
Efficiency	97
The Perils of Commentary	98
Mistaking the Horizon	98
Brainwashing	98
Hyper-professionalization	99
Reflections on the Job Commentary	100
John Rogerson	102

Chapter 9
SHEFFIELD UNIVERSITY III (SINCE 1990) 108
   Departmental appointments 110
   The *Dictionary of Classical Hebrew* 122
   The Distinctiveness of *The Dictionary of Classical Hebrew* 126

Chapter 10
WRITINGS AND SCHEMES [UNFINISHED] 130
   Methods: A Confluence 130
   Methods: A Taxonomy (2015) 130

Chapter 11
TEN THINGS I HAVE BEEN SAYING (BUT NO ONE WAS LISTENING)
[UNFINISHED] 131

PUBLICATIONS OF DAVID J.A. CLINES
(AS AT 1 NOVEMBER, 2022) 134

APPENDIX ONE:
AUTHOR'S NOTES
[UNFINISHED] 164

Index of Names 166

Preface

Yes, you have heard the title of this memoir somewhere else before. It is the subtitle of George Eliot's 1871–1872 novel *Middlemarch: A Study of Provincial Life*. And there is a volume by the South African novelist J.M. Coetzee, *Scenes from Provincial Life*, his fictionalized memoir of boyhood. Beyond those, I don't know that the phrase has been much used. But somehow provincialness suits my image of myself, and I will offer you here a heap of disjointed scenes—and certainly no grand narrative—in which I can remember playing a part.

Chapter 1

Early Years

From the lounge room of our house at 44 Frederick Street, Oatley, in Sydney, we could see in the distance, 200 m away, an arm of the Georges River,[1] Sydney's second river. Twice every day, the tide covered the sandbanks; the steep cliffs on every side gave the impression of a vast and deep stream.

The Georges River at Oatley was from our windows, however, not just a picturesque sight. What we saw every day was the focus of a characteristic Australian anxiety about the land. In that very spot, a horrific episode in which a young woman had been 'taken' by a shark was constantly recalled, especially by my mother, as a warning against ever approaching the river. We settlers on the land owned the land, I was taught, yet in another sense we were owned by the land, tyrannized by its arbitrary cruelty, its overwhelming droughts and fires that are still today beyond the reach of technological control. The land gave, plentifully, but it also was forever taking away.

The 'taking' of the young woman by the shark (it was not conceived exactly as an illegitimate seizure, but a symbol of the land's ownership of those who had dared to settle on it) was a powerful mytheme over many an Australian childhood, I suppose, but it was not imaginary. There was such a shark attack, I discover, in January 1946, in Oatley Bay,[2] when I was just seven years old and my brother Peter not quite two. The effect on my parents of this admittedly extremely rare occurrence must have been traumatic.

The name for the land as the unmastered, primeval, aboriginal Australia was the Bush. The Bush had always been there. The Bush had not been

1. We knew it as the George's River, but it was decreed in 1966 by the Geographical Names Board that no Australian place name was to include an apostrophe.
2. Sharyn Cullis, 'Living with Sharks on the Georges River', available online at https://dictionaryofsydney.org/entry/living_with_sharks_on_the_georges_river/.

cleared or developed or eradicated or lived in. The Bush in Australia was the given; everything else—houses, railways, towns, civilization—was superstructure.

And the Bush could be close at hand, even in the Sydney suburbs. Frederick Street, Oatley, with its 20 houses, plus the shops, between the railway station and our house came to a sudden end with an entrance to the Bush: a 100 m frontage, where a house or two could have been built, was a shallow cliff edge of the Bush. A few seconds from my front door, across the road, and I was in the Bush, suddenly deep down in the Bush, where all I could hear were the raucous sounds of the birds and the skittering of goannas in the undergrowth.

Suppose a bush fire caught hold in the Bush across the road. A flaming branch of eucalyptus or even a spark could fly over the road and settle in the gutters of our house. So when the wind was from the southerly direction, the garden hose would have to be trained on the roof and gutters and the suburban house became for a time a potential victim of the Bush.

So I think of myself as born, on 21 November 1938, at a juncture between a Sydney suburb and the anonymous Bush. Most days the Bush was a serene neighbour, but it could be roused without warning.

My father had planned and overseen in the early days of the War a very modest two-bedroomed house on a vacant lot of regulation size, 44 feet by 147. It was built in brick veneer, supposedly cooler in summer and warmer in winter than double-brick walls, but also cheaper than double brick because it is the inner wooden frame that supports the house, not the outer brick wall.

Among my earliest memories is guiding a visitor around the foundations of the house: here is the bedroom, and here is MY bedroom, and here are the bathroom PIERS—the last being shouted triumphantly, presumably because I had just mastered the word. The floors of the other rooms were all laid on piers too, of course, but the bathroom piers supported a solid concrete floor, which was much later to prove my favourite place in the relentless Sydney summers.

Most early memories are no doubt not my own, but the record of often-repeated family anecdotes. All the same, the scene on the front lawn where I was cavorting naked under the garden sprinkler sounds authentic. My mother's Come in this instant, young man; dancing with no clothes on is *naughty*, was met with the sadly characteristic, But I *like* naughty.

There is a scene too of drawing into a railway station and seeing soldiers and cadets on the platform: there are soldiers, cried I, and there are more soldiers, and there are BABY SOLDIERS—no doubt under the impression that soldiers were born, not made.

Chapter 1. *Early Years*

Provincial Oatley

Sydney today is a world city, with a hugely diverse population of 5 million. At the beginning of the 1950s, though, it had only 1.7 million, mostly of British descent. It had only been 50 years since the six Australian colonies of Britain had ceased to be part of the British Empire, and had become a dominion, the Commonwealth of Australia. Sydney, though an important hub, was still a remote and provincial place. Even within Sydney itself, there was a great difference between the inner-city suburbs like Kings Cross, and the outer suburbs like Oatley. We had a fast railway connection to the centre of the city, but in many ways our suburb was more like a country town.

Oatley gave the air of a somewhat randomly put together suburb: it had not been laid out or planned, and many houses had been built piecemeal by their owners. It gave the air of a place where hippies had put down roots. It wasn't ashamed to be thought marginal. It was a provincial adjunct to a provincial city.

As well, the very rhythms of life belonged to the provincial. Milk was delivered each day by horse and cart. I have a picture in my mind's eye of the huge milkman with his churn in hand running up our front steps three at a time, to pour our measly delivery of a couple of pints in a flash and be off to the neighbour's (no supermarket, no bottles or packets of milk). The iceman brought a delivery too, twice a week, a big chunk of ice the size of a bread bin; it would take some days to melt in the ice-chest, dripping down into the tray beneath.

The surest sign of the provinciality of our suburb, however, was the weekly visit of the nightsoil man (the demotic term was 'dunny man', though we were not allowed to use that vulgarity; 'dunny' is only a diminutive of the English and Scottish 'dunnekin', dung + kin 'house'). Up the side passage to the house would run the dunny man with an empty can (and a lid) on his shoulder. In the outhouse far enough from the back door for the smells to dissipate he would set down the empty can, clamp the lid on the full one awaiting it, hoist it to his shoulder, and swing down the side passage again. That can contained the family's product, liquid and solid, for a whole week. The sight, and smell, of dunny day was not quickly forgotten.

The outdoor toilet was not only disagreeable in the extreme; it was also probably the most dangerous part of any house, for the famed and venomous redback spider loved to lurk beneath the seat. Before seating yourself, lift the lid and slam it down again, giving any spider the fright of its life, and you as peaceable a time as you could hope for. It was not until about 1953 that our suburb was 'sewered' and we had the luxury of an indoors toilet. When I got to Cambridge in 1961, I found there was no toilet within 100 yards of my room, and it was a trip down two flights of steps and into the open air in the bitter British winter if one needed a toilet in the middle of the night (much further than that if you should happen to want a bath). Hardy Australians, especially provincials, did not bat an eyelid.

The Beginnings of Oatley

James Oatley (c. 1769–1839), a watch and clock maker, was transported to Botany Bay for life in 1814 for stealing shirts and bedding. Seven years later, in 1821, the Governor, Lachlan Macquarie, granted Oatley a conditional pardon and appointed him overseer of the Town Clock for his work in installing the clock at Hyde Park Barracks. Between 1831 and 1835, he received several land grants, including some of the present Oatley. Frederick, after whom our street in Oatley was named, was the third son of James Oatley.

Oatley began to be developed at the beginning of the twentieth century.

Chapter 2

First Schools (1943–1950)

I first went to school at Mortdale Infants, three-quarters of a mile (1.2 km) away. It was a weary trudge home in the summer afternoons. I don't think I liked the Infants school at all. There were stupid games, like Drop the Hanky, where I was always being shouted at for not realizing it had been dropped behind me, and then running in the wrong direction. I decided games in general were stupid, and not for me, and avoided them all my life whenever possible.

There were also challenges to my non-existent dexterity such as basket weaving—what a useless occupation. The shoddiest of work was carried home as if it were some achievement, but I knew I was a duffer, and have never improved. I am the worst typist in the world, and it is a miracle I can tie my own shoelaces.

And then there were girls. There were no girls in my immediate family or in any household I played with, no girl relatives except a cousin I rarely saw. Knowing so little about them, I felt excluded from their games and their giggles, but I didn't team up with the boys throwing themselves about either, so I must have been a bit of an isolate. I don't remember being unhappy, though.

Whether it was any different at the boys' school just down the road, where I went from age 6 onward, I no longer know, but I was from then on in a male-only environment for the next 11 years of my schooling. For the first year at University, after the flame-haired Julie smiled at me at the end of or first Latin class, I was probably perpetually tongue-tied.

One teacher of those early days whom I remember well was Mr Heard ('Sir Heard' he was called at our dinner table because he was always being quoted as an authority on the topic of the day). At a parents' evening, he said to my mother, He's a very nice boy to have in the class, Mrs Clines, but he does have a tendency to laugh at the other boys if they make a mistake.

Plus ça change, I reflect, though I have developed some more grown-up forms of laughing these days, sometimes muttering about unmasking the other fellow's ideology.

One day the class came back in after lunch to find an entire imaginary underground city with trains and escalators and all the paraphernalia of modern life (such as it was in the late '40s) depicted all around the classroom—the work of Peter Wellings and myself—this in the days before pupils' work was ever displayed in classrooms and when it must have been a very cheeky act to take over the class's walls. We were not reproved, as far as I remember, and I always harboured a yearning to be a town planner. You may still hear me ranting about the idiotic decisions of Sheffield City Council, especially about parking at the train station.

Peter

In February 1944 my brother Peter was born. I had been told nothing of the expected event, but I do remember waking in the night to a household convulsed by anxiety and frantic arrangements, the word 'hospital', and then the disappearance of my mother. I think five-year-olds are better prepared these days for such upheavals.

Anyway, when my mother came home, Peter was not with her. He was suffering from hypertrophic pyloric stenosis, a narrowing of the opening from the stomach to the small intestine. He remained in hospital for the first six months of his life, and obviously he became the focus of daily concern. I was taken to see him, and was distressed by what I remember as his protuberant eyes (actually, they are quite deep set). I have had since then a distaste for anything to do with eyes and cannot bear even to have drops put in them.

Peter survived those early months, and no lasting harm was done, as far as I know. He became the liveliest in our family, quick witted, smart, amusing, a bit mischievous. We got on very well together, though the five-year gap between us was a bit much at times. I will say more about him later,

Opportunity Class

A big change was in the offing when in 1949 my parents received a letter saying I had been selected to join the Opportunity Class at Hurstville, a few miles from Oatley, and nearer the city. In a burst of egalitarian nomenclature, the New South Wales education department had given the same name to special classes for the very bright and for the very backward children. My mother, who was a great tease, always maintained that she never knew which class I had been selected for. (I was a pretty dreamy kid, and no doubt gave an impression of not belonging to the real world.)

So 36 boys, two from each school around Hurstville, were going to a new class led by a super-teacher who would advance them prodigiously. It worked. We finished the two-year curriculum for 10- and 11-year-olds in six months, and ventured into dozens of new fields, from chess to world politics to languages, in order to occupy our busy brains. Our teacher, Joe Davis, was mentioned by the notable journalist and littérateur Clive James in his *Unreliable Memoirs* (Clive was taught by him a year or two behind me, and I never knew him at school).

A gang of boys would collect around our teacher at the end of the day, to walk with him the 15 minutes to the railway station in high-spirited chat, and often to have a milkshake at his insistence (and on his tab) before catching our trains. Today he might have to consider his position, but the world was a more temperate place then, and a teacher who lived for his boys and enjoyed their company to the end of the day was only to be applauded.

One thing I did not like about this high-octane regime in the classroom was that each week the seat where you sat depended on your highly competitive scores in mental arithmetic and spelling the previous week. Everyone changed position every week, and the highest achiever had the best seat. I don't believe I was ever in that seat, but I think I was pretty well always in the first row.

School was easy for me. I don't think I worked hard, but the lure of the new was a great incentive. One idea of our teacher was to embark us on the creation of 'projects', themes of our own choice that we could research and develop. In the first year I created an exhibit on wool, writing to various firms that specialized in the processing of wool (Australia still produces a quarter of the world's wool, and it must have been much more in the 1950s). I got samples of wool in its various stages of treatment, learned all I could about the industry, and became expert in the layout and design of my results. In the next year, my theme was wine, amazingly for the son of such abstemious parents. But it too was one of Australia's natural resources, and from the wine merchants there arrived dozens of wine labels and paraphernalia about wine production. Not a drop was taken, I hardly need say, since I was only 11. But those wine labels were an education in graphic design, still advantageous to a publisher with an eye to a snazzy cover.

When it came to the question of what high school we each should go to at age 12, those who were more scientifically oriented went to Canterbury High School, or Fort Street High, and the more bookish of us to Sydney Boys' High School, where we encountered a very different clientele.

Chapter 3

My Parents and my Church

My father

My father, Alfred William Clines, born in 1912, was by profession a draughtsman. He left school at 13, working first for the Sydney mapmaking firm of H.E.C. Robinson, later Gregory's, which produced the standard Street Directory of Sydney in many editions. When the War began he was transferred to a position in the Hydrographic Unit of the Royal Australian Navy, based at Garden Island, a Navy base on Sydney Harbour. His office, which I visited occasionally, on a knoll at the tip of the island, had a magnificent view of the Harbour, not unlike that from today's Opera House. He worked in a team of only six hydrographers (or, cartographers) for the whole of Australia; their immediate task was to prepare navigational maps for Australian troops to use in the protection of Australian waters and in action against enemy-held positions in the South Pacific.

When no suitable older map existed, naval personnel would survey the relevant waters, in small boats and occasionally under gunfire, dropping their lead weights into the sea and recording the depth of the water every so many yards in a fixed direction. Their results, consisting of many hundreds of depth records expressed in one of their charts in fathoms and feet, would be passed to the cartographers, who would create an edited version of the raw data. Of course, the mapmaker was always looking out for uncharacteristic depths, for the master of any vessel needed to be aware of the places where, for example, a normal depth of 10 fathoms was suddenly reduced to 4 by some underwater reef or obstruction. (A fathom, by the way, is six feet.)

After the editing of the data came the drawing of the map itself, in the impeccable style of the British Admiralty Hydrographic Office, which the Australian cartographers imitated. Everything, from contours on the land, ocean depths and place names, was drawn by hand, and the cartographers had to be fine penmen. A complex chart (like that of Port Jackson mentioned below) would take my father six months to complete.

The family keep several rolls of his charts, some of remote Pacific islands, and—most famous of his productions—his *Approaches to Port Jackson*, Port Jackson being the proper name for all the waters popularly known as Sydney Harbour (which has a much narrower reference). My father's chart of 1946 (updated) is still carried by every ship entering or leaving the Harbour, though most vessels of any size are being piloted in its waters by local pilots, who have all its details by heart. A novelty he introduced to the hydrographic art was to add at the foot of the chart a line drawing of the view of the opening from the sea to Port Jackson. Studying that drawing one will quickly see why the earliest British explorers in the eighteenth century were unaware of the very existence of the harbour, and consequently planted their first settlement at Botany Bay, some eight miles (13 km) south of what was to become the site of the city of Sydney. Botany Bay was a most unsuitable site for many reasons, but the location of Sydney, as every traveller knows, is exceptional.

I have often compared my unusual lexicographical work on the ancient Hebrew language with my father's highly specialized cartography. We evidently shared the same ideals of precision and concision and a concern for the overall aesthetic effect of the production, as well as a taste for the distant horizon.

My father believed in the value of his occupation, and was pleased to have a distinctive and unusual role in the modern world. But that was the day job, which he never carried home. His real life was his study of the Bible and his preaching, of which I will say more in this memoir.

I should not omit mention of my father's athleticism. He was selected for the New South Wales Under-19s cricket team, but gave it up when they began to practise on a Sunday. He could still be observed miming the athlete while preaching on the Christian's race (Hebrews 12.1), for example, crouching down on the speaker's platform like a runner about to sprint off into the distance.

My father passed away in 1986.

Chapter 3. *My Parents and my Church*

My mother

My mother was born Ruby Coral Wells in 1913 (8 August, d. 25 Jan 2011), in Goulburn, an agricultural town 120 miles southwest of Sydney, with a population today of some 20,000, but rather smaller then. Her father worked for the New South Wales railways, and moved the family to Sydney in the 1930s. My mother was a true Australian pioneer, having grown up in a house, still standing, with a dirt floor. In later years, we often drove a little out of our way when passing through Goulburn in order to glimpse the house and the charming primary school she attended as a child. Later on, my daughter Miriam, after a visit to Ruby, wrote her first book, *Four Bush Girls*, which told their story. We had it professionally typed and bound.

My mother had four sisters and a brother; when I was growing up she was especially close to one of her sisters, Flo (Florence), who lived a couple of streets from us in Oatley. Ruby was a milliner by profession, and for a period, though my father disapproved of women going out to work, she got a job finishing hats at home. I would carry semi-completed hats from some workshop in Pitt Street in the centre of Sydney, and then return them when she had perfected their final form. (I seem to have been always carrying things home, whether hats or oranges or second-hand books or lessons for Emmaus Bible School or my own school case, which was always overloaded with books in case I ran out of 'reading matter', as it was called, on my train trips. My right shoulder today is noticeably lower than my left, which I attribute to the incessant carrying in my youth.)

Like many Australian women of her time my mother became a full-time homemaker at her marriage, applying her intellectual capacities to the logic of family debates and the hunting out of fallacies. A dictionary was an essential element in setting the table; I remember a controversy that rumbled on for years about which syllable in 'controversy' should be accented.

Ruby was far-sighted and adventurous, planning the family holidays, including more than 12 trips to the UK and Europe, some by sea (even bringing their Australian car with them on one occasion), and others by air. She hated planes, but devised an effective preparation for flying: in the days before the flight she would drive to a vantage point overlooking Sydney airport and watch the planes taking off and landing, for hours, without incident. So fortified, she could climb aboard her jumbo jet without excessive trepidation. She passed away in 2011, at the age of 97.

My grandparents

Little Grandpa and Little Grandma were what we called my father's parents; Big Grandpa and Big Grandma were my mother's parents. You had only to see them to know how inevitable the titles were.

Little Grandpa and Little Grandma lived in a small terrace house in the inner-city suburb of Leichhardt, Grandpa being a bootmaker who was displeased to be called a cobbler (who was not a craftsman but only a repairer). Through prudent investment, he had built up before the Great Depression of the 1930s a holding of almost 20 houses like his own; but one by one he lost them in the Depression. He did not seem bitter about it, and loved to take me to his long low workshop in the backyard of his house where all his tools had their place. There was a cast iron 'last' (in the shape of human feet) for every size of men's and women's shoes, different for left and right feet, naturally; onto the last the shoe for repair would be fitted, upside down, so that he could replace the sole, and finish off the repair with new sweet-smelling leather, waxing it so that it looked like new.

My paternal grandparents were fifth-generation Australians, and it was probably Little Grandpa who taught my father to refer to England as 'the old country' or even 'the home country' though neither of them had ever visited it. Researching the family history, my mother believed she had identified a Welsh ancestor who had worked in London in the mid-nineteenth century as a plasterer—which will no doubt have meant a person skilled in applying elaborate decorations to ceilings and walls such as were fashionable at that time. The name Clines may be connected with a word for the slope of a valley. It is unlikely to have anything to do with the German *klein* 'little', even though we called these grandparents Little Grandpa and Little Grandma.

My mother's parents were also fifth-generation Australians. My mother believed she had located one convict among our ancestors on her side, one of two brothers from Cornwall who had been 'transported' to Australia for the crime of stealing a sheep. We forgave them, since people do not steal sheep for fun but from necessity. And in any case there is in Australia a certain cachet in having one ancestor or two who came to Australia at the recommendation of the best British judges, as the saying has it. It is not advisable, however, to have too many ancestors of this type.

My mother's mother and her family, the Wellses, lived in Albany Road, Stanmore, another inner-city suburb, in a terrace row of white houses. My mother's sisters were Vera, Thelma, Flo, and Marjorie. Thelma, to whom Ruby was closest, and Ruby were pregnant at the same time, Thelma with her first, Ruby with her second child. Thelma's death in childbirth was a traumatic event for Ruby. The boy Ted was brought up by the other sister Flo, and Ruby and Flo, who lived in Oatley just 100 yards away from us, saw each other almost every day for tea and chat.

I liked to visit Big Grandma's house, where I only remember being spoiled. This was the only house of our extended family that had a pet (was that uncommon in the Australia of my youth, I wonder?). It was a large white cockatoo (an Australian parrot) with a yellow comb, and he was known as Cocky Wells. He was much given to imitating human voices, often calling out to the next-door neighbour as if he were Big Grandma initiating a conversation. The neighbour would rush out into the backyard, only to find a cockatoo awaiting her.

When we would arrive at the house he would invariably say, Here's Jinx (his name for me), and, as always, Cocky want a bit of butter—and continue saying it, bossily or plaintively, till he got it. When one of my mother's sisters would creep in late at night, he would say in the loudest of hoarse stage whispers, Who's there? Is that you, Thelma? (or whoever), thus alerting the household to the entry of the latecomer and spoiling her attempt at secrecy. He didn't like Vera, because she would sweep him up into his cage with a broomstick. Cocky had a cage as his own dwelling, but he was not confined to it: he was usually to be found outdoors, perched by choice on the clothes line in the back yard. Sometimes he took to tearing the sheets drying there with his beak, and when reproved would say, Pinky did it, Pinky being a galah (a grey and pink cockatoo), non-speaking and so always the scapegoat. Cocky would say, The crowning day is coming, a Salvation Army favourite.

On a Saturday evening, it was time for Cocky's 'tonic', which made him lose what little inhibitions he had; he would swing round and round the clothes line like a dervish. It was a long time before we realized that the tonic was in fact hemp (hemp seeds are recommended for birds), but we wondered if the dose was a little too liberal. Anyway, he enjoyed it, and we enjoyed his performances.

My church

Another given of my early life, which accompanied me at least to my late thirties, was the family's church affiliation. My father and mother, and hence our family, belonged to an 'assembly' of the Brethren in Oatley. If ever we used the word 'church', we were careful to make it refer only to the congregation and never to a building—following the New Testament usage of *ekklesia*. The Methodist Church in Frederick Street, for example, would be transmuted in our language to the Methodists' church building.

Brethren assemblies were independent congregations, friendly with similar groups in other suburbs and towns, but with no formal connection to them, and no hierarchy governing the individual churches (there were about 40 such churches in Sydney in the 1950s, many of them much larger than ours). They differed from most other Christian groups mainly in the fact that they had no paid ministers. Services were run by the willing and capable (male) members of the congregation. The theological beliefs of our Brethren were more or less identical with most Protestant churches of an evangelical nature, such as the Baptists.

Small assemblies such as ours could not afford to build a chapel (they were usually called Gospel Halls), and had to rent a meeting place. In Oatley, the only such venue available was the Masonic Hall, most unsuitable though it was. On a Saturday evening, it would probably have seen a gathering involving beer and probably dancing, so for our Morning Meeting at 11 am on the Sunday, it had to be thoroughly aired, though never with total success.

The Morning Meeting was a service of worship. That meant that the focus was on adoration of the deity, his attributes and qualities. Adoration was different from thanksgiving, though it could include it; for thanksgiving tended to shift the focus on to the thankful recipient of blessings and so away from the object of adoration. The aim of the gathering, its hymns, prayers and Bible readings, was simply to extol the deity. It was an unusual feature among Christian churches I later became acquainted with, and an art form that participating members of the congregation needed to become practised in.

The Meeting would always begin with a hymn, chosen and announced by any 'brother', a (male) member of the congregation, and sung without musical accompaniment by all (in the Gospel Meetings on a Sunday evening, a piano or organ was used). There would follow an extempore prayer, and then another hymn or a Scripture reading to enhance devotion. Since none of the contributions had been scripted, there was often a considerable pause between items, which was acceptable (as with the Quakers) as a time for personal reflection (though a sensitive participant could tell the difference between such a meaningful pause and what were called 'poverty pauses' when clearly no one had any idea what should be said or done next). At its best, a Morning Meeting could develop a theme of its own, and the contributions of various pray-ers and choosers of hymns could create an ad hoc unity for the whole event.

The congregation, no more than 30 or 40 at Oatley, sat in a large circle. Those who had not been baptized, and were therefore not members of the congregation, sat at some distance around the walls of the cavernous hall, and amused themselves as best they could for an hour and a half. Obviously, secular reading material was inappropriate for children on such an occasion, but I had come across some suitably sanctified volume of Bible trivia which kept me entertained. I learned which was the longest verse in the Bible (in Esther), and which the shortest ('Jesus wept'). I could have memorized the names of the Israelite judges and the kings of Israel and Judah if I had been so inclined. Naturally, this handbook omitted any amusing trivia, like Where is tennis mentioned in the Bible? (Moses served in Pharaoh's courts), and my particular favourite, Who is the first man in the Bible? (Chap. 1).

The service generally ended with a Bible exposition, addressed (unlike the preceding part of the service), not to the deity but to the congregation as their takeaway from the event. With the collection and the notices, it was all over, and the chairs were rearranged in the usual pattern for the evening service.

From the age of 5 until I was baptized (and so became an adult member of the assembly) I probably sat through 500 of these Morning Meetings. It was a kind of cruelty, but my 750 hours of compulsory silence with only a Bible, a hymnbook and my Bible trivia book left me very familiar with the contents of the Bible, and proved an excellent foundation for a biblical scholar. So I am not complaining.

The church and the world

I have begun with the meetings of the 'assembly', but it would be wrong to give the impression that these meetings made a strong mark on my life, not, that is, compared with the omnipresent control that the religious outlook that the Brethren lifestyle had over us.

I would characterize this control in terms of the dichotomy we lived with, between the church and the 'world'. Life within the norms of our religious ideals was what was required by God; all other activities, impulses, desires, objects, were of the 'world', which was by definition opposed to God. One had to exist in the world, indeed, but one should always be striving to be as little contaminated by it as possible. Perhaps I exaggerate, for we ate what our non-religious neighbours ate, we went to secular schools, we associated with our non-religious relatives (though my father was always uncomfortable in their presence). But, for a true believer, the world was essentially to be shunned.

I think the saddest hymn ever written, by John Nelson Darby (1800–1882), one of the early Brethren, is one that was in our hymnbook, *Hymns for the Little Flock*, and not infrequently sung by us:

> This world is a wilderness wide;
> We have nothing to seek or to choose;
> We've no thought in the waste to abide;
> We've nought to regret nor to lose.

Now there was a certain attraction to an impressionable teenager, I have to confess, in this extreme asceticism, but I think I knew it was deeply wrong even if I couldn't have said how and why. How this outlook could be squared with Genesis 1's depiction of the world God created as 'very good' always defeated me; was it truly believed that one human sin in the Garden of Eden had completely negated the divine purposes? I must add that I never saw much sign of adherence to the 'wilderness wide' theology among the members of the assembly, however much they may have paid it lip-service when at their pious hymns. They all had secular jobs, drove cars, took holidays and lived in the world very much like non-believers; but in their recreations they were certainly out of line with their fellow Australians.

If anything could be categorized as 'worldly', whether radio, television, the cinema, ice-skating, makeup, it was *ipso facto* beyond the pale for a 'godly' person. Dinner-table debates often revolved around the question: Is there a Scripture for it? Curiously, though there was no Scripture for cars or trains or electricity, they did not seem to be proscribed. Nor was making money.

Politics and voting were of course 'worldly', and although I formed the impression that the Liberals were preferable to Labour, we were strictly non-partisan. At each election, voting being compulsory in Australia, and non-compliance punishable with fines, my father and mother would trudge the weary mile to Mortdale school, where the ballots were cast, and dutifully vote 'informal' (i.e., in British English, 'spoil their ballot papers'), thus obeying the law about voting but not participating in the voting itself.

The cinema was of course quintessentially worldly. Not only was it outside the realm of the godly, it was built on deceit, like every form of fiction. And as for the morals of Hollywood, the less said the better. So it was a matter of high drama when my school was to visit the cinema to see *Julius Caesar*, with Marlon Brando (1953). This was our Shakespeare set text that year, and there was no explicit objection to *reading* Shakespeare (literature was a permissible evil), so what was the problem with *seeing* a production of Shakespeare, who had self-evidently been writing for the stage and not the bound volume? I won my case on the home front, but felt guilty that I had displeased my father, and did not visit the cinema again until I left home at the age of 22. Lacking a decade or more of childhood experience of films that most people have, I still struggle with film plots, and find it immensely difficult to distinguish characters from one another.

Bible readings

Another feature of our church life were the 'Bible readings', which were mid-week meetings held in the home of one or other of the congregation. The idea was to study a biblical book, one verse at a time, in order to understand what was being said. There was no designated leader at these meetings, and anyone (male) was free to contribute a thought or ask a question. It was a kind of seminar. I think it was the German theologian Adolf von Harnack (1861–1930) who found that his grandmother was one of such a Bible reading group. When he discovered that they were studying the Book of Revelation, he asked in astonishment, So what do you do when you come to something you don't understand? Oh, she is reported to have said, We just sit around and explain it to one another (this is a sexist story, which I should probably not repeat). Now the Brethren Bible readings were not like that, for some at least of the participants (like my father) had become quite capable exegetes over the years.

But there were hazards. One evening, Mr Croucher, father of my pal Rowland, said, à propos of John 3.16 ('God so loved the world'), 'No doubt our young brother here will confirm that in the Greek the word for "so" has a depth of meaning that cannot be reproduced in the English language' ('in-the-Greek' in such sentences was always pronounced with a special, reverent intonation, analogous to the British phrase 'we are holidaying in-Scotland'). I was the young brother, and was much tempted to say, Well, it means just the same as 'so' in any language, I suppose; I managed with difficulty to side-step such a faux pas.

Nonetheless, despite the longueurs and the misdirections that had to be endured, the patient wrestling with the biblical text week in, week out, was formative for me. It was my first seminar on the Bible. There was no hurry, no timetable; it took us three years, I believe, to get through Hebrews.

Along with the Bible readings, I was learning by heart some of the key biblical texts, Romans and Hebrews especially (in the KJV, I have to confess). I had bought from the British and Foreign Bible Society what they called 'portions', little booklets containing just one book of the Bible, and carried them with me, reciting the text and testing my memory as I walked the 20 minutes from Central Station to school (if I did not hop on a tram in the bad weather). The elaborate rhetoric of Hebrews with its seemingly never-ending sentences and infinite subordinate clauses was compelling: 'God, who at sundry times and in divers manners, spake in time past unto the fathers by the prophets, hath in these last days spoken unto us by his Son, whom he hath appointed heir of all things ...' (and five more subordinate clauses). When I began learning it by heart, Hebrews was impenetrable to me; but as I committed more and more of it to memory its structure and its sequence became opaque.

Church activities

The only social activity at Oatley assembly I can remember was the annual Sunday School picnic. The 50 or so children and assorted parents would travel in a hired bus to a park where various hateful sports could be enjoyed, and a great banquet of sausage rolls and cakes consumed.

It was traditional in the days before the picnic to have prayers for its success, fine weather being especially requested from the Lord (who probably remembered how dismal rainy picnics held entirely in the 'shelter sheds' at the chosen park could be). Early on, I became very doubtful about suggesting to the Almighty that he should personally arrange the weather for our picnic, when farmers and weekend gardeners were crying out for a shower of rain. What had we done to deserve special and discriminating treatment? It was the beginning of a long wrestle with the idea of prayer, so esteemed and so unquestioned not only in our circles but across the Christian denominations (and for that matter, in religions generally).[1] When I was older and found that in the War both the Allies and their enemies had invoked divine aid, the problem only got worse. It seemed an invitation to the deity to exercise favouritism, but it put him in an invidious, not to say impossible, position. I must say, though, that when one of our former Sheffield students reminds me that he prays for me every day I do not take it amiss, for I take it that he has warm thoughts of me and wishes me well; I have no quarrel with that, and even feel more important and nurtured than I have a right to be.

Conferences

One way in which members of the various assemblies met each other, and not just with their own congregation, was through the institution of the 'conference'. Some of the larger assemblies would arrange an annual

---

1. I was fascinated to discover by accident recently that this is still a live issue among Christian theologians; see Jason M. Smith, 'Praying to Win: Reflections on the Involvement of God in Outcomes of Sport', *Theology* 123 (2020), pp. 329-36.

conference day, in which they organized a Bible teaching afternoon and evening in their chapel. Visitors from other assemblies would come. Typically, two well-known Bible teachers would be invited to speak on topics of their own choice, once in the afternoon, once again in the evening. In between there would be a buffet tea where one could circulate and chat. Parents were glad of the opportunity for their offspring to mix with other young people from Christian homes (rather from the dubious families of their school friends).

Each year, at Easter, there was in Sydney a grand conference of all the Brethren folk, with up to 1,200 in attendance. On Good Friday, it was held in Petersham Town Hall, in one of the inner suburbs, and on Easter Monday in Scots Presbyterian Church, Margaret St, in central Sydney. Into the carpets of Scots Church was woven the emblem of the Church of Scotland, Moses at the burning bush with the slogan *nec tamen consumebatur* ('and yet it was not consumed'). I was grateful to be a Latinist, and suppose I felt superior because I could translate it instantly; the Scots Church was decidedly a different atmosphere from the Oatley Masonic Hall. Getting into the spirit of the event, I would always volunteer to serve cups of tea and hand round sandwiches and scones in the interval.

During the sessions, I would be busily taking notes of all the addresses. My mother would have mischievously warned me about sitting next to 'girls with weak spines', who might lean against me, as also against those with batteries up their arms to give me a thrill if I held their hand. Even if those warnings were not necessary, it was always a convivial occasion, despite the high seriousness of the ostensible purpose.

Conscientious objection

Compulsory military training was established in Australia in 1951 during the Korean War. All males above 18 were required to complete up to 176 days of 'National Service'. I was a conscientious objector to military service, and I remain a pacifist, but I am to this day disappointed that my church gave me no support in my stance. Others in the church would mutter that it was a matter of 'individual conscience' and change the subject. I now believe that they were in fact opposed to conscientious objection, but did not want to dispute the matter with me. I think the Brethren of that period were largely right-wing; I know they were opposed to the Labour Party, which had strong Catholic roots and possible contamination by godless Communists. In my innocence, I did not realize that there must have been support groups for objectors, and I went to the appointed hearing of my case without any preparation at all, as far as I recall. I was grilled in a hostile fashion by a military man in a court-like setting. I suppose I came across as, at least, naïve and sincere though misguided, since I was assigned to 'non-combatant duties'. I was able to defer the fulfillment of those duties year by year while I remained a University student, and in 1959 National Service was abolished and I was free of the obligation.

Exclusive Brethren

As a dark shadow of the Open Brethren, the term we would use of ourselves if pressed, there was the network of Exclusive Brethren assemblies, which had split from the Open Brethren as long ago as 1848. Unlike the Open Brethren's insistence on the autonomy of individual churches, the Exclusives had a centralized structure, headed by a leader of all the congregations worldwide. I was once invited to meet with a family of Exclusive Brethren with a view to defecting to them; the meeting was arranged by Ron Emmerick, a classicist in Sydney who had joined them, though he later became an ardent atheist.

Though they were living a luxurious lifestyle and were very keen to attract talented people to their company, I was repulsed by what I encountered. Subsequently, their movement was rocked by scandals, and yet nevertheless apparently survives. They now refer to themselves as the Plymouth Brethren Christian Church.

The Open Brethren

Partly in order to distinguish themselves from the Exclusives and partly to be rid of the sexist and dated term 'Brethren', many of the Open Brethren churches to which my family and I belonged are now known in Australia (since c. 2006) as the Christian Community Churches of Australia. There are said to be some 320 congregations affiliated to this group, with c. 46,000 members.[2] Worldwide, the number of Open Brethren churches has been estimated at 40,000.

Open Brethren and biblical scholarship

Despite lacking an ordained ministry and colleges for theological education, the Brethren have produced many biblical scholars. In the nineteenth century, George Vicesimus Wigram (1805–1879; he was the twentieth child of his parents, as his middle name indicates) prepared *The Englishman's*

---

2. The Wikipedia article 'Christian Community Churches of Australia' is especially helpful and balanced.

Greek Concordance to the New Testament (1839), and before long *The Englishman's Hebrew and Chaldee Concordance of the Old Testament* (1843). The plan of each volume was that under each Hebrew or Greek word were listed all occurrences, with the biblical reference, and an extract from that verse. Samuel Prideaux Tregelles (1813–1875) was a textual scholar who published a major critical edition of the text of the New Testament (1857–1872), as well as translating the Hebrew lexicon (1846) and the Hebrew grammar (1848) of Wilhelm Gesenius. J.N. Darby, one of the founders of the Brethren movement, translated the New Testament into English, and with collaborators, the whole Bible into English and French and German.

In our own time, among Brethren biblical scholars I may mention the foremost, F.F. Bruce (1910–1990), and, among Hebrew Bible scholars, David F. Payne (b. 1931), Leslie C. Allen (b. 1935) and Robert P. Gordon (b. 1954), and also the Septuagintalist David Gooding (1925–2019).

Chapter 4

Sydney Boys' High (1951–1955)

At age 12, in February 1951, I enrolled in Sydney Boys' High School, a selective grammar school located a mile and a half (2.3 km) from the city centre. I would take a train from Oatley station a bit before 8 am for a 30-minute ride to Central Station and then a 10-minute tram ride to school. If I was early, and could walk from Central to school, I could keep the fare for my own purchases later (see below).

Sydney High was just across the road (Anzac Parade) from the Sydney Cricket Ground. When a match was on, I could be watching it minutes after the end of classes, for free, since the gates were opened by about 3.30 in the afternoons. Mostly I saw matches between the first-class teams of the six Australia states, who were competing for the Sheffield Shield, a trophy donated by Lord Sheffield, 3rd Earl of Sheffield, an English Conservative politician known best for his patronage of cricket. I saw the West Indian Gary Sobers in action in a test match, thought by many to be cricket's finest all-rounder.

When I arrived at Sydney High, I had not, as far as I know, ever met a Jewish person. In my class, however, a good third of the pupils were Jewish, since Sydney High recruited many of its pupils from the Eastern Suburbs with their many Jewish families as well as from the southern suburbs like Hurstville and Oatley from which I had come. A rapid updating was in order since the Old Testament, with which I was pretty familiar, was not the best resource for the present day.

There must have been sporty Jewish students, but those I came to hang out with were, like myself, more given to conversation and debate. We became adept at devising means of avoiding physical exertion while exercising our brain cells to the top of our bent. A group of us became skilled scorers of cricket at the Wednesday afternoon intra-school matches, and our decisions were acceded to by players and teachers alike, though we had in actuality spent much of the afternoon in philosophical discussion.

Of my group were Harvey Cohen, later professor of medicine at Sydney, Peter Wilenski, who became a senior public servant, Secretary of the Department of Foreign Affairs and Trade, and Marcus Einfeld who became a federal judge and president of the Human Rights and Equal Opportunity Commission, but in a bizarre case in 2008 stemming from a $77 traffic fine was convicted of perjury and perverting the course of justice, and served two years in prison.

Teachers

With few exceptions, the teachers at Sydney High have left little mark upon my memory. My favourite teacher, Mr Edmonds, taught me French throughout my five years; we called him Scraggs, for some unknown reason. His exact and exacting French was learned entirely from books and magazines; he never visited France or any Francophone country. He made us keep a notebook of French phrases, many of them gleaned that morning on his train ride to work: Here's another for your phrase-book, gents, he would announce, and everyone's notebook would be hauled out from their desk. Scraggs was famous for his ability with a thrown piece of chalk: a boy talking to his neighbour behind him would get a short sharp shock in the ear, to the applause of the class.

There was Mr Beck, who first entered the Greek classroom bearing the massive lexicon of Liddell and Scott on his head. He did not seem to last very long; a much better Greek teacher was Robert Maddox, who became a noted New Testament scholar and principal of Leigh College in Strathfield, Sydney, the Methodist Theological College. He came to Sydney High in his first year of teaching, and we tried to make life difficult for him. In the opening scene of Aristophanes' *Clouds*, a night-time scene has a young man farting in his sleep. The verb is *perdomai*, and our class is innocently asking why that is being translated 'snoring'. Mr Maddox blushes, replies that such is the standard translation, but reminds us that according to Grimm's Law *p-* in Indo-European (and so Greek) becomes *f-* in Germanic (and so English), and *d-* becomes *t-*, so work it out for yourself.

I also remember our Latin teacher, Mr (Edgar) Bembrick (b. 1890), who had written the introductory textbook (and 40 other cribs) and knew it by heart.[1] A bored voice would drone: Clines, Exercise 11, Sentence 7. Translate, and Clines would recite some guff about the girls giving roses

---

1. A fellow sufferer from about my time has written on his blog: 'He, I suspected, personally knew Julius Caesar, in fact probably taught him ... He ... claimed to be able to complete [from memory] any line of Latin or Greek verse we could throw at him.'

to the sailors (first declension nouns, first conjugation verb, you may have noticed). It was the same in Second Year, when we read with him Caesar's *Gallic Wars*. He knew exactly where we had left off the previous day and what the next sentence would be. So stimulating.

I did not get on well with the physics teacher, Mr Basser, in my first year. We were supposed to keep an Experiment Book, reporting our doings in the lab under headings like Aim, Equipment, Method, Result. I must have got the wrong end of the stick, because most of my experiments, due to my clumsiness and inability to follow instructions, were failures: water flooded the Experiment Book, glass slab fell to floor, nothing happened, forgot next thing to do. It appeared that these did not count as experiments, and the only experiments that were to be inscribed in the Experiment Book were experiments that reached the predetermined conclusion. Though I didn't know the word 'totalitarian' at the time, I suppose I thought it, and perhaps this conveyed itself to the teacher, who was pretty angry. Anyway, I got a score of 30% in the exam, the only time I ever failed in an exam. I don't know how the impasse was resolved, except that I was perhaps moved out of the class.

The Curriculum

My subjects were English, Maths, Physics, Chemistry, French, Latin, Ancient History (in First Year). There was nothing unusual about the curriculum, which must have been replicated in thousands of schools throughout the British Empire and Commonwealth. But it was an awful education.

It had been transmitted over generations from the classical education the future rulers of Britain would receive in their public schools, with a few recent additions like the sciences. But it had never been thought through from scratch, and it had little relevance, or none, to the future life of the pupils. I can see how much the curriculum has changed in the last 70 years since I was a boy by looking at the school's current website, where drama, industrial arts, music, personal development, social sciences, and visual arts now feature.

But the curriculum of my day, in the 1950s, was locked in the past. The chief omission, in my view, was biology. At Sydney Girls' High School, next door to Sydney Boys' High, biology was on the curriculum from Second Year, in place of Greek or German in the boys' school. I was never taught a single thing about my body, and have a lamentable ignorance about it to this day. In my case, the Pauline recommendation, 'I keep under my body, and bring it into subjection' (1 Cor. 9.27 KJV), only served to reinforce this attitude, which made women the responsible bearers of the knowledge and experience of the body, and men the insouciant users of the body (as of everything else).

The second omission was the preparation of boys for adulthood, as citizens, householders, fathers, employees. Within a few years of leaving school, many boys would be married, voting in elections, negotiating a mortgage, dependent on government services and facilities, subject to the misinformation of newspapers and the media, ignorant of Australian history and the nature of Australian society. For these vital aspects of their daily life they would be left to their own devices, and no amount of Latin or Physics would serve them. What we endured was almost a systematic anti-education, and many generations were wronged by the carelessness of educational policy and its implementers.

It did puzzle me why politics, party politics, were not taught in school. We had representatives of various churches coming into the school to give religious instruction once a week, so why not Labor Party and Liberals hawking their wares?

Galleys

One job at the school that fell to my lot was proofreading the galleys for the annual School Magazine. A classmate and I were designated to this task and sent to a large cupboard under the stairs for a couple of days with the feet-long proofs. It was an exciting event to be responsible for the final form of the magazine, and exactly the work experience a future publisher needs to have in one's CV—not that I ever dreamed what might become of me!

Sports days

Sydney High School (SHS) was unusual in that it was a member not only of the league of major Sydney high schools (CHS, Combined High Schools) such as Fort St and Canterbury, but also, because of its age (founded in 1883), of the Great Public Schools (GPS) although it was not a private, fee-paying school. Consequently, SHS had two annual interschool sports days at the pinnacle of its sporting calendar.

Whether because of my prowess at reporting the cricket scores from the weekly matches or for some other reason, I became a trusty carrier of results from the track or field events at the annual sports days to the official headquarters in the centre of the sports arena, and so a source of the latest knowledge about how our school was doing in the competition of the day.

My favourite sports day memory from one of the swimming carnivals was of a teacher screaming through his microphone, That boy coming down the slippery slide, STOP!

Lunches

Usually I took a packed lunch to school, but when I was in funds I would treat myself to the quintessential Australian lunch, a round meat pie with lashings of tomato sauce squirted into it. A Sydney handbook recommends visitors to ask for 'pine saws' (say it for yourself); it was hot and tasty and sustaining for a whole afternoon. In later life I am always sure to get one whenever I go to Australia.

Knife game

There was one game that I was half good at, which we perhaps called Territory (it has some resemblances to Mumbley Peg, but we never knew it by such a name). You and your partner/rival found a piece of smooth earth in the playground, drew a circle a metre or so in size, and then in turn threw your knives into the soil so that the knife stuck in the ground. You drew a line across the circle in the direction your knife had entered the soil, and claimed the larger piece of the circle as your territory. You repeated the same moves with increasingly smaller bits of territory. There must have been complications in the game that I no longer remember, but it certainly confirms that a knife carried to school in the 1950s was part of a schoolboy's daily accoutrements, and not an offence in the eyes of the police.

Saturday work

In our house, Saturday was devoted to jobs around the house, and I was expected to pull my weight. Many of these jobs seemed to consist of moving bricks or piles of rubble from one part of the backyard to another, and given that my father seemed more eager to begin works than complete them, I did not always see why we were doing what we were doing. So I was always inventing dodges for getting out of Saturday work, like buying and reading the *Sydney Morning Herald* (bought because there were church notices on a Saturday).

The biggest and longest lasting challenge was the excavation of virgin rock at the front of the house to create a garage for a hoped-for future car. Today one would hire a gang with some compressed air and have it out in a morning, but then there was no money for such enterprises, and everything had to be done by hand. There was never a time, in many years, when the excavation was not begging to be continued, pleading with me as I came in and out the front gate.

One day it was done, and even before there was a car, there was a garage with a table tennis table, with a hardboard top, but full size. I and my mate Rowland Croucher could bash away all day during the holidays there. He was an all-round athlete, and won virtually every match, but I kept on playing, for what else was there to do?

Quite apart from Saturday work, there were bookshelves to be made, not only for my father, who would bring his book purchases up the front steps before entering the house from the back, so as to retrieve the new books from the front step later in the evening without anyone knowing he had been buying. He was a very capable carpenter, and prepared every shelf from roughly sawn timber he brought home on his shoulder; they all then had to be planed—a back-breaking job. But that was the way I got my bookshelves as well as he his, so it was worth it in the end.

He had the system of arranging his books by size and colour, for, he said, you always remember whether the book you are looking for is a small green one or a fat red one. Also, it saves space if the bottom shelves are taller than the top ones, and I have followed that principle in all the bookcases I have made (or caused to be made) in all my life. Each book bore a coloured tape around its spine, showing which shelf the book had come from.

My father was out preaching most Sunday evenings, and it was a treat to go with him in the train (a car came late to our family). On the way to one distant church or another, perhaps an hour each way, he would be occupied with reading over his notes, getting his sermon in mind so that he could deliver it extempore, but on the way home that could all be put behind him and our conversation never faltered. Today this would be called bonding.

Bookshops

After school, perhaps once a week, I would not take the tram directly to Central Station to go home, but another into the more commercial heart of the city, where I could visit the second-hand bookshops. There must have been five or so shops with the same pricing system. Laid out on vast tables were the shilling books (or 3 for 2/6), or the sixpenny books (3 for a shilling) or the threepenny books (3 for sixpence). It was a rare week I did not come home with a haul of at least 3 books.

Some afternoons I did not go book buying but to the City Library, a musty many-storied place in the Queen Victoria Building in George Street with a rickety lift, to get my literary fix. The Building, occupying a whole city block next to St Andrews Cathedral and the Town Hall, is said to be the finest example of Federation (i.e. Australian) Romanesque, and, happily, it has been sympathetically restored in the 1980s. I was thorough with Shaw and Wilde because I was always a sucker for an aphorism or a witty remark, and I loved Shaw's socialism and feminist impulses. Any French novel that came to hand rode home with me, and so did magazines like *National Geographic* and *Paris Match*.

Unless I had squandered all my cash, I would still have enough for a milkshake (pineapple was always my favourite flavour) at the bar in whatever underground station I was using, Wynyard or Museum. Sometimes, if I was coming home from school through Central there would be for sale great cheap bags of oranges shipped up from the Riverina, a fruit-growing area in south-western Australia that was then being developed. If I hauled one of these bags home, I would be met with plaudits.

Shopping in Oatley

Very differently from today, when the shops in Oatley village (as it now likes to think of itself) are multiracial and cosmopolitan, Oatley in the 1950s was exclusively Australian. I don't think we ate a single thing that was imported, and there was no fancy fruit and vegetable like avocado or broccoli. I loved the humble choko, a green cucumber-like fruit of a climbing plant; everyone had one of their own in the backyard, and it would produce hundreds of fruits each season. Perfect with pepper and loads of butter. Pink pumpkin grew in the backyard too, but it is never seen on English menus. I think that all the vegetables at our house were boiled, little was eaten raw, and culinary adventures were not entertained. We had heard of pasta, but never tried it (foreign muck). But meat was plentiful, cheap and tasty, and the meat, usually grilled, made the meal.

Often I would be sent to the butcher's at five in the afternoon just before he closed to ask for 'four nice lamb chops'. A boy of 12 can hardly ask a butcher for 'nice' chops, so either that requirement would be dropped or re-phrased: My Mum wants four nice lamb chops (sotto voce: but I'll take anything you give me).

Cheese came in just two varieties: mild and tasty, and I don't think there was a single shop that sold hot takeaway food. Supermarkets had not been invented, and every grocery item you bought was personally fetched by the grocer. A string bag was a luxury shopping item.

Chapter 4. *Sydney Boys' High (1951–1955)*

Chickens

I have said we had no pet, but at one point we did keep chickens. They were bantams, smaller than most hens, but they laid tasty eggs. My father had built an enclosure for them, perhaps 30 feet in length and six feet wide, against the side fence at the back of the yard. There was plenty of space for the twenty or so hens and their cock, but some afternoons I could let them out to forage in the rest of the garden as well. Their wings had been clipped, so they would not fly over the fence, but it could still be a problem to round them all up and get them back in their pen safely.

It was my job to mix their morning feed with hot water and set it before them. I was very proud of my flock, and loved their fearlessness as they gathered excitedly around my feet when I brought them their feed. It was good for me to learn to be a servant to them, being consistently on duty even in the coldest mornings, and praising them for their excellent products. Oh, and having to carry their feed from the produce store in Mortdale every few weeks.

House extension

In the 1950s, there was money enough to have our house extended. The bedroom of Peter and myself became my father's study, two rooms were added at the back, a bedroom for the boys and a 'sunroom', which became the family living room; the kitchen too was extended with an 'ingle nook' where we could breakfast and, incidentally, get an even better view of the river. It was about this time that the house was attached to the sewage system, a new washing machine was installed (though I mourned the loss of the 'copper' in which the clothes were boiled and the wringer that I often was allowed to turn so as to squeeze most of the water out of the washed clothes). Before long, in about 1953 or 1954, I think, I mounted a struggle to take over half the sunroom so as to have a den or space for myself and my books and my studies. Once I was successful, I installed the radio there, and had classical music as my background to work (as I still do).

Politics

My first political act was to tear down posters that had appeared overnight on our suburban lampposts. During the Cold War, the influence of communism in the Australia trade unions had for long been a bone of contention, and the Liberal (i.e. Conservative) Prime Minister, Robert

Menzies, called in September 1951 for a national referendum to outlaw the Communist Party. Picking up the vibes from home and church, no doubt, I was affronted by the posters protesting against the outlawing proposal, so I ripped down as many as I could one dark night. It never occurred to me to doubt that suppression was the best way of dealing with bad ideas. To everyone's surprise, the outlawing of the Communists was defeated by 50.6% to 49.4%, and Australia remained true to its commitment to free speech (actual support for the Communist Party itself was minimal).

My next incursion into politics was more serious, and more sustained.

Radio and Politics

In the mid-1950s, our family acquired a radio, ostensibly for the health of my mother who was suffering from depression. But she was not much interested in the radio, and it fell into my hands. In my den, I had in the background through most of my work days the cricket, classical music, or Parliament on the radio. I became so familiar with the parliamentary debates that when I discovered I could have Hansard (the printed record of Parliamentary business, issued daily when Parliament was sitting with a complete record of the previous day's business) delivered to my house for a trifling four shillings a year, I became a devotee.

Sydney Heat

There would be two weeks at least in the Sydney summers when the temperature would be above 100° F every day. I hated it. Despite the cross-draft from the windows in my den, I would give up working when the pen kept slipping from my fingers because of perspiration, and I would lie down on the bathroom floor, the coolest spot in the house because it was made of terrazzo. I would sleep fitfully during the day, and then work all night, especially if the Southerly Buster had arrived.

The Southerly Buster (some called it Dr South) was a cool wind from the southeast that would blow in to Sydney in the evening after a very hot day, reducing the temperature by 20° F or more in a few minutes. You could hear it coming, in the tree tops, more than half an hour before it actually arrived, and we would sit on the front steps waiting for it. Many people went to one of Sydney's many beaches, to be either near or else in the water. When the Southerly arrived, there would be a mad dash for the cars, and then awful congestion on the roads, so I think we never took that option.

Sometimes, when asked why I left Sydney, I say I ran away from home because of the heat. It is not the whole truth, but there is truth in it.

Affording University

One evening in my last year at school my father called me into his study and said solemnly, I'm afraid we can't afford to send you to University. I think it was just about as blunt as that, and it was a shock. I had long imagined that this was where I was headed.

I didn't doubt his word, and I knew what I had to do. I had to sell myself to the New South Wales Department of Education as a trainee teacher. They would pay my fees if I would agree to serve them after graduation for five years as a teacher. That was what my mate Rowland had done. I visited him later in his first posting, at Captains Flat, a small town of some 600 inhabitants, and formerly a lead, zinc, and copper mining town. It was at the end of the railway line from Canberra, 64 km (40 miles) away, and 327 km (200 miles) southwest of Sydney. It was later used as the location for the movie *Ned Kelly*, starring Mick Jagger as the Australian bushranger. Rowland enjoyed Captains Flat, but I could not have imagined myself in such a place. Still, there were plenty of other schools in New South Wales to which I might have been assigned. But it was not a welcome prospect.

As it turned out, though the Department of Education thought they would have little use for a teacher of the classics, they funded me through my five years at Sydney University, and allowed me, once I had a job in Sheffield, to pay back my bond at very reasonable terms over quite a number of years. It was a very humane means of getting an education.

Chapter 5

Sydney University (1956–1961)

To enroll as an undergraduate in the University of Sydney in the 1950s, your first and only transaction was with the Fees Office. You filled in a form of the courses you would take, and paid the appropriate sums. The Office must have known that you were entitled to enroll, of course, but that was very straightforward: everyone who took the final school examination either matriculated or didn't matriculate. The University did not care what you studied, and there was no advice (though I have a faint memory of a brief consultation with a person about my choice of subjects, who thought it was very odd, but perfectly legitimate).

After that, my first memory of the University was of attending a mass gathering of all First Year students in the Great Hall, built in 1859 in the Gothic Revival style (Trollope called it 'the finest chamber in the colonies'). The robed presenter began his speech by inviting us to look at the person at our left, and then to the person at our right, and then at ourselves. Only one of the three of you will be here next year, said he. Will it be you? To understand this chilling statement, one needs to know a little more about the Australian system of higher education.

In the 1950s, the final state examination was called the Leaving Certificate (it is now called the Higher School Certificate, HSC). A pass in a certain number of subjects constituted matriculation to university. Australia being one of the most urbanized countries in the world (89% today), most students went to university in their own city, and most lived at home. So a student like myself, matriculated, would naturally go to the University of Sydney (there were only eight Australian universities in 1951).

Naturally enough, since there was no selection for a university place there was a high dropout rate. It was wasteful of resources, but it can be argued that it was a good system for separating those who could benefit from a university education from those who couldn't: give all with the basic qualifications an equal chance.

Chapter 5. *Sydney University (1956–1961)*

At Sydney University, you could do three subjects in each of your three undergraduate years, or four in the first, three in the second and two in the third. I chose the second pattern, with Latin and Greek as my core subjects, adding Ancient History and Hebrew in the first year, Hebrew in the second, and continuing Hebrew in the third year though I didn't need to. If you wanted an Honours degree, you did an extra year for that. I did two extra years, in Greek and Latin, because I was awaiting a Cooper travelling scholarship to the UK, which became available only every two years.

Latin

The professor was A.J. Dunston (1922–2000), who came from Reading University in 1953 to the chair of Latin. When he first entered the classroom, he called on someone from his list of students to translate some nominated lines from our set text, Virgil's *Fourth Aeneid* (Dido and Aeneas), spreading havoc among the class as we all wondered who would be the next victim of such unprepared public performance. Dunston's bite was not as bad as his bark, however, and it was he who arranged for me, later on, to be accepted into St John's College in Cambridge. As far as I can remember, I made no formal application, and everything was handled by him and his former colleague at Reading, John Crook, an authority on Roman law, who had become a Fellow of St John's, and was to become my personal tutor.

For my fifth and honours year in Latin, I devised with Dunston a dissertation on Silius Italicus, a first-century CE Silver Age Roman poet few had heard of, though his 17-book *Punica*, an epic poem about the Second Punic War (218–201 BCE), was the longest surviving poem in Latin, c. 12,000 lines. Silius has long had a reputation as the worst Latin poet ever, but in recent times he is being rediscovered. Silius took his inspiration from Virgil and Homer, and my undertaking was to compare his many extended similes with those of his predecessors, which he borrowed, adapted or imitated. There was no literature on the subject, and I had to make up my own approaches as I went along, working with nothing but the text itself. *Ad fontes*, back to the sources, has long been a motto for me, and such was my first foray into a purely literary topic, a theme that I reverted to on numerous occasions in Hebrew Bible studies.

Greek

The professor of Greek, George Pelham Shipp (1900–1980), another Sydney High old boy, who had been born, as had my mother, in Goulburn, was a different kind of scholar. In his fine high-ceilinged study on the ground floor of the University's frontage, there were at least four tables, one of them laid out with the recent issues of all the major classical and philological journals. When I first saw that table, I felt I was in the presence of a true scholar, and Australia became suddenly much closer to Europe than it had ever been. Gradually I followed his example, and by the time I left Sydney for Cambridge I was subscribing to *Vetus Testamentum, Journal of Theological Studies, Journal of Biblical Literature, Revue biblique, Bibbia e oriente, Zeitschrift für die alttestamentliche Wissenschaft* and others, and accounting myself a distant and very minor member of the world of scholarship.

With Shipp I studied the Greek dialects, as laid out in Buck's handbook. My exam in that subject was the only exam I have ever done orally, and I completely fell at the first fence, losing my nerve at the simplest question. Shipp and his co-examiner Professor Treweek were sympathetic and pulled me out of my funk, and I must have made a good showing in the end.

Shipp himself was a notable philologist, with early work on the language of Homer and the Mycenaean language. Knowing my interest in the New Testament he created a course for me in 1960 or so which he (not remotely religious) and I would read the Gospel of John as a witness to the changing of the Greek language from Attic to the Koine on its way to modern Greek. He was a lover of all things Greek, spent his holidays in Greece and spoke modern Greek; he got much pleasure from showing me how the normal Greek for 'fish', *ichthys*, a famous Christian word, appeared in only one context in John, its place otherwise being taken by *opsarion*, which ultimately became in modern Greek *psari*. All this and much more appeared in his *Modern Greek Evidence for the Ancient Greek Vocabulary* (1979).

Another Greek teacher was Bill Ritchie, who came back to Sydney in 1958 after his Cambridge PhD on the authenticity of the *Rhesus* of Euripides (published 1964). He was a shy man, who would glimpse a gaggle of his students for the 9 am lecture slot gossiping in the south-western corner of the Quadrangle as he crossed by a different route. He knew we were there, and we knew he was ready, but we cruelly delayed shifting ourselves to the classroom as long as possible. When settled, some of the women would sit in the front row to make eyes at him to embarrass him, another cruelty. In the next year he took a few of us through a learned tour of the Oresteia material as it appeared variously in Aeschylus, Sophocles and Euripides. It was a great idea that could have been riveting, but it needed a bird's-eye view of what was going on with each dramatist, and, getting bogged down in the detail, it turned out to be turgid.

Chapter 5. *Sydney University (1956–1961)*

The best Greek teacher I had in Sydney was the Oxford-educated J.H. Quincey, of whom it was alleged that he believed that if you shut up a roomful of fresh air tight in the autumn it would stay like that to the spring (Sydney winters were perishing, even for an Englishman). Quincey was an exceptional teacher because he made us engage with the content of our text, and not imagining that translating it was the end of the matter. We were reading Plato's *Republic*, Book I. There were just three of us in the class, one of the others being Paddy (Padraic) McGuinness (1938–2008), a contrarian who became a noted Australian journalist and editor. We probably read only a dozen pages of the Republic in the whole term, because Quincey would say after we had translated a speech of Socrates, for example: Now, Clines, how would you reply to Socrates? There would follow a freewheeling discussion about justice or whatever, stretching the mind and making us feel we belonged to the gang of Socrates in the Stoa. Then we would compare our feeble response to what Socrates' interlocutor actually said in the next lines.

For my fourth and final year in Greek I undertook to write a dissertation on *Words for Good and Bad in Demosthenes and the New Testament*. The dissertation was the almost the sole activity of one's honours year, and you worked on it more or less by yourself. Shipp had introduced me to the new science of semantic fields, as promulgated by Jost Trier, and I decided to investigate one such field in Greek, words for good and bad. My study was first synchronic, as I analysed the uses of these words in two sets of texts, the speeches of the fourth-century orator Demosthenes and the New Testament, five centuries later. Secondly, the study became diachronic, as I compared the changes that had taken place between the first and the second synchronic states. Unlike the writers of most dissertations, I did not get hung up on theoretical issues, but plunged straight into the textual evidence. Strangely, I don't remember ever discussing my work with Shipp, but I do remember my mad rush to get the manuscript delivered by 12 noon on the due date. I have mislaid the manuscript now, but I remember discovering how *kalos*, an ethical word in Demosthenes, had became in the New Testament 'beautiful', and how *agathos* had taken its place as the regular term for ethically good.

Hebrew

The Department of Semitic Studies in Sydney in 1956 consisted solely of E.C.B. (Colin) MacLaurin, whose office and only teaching room was in an ex-army hut located in a car park in the shadow of the University Library. This office accommodated nothing but MacLaurin's desk and chair and six chairs for students. The miniature blackboard could hold only 10 Hebrew characters on each of its 6 lines. When we did translation into Hebrew, one student would call out the Hebrew words, and MacLaurin would write the consonants on the board; the next student would be invited to supply the vowels, starting with the last word written. Hebrew was thus written right to left, but pointed left to right, from the end of the sentence to the beginning. Sometimes when rewriting Hebrew on the blackboard I have negligently fallen into this system, to the general consternation of the class, who have rightly thought it bizarre to vocalize a whole sentence at one time, and backwards at that.

It is hard not to believe that the humiliating circumstances in which Hebrew was taught in Sydney in those days were not the result of some vendetta against the subject or its teacher. MacLaurin was very outspoken in defence of his (Liberal) party political views, which may not have been welcome in the university, but he never hinted at any such background to the department's dire state. It is a matter of fact, nevertheless, that some ignorant skullduggery was in play when a proposal to add the teaching of Arabic to the work of Semitic Studies.[1]

MacLaurin's scholarship was of the kind known as 'independent', circling around contentious issues such as the origin of the tetragrammaton with striking proposals. A number of his articles were published in *Vetus Testamentum*, and as self-published monographs. I will always be grateful to him for his standard response to any clever suggestion from a student: 'Mr X, you should write that up and send it to *Vetus Testamentum*', half-seriously at least putting into the minds of more than one of us a dim possibility that one day would come to fruition. (*Vetus Testamentum* had been founded only a few years previously, in 1951, and was clearly the cool place to publish.)

We had another part-time teacher as well, Rabbi Dr Israel Porush. senior rabbi at the Great Synagogue, Sydney. At the inauspicious hour of 5, one afternoon a week, he would take a handful of us through the *Sayings of the Fathers* (*Pirqe Aboth*), which I am afraid I did not greatly appreciate at the time, probably because they were non-biblical (youth can be so short-sighted). But they stuck in my memory and made a lasting impression on me, appealing to my love of aphorisms and pithy sayings. My favourite has always been the saying of Ben Bag Bag about the Torah: 'Turn it over, and turn it over again, for everything is in it. And gaze on it; and become

---

1. See the article by E. Stockton, editor of the *Australian Journal of Biblical Archaeology*, 'E.C.B. MacLaurin and the Department of Semitic Studies of the University of Sydney', *AJBA* 1/5 (1972), pp. 1-8.

old and worn out in it, and do not deviate from it, for you have no better portion than it.' It is a fine motto for a biblical scholar, and can so easily bring me to tears. But I also reverted many times to the more enigmatic saying of Hillel: 'If I am not for me, who will be for me? And if I am only for me, what am I? And if not now, when?'—applicable to a myriad of life situations.

I should add that Hebrew was a great struggle for me in my first year, and I often feared I would never succeed at it. At the end of the second term I was still disconsolately looking up every verb form in the back of the textbook (Wood and Lanchester, a pretty dismal grammar). But a couple of weeks before the exam there was an unexpected sea change, and I became more confident. I many times encouraged flailing students with my early experiences of the language.

Ancient History

My fourth subject in First Year was Ancient History, which seemed to begin with primeval protoplasm but before long entered the more familiar world of the pyramids and the Graeco-Roman world. This was a class of over 500 students, held in the Wallace Theatre, a smart new building (65 years ago, I mean). I had never been at a proper lecture before, and no one had given me any tips on how to take notes. Long since, I had invented my own system of shorthand (mainly leaving out the vowels, but with various other ingenious devices as well), which I had practised on sermons many times. So I attempted to write down every word of the lecturer, and was pretty successful. What I had not foreseen was the matter of what I was to do with these transcripts. Going over a whole hour's lecture while it was still fresh in my mind was not a very exciting prospect, and what was the point of doing it a month later? So that project came to a natural end after a few weeks, and I began to take real notes, like anyone else.

Often I found myself sitting somewhere near Robert Hughes, who became a famous art critic with his BBC television series, *The Shock of the New* (1980) and his history of the settlement of Australia, *The Fatal Shore* (1986). A public school boy, he did not seem particularly interested in ancient history, spending his time in the Wallace sketching other people.

The lecturer, who would arrive with a vast carry-all in which he could barely locate the script of his lecture, and gave all the appearance of total disorganization, turned out to be, I later discovered, Geoffrey Evans, a distinguished Assyriologist. I wish I had known it at the time; I would not have sniggered like the others. Evans marked my essay on the Hittites (I suppose I chose the topic because they are mentioned in the

Old Testament). His only comment was: Should have used Gurney. I was mortified. Of course I had used Gurney, whose Pelican volume was the best resource on the Hittites. I had just left it out of my bibliography by mistake. Lesson learned. Now I am more likely to be accused of not leaving *anything* out of my bibliographies.

I have one story from that class, filed in my mind under Be slow to believe. The results of university examinations were regularly published in the *Sydney Morning Herald*, and early one morning my mate Rowland appeared at the door with his copy. You're OK in Greek and Hebrew, he said, but I'm afraid you've dipped in Ancient History. I was very put out about that, for though I didn't think I had written a brilliant paper, I didn't think it was all that bad (and apart from a disaster in first year Physics at school I hadn't made a habit of failing exams). Much later in the day I got my own copy of the paper and found that while Rowland was right and I was not in the list of Passes, I was in the list of Credits. Ever since, when I don't like what I am told (medical news, for example), I am slow to believe the worst.

Emmaus Bible School

An important new development among the Brethren in Sydney (and crucial, as it turned out, for my own career) was the creation of a Bible school for training of missionaries and other church workers (no paid pastors, though, among the Brethren). It was an affiliate of Emmaus Bible School in Oak Park, Illinois, in the Chicago region (and now in Dubuque, Iowa), which had begun as a correspondence school for soldiers in World War II seeking systematic Bible teaching. An outpost of the correspondence school had been established in Sydney in the 1950s, and I had played a small part in it. In this way: the modules of instruction were cyclostyled (mimeographed) in the offices near Central Station, Sydney, and I was one of those who carried the materials home in order to compile the sets of booklets that were to be sent out in each mailing. Like the oranges from Central, the Emmaus papers were a heavy burden to get home, but they were something to occupy me (sometimes a party of us) on wet Sunday afternoons (not all occupations were suitable for a Sunday, you may remember).

When the Bible School proper began in the late 50s, my father, being one of the leading 'ministering brethren' in Sydney, was naturally invited to do some of the teaching (gratis of course), and was happy to transfer his verse by verse Bible teaching from the setting of the local churches to the even more appropriate setting of the Bible school.

Chapter 5. Sydney University (1956–1961)

By the end of the 50s, perhaps in 1959 or 1960, I was added to the roster of teachers, in the first place to teach Greek and Hebrew (I was the only person among the Brethren in Sydney who had studied those languages at university). Later I added Old Testament Theology and Church History (the latter in the steps of F.F. Bruce).

Old Testament Theology was my favourite course, for I was teaching myself each week ahead of the class wide areas of Hebrew Bible knowledge. My handbooks were Norman Snaith's *Distinctive Ideas of the Old Testament* (1944), and G.A.F. Knight's A *Christian Theology of the Old Testament* (1959). Von Rad's *Old Testament Theology* would not appear in English until 1962 and 1965, and Eichrodt's similarly entitled volume until 1967, by which time I had left Australia. I loved the linguistic foundations of the treatments by Snaith and Knight of these overarching themes of the Hebrew Bible, and felt that my students were beginning to experience the deep resource these biblical books could prove for their theological reflection (hitherto among the Brethren the Old Testament had been very largely treated as allegory, with special focus on the structure and contents of the tabernacle, or as moral instruction, with the lives of the patriarchs never quite getting the critical attention they deserved). If I did one thing at Emmaus, it was to introduce the students to the Old Testament as a book about God.

As for Greek and the Hebrew, there was no dumbing down of these biblical languages, nor could there be. But in dealing with students of various ages, from many backgrounds, who were sitting in my class not for academic reasons but because of their desire to understand their scriptures more exactly, I came to formulate different goals in language learning than those I had been subject to at school and university. The focus at Emmaus had to be the students and their needs and capacities, and a lot of the traditional content of biblical language courses, like learning verbal paradigms, had to be junked. I wanted to get them reading the biblical texts, and it was no shame for them to use interlinear translations or to make intelligent guesses about where a sentence was heading.

I learned at Emmaus the rewards of teaching mediocre and below average students. Brilliant and averagely capable students did not need me; they would succeed without my input. But the floundering students could become with timely help flourishing students. I remember one, a former pig farmer from Victoria, whom the IQ test the principal had unwisely subjected all the students to (and, even more unwisely, told them their results) marked out as distinctly unacademic, was determined to persevere. It was his Bible, and he was going to teach the Bible to others, so he would get hold of the Greek if it killed him. He knew I was on his side, and not his judge, and he stubbornly stuck to his last. He never became a scholar of any kind, but he passed the exam, and, though it was the only foreign language he knew, he could certainly say he knew (some) Greek.

Christian Youth Camps (CYC)

Quite another activity of my Sydney schooldays was my involvement with the youth camps the Brethren in Sydney ran. They had two main sites, one at Toukley on the Central Coast between Sydney and Newcastle, the other at Mount Victoria, one of the Blue Mountains communities. In this village, 1000 m above sea level, and 75 miles (120 km) west of Sydney, a holiday venue of cabins in the bush for children and young adults was being used while still under construction in the 1950s. Much of the work on the site was done by voluntary labour; groups of 10 or 15 from local Brethren churches in Sydney would drive up on a Saturday, spend the day in building work (every able-bodied Australian male could at least run a cement mixer or nail weatherboard planks on to the wall of a cabin), and drive home after dark.

Some years I would be a staff member on one of these adventure holidays for children between 8 and 16 years. Other years, I would be a kitchen assistant to two delightful elderly women, one stout, the other thin as a rake, peeling potatoes from morn to night and washing up pots and pans and dishes at all hours. The mountain air, the freedom of the bush, the camaraderie, made these weeks into five-star holidays for me.

One of my most shaming moments was at such a camp, where I had to deal with a young trouble-maker. With all the force of my office, I told him to stand in a corner until I came back. But I quite forgot about him, and when I went back hours later he was still there. He got his praise for his fidelity to his post, but to that day I have never forgiven myself.

Classical productions

The 1950s and 1960s were a good time for classical studies in Sydney; for 13 years the undergraduate Classical Society mounted each year a Greek or Latin play in the original, which was attended largely by school audiences. The greatest excitement was the production in 1959 of Menander's *Dyskolos* (*The Old Curmudgeon*).

Menander, a fourth-century BCE Greek dramatist and the best-known representative of Athenian New Comedy, wrote over 100 comedies, almost all of which have been lost (Paul quoted Menander in 1 Corinthians 15.33 'Bad company corrupts good character'). But in 1959, a Greek papyrus from Egypt was published containing an almost complete text of his *Dyskolos*, first performed in 317–316 BCE. The story of how the play was given its first performance in Greek in modern times by the Sydney student society is recounted breathlessly by two of the participants in the production, Christopher Flynn and John Sheldon, my contemporaries (Sheldon was my companion on our voyage to Europe, of which more anon).[2]

Copies of the play reached Sydney in March 1959, and the performance was scheduled for July. The academics got busy on mending (which is to say, emending) the papyrus text, which was not at all pristine (one of the original characters had to be restored, and the text was improved in some other 90-odd places), while the producers and cast were becoming familiar with the play itself. Everyone in the Greek and Latin departments seemed to have been involved in the production. While scheduled lectures went on, no one was expecting essays and class work to be handed in. As for the *Dyskolos* itself, even getting hold of a copy of the text was a hurdle, for photocopiers were unheard of, and people had to rely on faint carbon copies of the play typed out by the departmental secretary until someone managed to get actual photos of the pages made for the actors.

It was only at the time of the performance that we learned that our production of *Dyskolos* had been anticipated by another, four weeks earlier in Geneva; but since that production was in a French translation, Sydney retained the honour of the first performance in Greek in the modern world.

I was one of the prompters for *Dyskolos* (I never played a part in any of the productions, too shy perhaps, or else, more likely, patently unsuitable).

For our next play, in 1960, the comedy *Rudens* (*The Rope*) by the Roman playwright Plautus (254–184 BCE), I was also a prompter, but I had as well prepared a translation of the play, typed it on waxed stencils for cyclostyling, duplicated 300+ copies, and collated them for sale to the mostly school audience so that they could follow the plot. That 43-page foolscap production became the first item in my list of publications. It was not a stuffy nineteenth-century translation such as you might find in the Loeb Classical Library, but modern and amusing, so I hoped. I wish I could lay my hands on it now, to see how I would judge it today.

---

2. Christopher Flynn and John Sheldon, 'Menander's Dyskolos at Sydney, 1959–2009', *Antichthon: Journal of the Australian Society for Classical Studies* 44 (2010), pp. 111-27.

Travel to Cambridge

Since at least the 1920s, the Cooper Travelling Scholarship has funded a number of young classicists to travel to the United Kingdom for postgraduate study. It has been available only every other year, so although I knew in 1959 that I had a good chance of being awarded it, I had to wait until 1960 for it to eventuate. I used the spare year to add a Honours degree in Latin to my Honours in Greek.

The scholarship, which was for two years, would pay for my tuition and lodging in Cambridge, and give me a maintenance allowance of about £1000 per year, a handsome sum even more (I think) than I was to receive as an Assistant Lecturer in my first teaching job in Sheffield.

I left Sydney on 2 September 1961, in time for the start of the academic year in England in October. In future years, my mother would ring me on that very date, saying, I thought you would like to be reminded, David, that this is the day you ran away from home. She was teasing, of course, but her language was not unserious. When I left, it was only for two years, since I had no funding and no prospects beyond that time. My brother Peter was my best friend, and the separation was a wrench for us both. It was only gradually that it became obvious that it was going to be a permanent move. My father and mother and brother had known only of our tight-knit family of four.

It was long before I could afford to travel to Australia to see them, but my mother organized between then and her death altogether, I think, 13 expeditions to Europe, always in order to see me and my family, and we had many good times with them on the continent of Europe and in the UK during their visits.

Chapter 6

CAMBRIDGE (1961–1964)

Sailing to Europe

As I have said, I left Sydney at the beginning of September 1961 for Cambridge. In those days, only very rich people travelled between Australia and the UK by plane, and almost everyone went by ship, in First or Tourist berths.

It happened that the most convenient passage was on board the rakish S.S. Oriana, only nine months since its first voyage, and the largest and fastest of the ocean liners on the Australia–UK run. Oriana could sail at 30 knots and weighed 42,000 tons (the modern cruise ship Royal Caribbean's Symphony of the Seas is more than five times bigger at 228,000 tons). But in 1961 Oriana was the last word in technology and sophistication.

What is more, bookings for travel from Australia would fall off in the European autumn, for who wanted to be in Europe during their awful winters? There were cabins going empty. The Orient Line was therefore in the habit of giving free passages each year to 25 Australian students travelling to the UK for postgraduate study. And since the unoccupied cabins were mostly in First Class, they were the cabins we were assigned, dining in style each day. I had hardly ever eaten in a real restaurant before, so the voyage was nothing if not an education.

My companion in my travel to Europe was John Sheldon, a Sydney classicist like myself. After his degree at St John's in Cambridge, John became Master of the Lower School at Sydney Grammar School (one of the Great Public Schools) from 1969 to 2001. He has been by all accounts a charismatic teacher, not only of Greek and Latin but also of Sanskrit (not elsewhere taught to school pupils in Australia, I imagine), a language we had both begun in Sydney with Professor Treweek. After his retirement John devoted himself to Indo-Iranian and other exotic languages, a study that issued in his magisterial *Texts of Greek and Latin Authors on the Far East* (2012).

The route from Sydney was to Melbourne, Fremantle (the port of Perth), Colombo (Ceylon, now Sri Lanka), Suez, Port Said, Naples, and Southampton. John and I had decided to leave the ship at Naples and travel overland by train to the UK, our first taste of Europe. John, whose family had some experience of European travel, had organized, as I remember, the whole of our itinerary, and I was happy to fit in with the plan. After Naples, the Oriana continued on its way to the UK, and our luggage would be sent up from Southampton to Cambridge.

The ten-day trip from Naples to Cambridge was an unforgettable adventure, and decidedly the best introduction to Europe we could have designed. Of Naples I recall only the offer on the quayside of an idler's sister, very clean—which confirmed the depth of depravity of the Europeans I had suspected.

Rome was remarkable to me for the compactness of its ancient centre. Even after ten years of Latin study, I had acquired no idea of its layout (it was not necessary for translation!), that the Colosseum was at the foot of the Palatine Hill, and the arch of Titus only a stone's throw away, and so on. I so much wanted to master the antiquities, and linger among them, but never to this day have I found myself in Rome with enough spare time.

In Milan and Cologne we climbed to the cathedral roof, at sunset, and felt quite grand as we took in the view of these close-packed and rather treeless European cities. In Switzerland, we had paused overnight in Lucerne, with its views of the Rigi and its ancient covered bridge over the Reuss. It was everything I imagined Switzerland to be, and I would come back many times.

I think that of all the European cities of this whistle-stop tour I was most taken by Paris, to which I could not wait to return. Perhaps it was to do with my comparative facility with the language, but I even now feel, though I have been there rarely in recent decades, that I am more at home there than in many great European cities.

On this journey, I barely noticed London, for I was eager to get to Cambridge, and knew I would be able to visit and explore the city many times in the future.

Setting foot in Britain

John had business to do in Paris, so we parted there, and I took the train one morning from the Gare du Nord to London via the ferry.

My first experience of England was troubling. Arriving in Dover, I went to the station for a London train. Having nothing with me to read, I thought I should buy a newspaper, but when I got to the newsstand and saw a plenitude of titles, I was frozen for a moment. The only English newspaper I knew the name of was *The Times,* and so I asked for it. The man in the booth said, Oh, one of the toffs, are we?—which was a great shock to me. I hadn't realized that your choice of newspaper was a signal of your social status, or class—or, as in this case, your claimed or alleged class. In Australia, there were morning papers and evening papers, and nothing was signified by which you chose. In Britain, I learned that day, it was a marker of class. On other days, I learned that almost everything else also was a marker of class.

My second experience was a curious inversion of the English class system: it was an experience of Australian snobbery, strange though that concept may seem. As we were approaching London, I judged that we were still 15 minutes from our terminus, and so perhaps 12 or 15 miles from the centre. Looking out the window, I saw nothing but semi-detached houses and terraced houses, and I thought, Isn't it amazing how far out the London slums extend? In Australia, in the 1950s at least, the ideal home was a detached house on its own block of land. Terraced and semi-detached houses (there were virtually none of either type in Oatley) belonged to the older inner-city suburbs, which I thoughtlessly called slums.

I tell this story against myself, for the suburb I was passing through was Purley, where properties today like those I saw from the train are in the range of £500,000 to £1m, certainly no slums. In fact I live now in a terraced house, and I am not slumming it.

Another class story is from my first evening meal in College. In the dining hall, we sat on benches at long refectory tables. As I sat down, I mouthed some greeting to the chap already sitting opposite me. He replied, I don't believe we have been introduced. I'm sure we will be at the right time and in the right way. A fellow undergraduate! Perhaps he was pulling my leg, but it was the end of the conversation, as you can imagine.

Yet another class story comes from my first weeks in Cambridge, where I was talking to the cleaner at the faculty building where I took my Hebrew classes. She asked me if I would lock the back door after she had gone, which I was happy to do. But, I asked her, Why don't you lock the door yourself and go out the front door? Oh no, she said, I could never go out the same door as the professors come in.

Oh, and a final class story, from my first visit to the hairdresser in All Saints Passage opposite St John's. Do you go sometimes for a walk on the Backs?, I asked him (the Backs of the colleges being where the colleges abut the river Cam, various paths criss-crossing the area). Oh no, he said, that's not for the likes of me. So he had never been 200 yards from his salon to a picture-postcard view of Cambridge which was accessible to all and sundry (later on, the colleges excluded visitors from their precincts at certain times of the day)—on the ground of his class. He never failed to ask me, however, at the end of our session, whether there was anything I wanted for the weekend, a puzzling question from a hairdresser, I thought, but when I came to understand it, a source of bemusement at the thought that the English had sex only at weekends.

Living in Cambridge

I arrived in Cambridge. I entered by the Great Gate of St John's College, with its massive wooden door that would be shut at 11 at night, made myself known at the old Porters' Lodge on the right, got the key to my room, crossed First Court with the Victorian chapel on the right, and immediately came to the staircase that would lead to my room. There was no interconnection between the staircases; each led only to 10 or so rooms. At the foot of the staircase, the names of its residents had been freshly painted in white on a black background, and there was D J A Clines. I had arrived.

My room was on the second floor, above the kitchens, as it happened, though I never caught sound nor smell from them. From the window I looked into Second Court, in some ways the most perfect of Cambridge courtyards, sometimes called the finest Tudor court in England. First Court had been constructed in the sixteenth century, Second Court at the very beginning of the seventeenth, Third Court with its Old Library later on in the seventeenth. Directly opposite me, on the western side of Second Court, was the imposing Shrewsbury Tower, a gatehouse leading to Third Court, and a mirror image of the College's Great Gate. Everything was so astonishing that I don't think I properly realized what a prime piece of real estate I was to inhabit that year.

The bed-sitting room itself had been recently modernized, with a gyp (a small kitchen) and background central heating. There was a gas ring in the kitchen, and I could heat a tin of baked beans on it. But I was never warm enough in the winter, and always sat at might desk with my feet on a hot water bottle replenished every hour.

On my way back to my room from morning classes in the Oriental Institute, I would walk through the market square and always buy a secondhand book for lunch. Later, my family would laugh at my acquisitions: Why did you ever buy a book called *The American Christmas*? As I would near the college, the little shop opposite St John's would supply a pork pie (replacement for the Australian meat pie) and a loaf of bread, and I would have my lunch, and finish my book before getting back to work.

Dinner was in the Hall. You were charged for it whether or not you showed up, so there was every incentive to eat there, usually, in my case, at the 6.30 sitting. Afterwards, I tended to socialize with other Australians, which was a very short-sighted thing to do, I know, but it was a way of relieving our frustrations at the quaintness or idiocy of the local population.

The Junior Common Room had a good collection of classical records for borrowing for a month or so, and I kept renewing the Bach unaccompanied cello suites that I couldn't get enough of. I was happily self-sufficient, working quite hard at my set texts.

Every month or so I would go to London for the day to trawl through the National Gallery or the Tate. I bought all the guidebooks, but they invariably disappointed me because they said nothing about the paintings themselves but only gave information about their date and provenance. It was just like biblical studies, I came to realize: the historical criticism had overwhelmed what should have been (I thought) the true object of study. The average visitor to an art gallery, I calculated one day, spends an hour viewing 10 paintings in each of 20 rooms, and so 15 or 20 seconds in front of each painting. Against the norm, I would find a seat in a gallery, take out my notebook, and record my impressions of my chosen works, no more than three or four in an afternoon. I had invented my own version of reader-response criticism, as we call it in biblical studies, before the term was created. As for synchronic reading of texts, that was a hobby I was preparing for on fine Saturdays, when I would explore inner London on foot, getting a good sense of how it was connected together, what its parts were and how one street led to another, a synchronic reading of the city.

Hebrew in Cambridge

My five years of undergraduate study in Sydney and my first-class honours in Latin and Greek counted for little in Cambridge. I was obliged to become an undergraduate again, wear the short gown of undergraduates, and recognize that I would be for yet another two years *in statu pupillari*. Admittedly, I was changing subjects, from Classics to Hebrew and Aramaic, so it was perhaps not entirely surprising that I found myself reading for Part II of the Tripos in Oriental Studies (skipping Part I). Anywhere else, though, I think I would have by now been a postgraduate student.

Hebrew meant the whole range of pre-modern Hebrew, so it was not just Biblical Hebrew that I was to become proficient in. The curriculum included, as far as I remember, Isaiah 40–55, Jeremiah 1–20, Semitic

Epigraphy, Mishnah *Berakot*, extracts from Maimonides and Rashi, and no doubt other texts I have forgotten.

Most of the teaching of Hebrew took place in the Oriental Institute, the ugliest building in Cambridge, I claimed, on Brooklands Avenue out beyond the station. A three-storey edifice, it was built of a dirty grey Cambridge brick (it still stands). It was a good 20-minute walk from St John's (I didn't ride a bicycle; see later), but the bus to the station stopped right outside the college and took me to within a block of the Institute. The Spartan classrooms were on the ground floor or else in the basement; I would not have travelled across the world for such a destination had I known about it.

Teachers

D. Winton Thomas

Winton Thomas, as he was known to everyone, used his second given name to distinguish himself from the many Thomases of his native Wales; his surname was Thomas, not Winton Thomas, and I have had to correct many a bibliography or index to that form. A well-built man, he had played rugby for Wales. He was to my mind an ideal scholar, very learned, totally clear, and modest. He took us through the set chapters of Second Isaiah, introducing us to many proposals for new interpretations of the Hebrew in the light in comparative Semitics. He had been a pupil of Geoffrey Driver of Oxford, and followed his methods, entitling his inaugural lecture in Cambridge *The Recovery of the Ancient Hebrew Language* (1939). Driver and he felt they were embarked on a mission to re-discover the genuine ancient Hebrew language, which had been, to a significant extent, misunderstood by the Masoretes who preserved for us the text of the Hebrew Bible.

Of Winton Thomas I came to realize that If philology was his focus, it was also his horizon. That was never more evident than when we got to Isaiah 43:18-19:

Remember not the former things, nor consider the things of old.

Behold, I am doing a new thing; now it springs forth, do you not perceive it?

These to me were stunning sentences, which put the Exodus and all the events of past 'salvation history' (as we called it in those days) in a category subordinate to the 'new thing' the prophet was announcing. But when we reached the verse in class, Winton Thomas calmly remarked, 'Well, there's nothing of interest there', and moved on immediately to the next verse.

Chapter 6. *Cambridge (1961–1964)*

He meant, of course, that there was no philological or textual problem in need of solution, nothing that Driver and he could improve, and so he was speechless.

Some days he would come into the classroom waving a postcard he had just had from Driver, with a new suggestion for some crux, perhaps in our very text. Not all of Driver's suggestions were inspired, but I cannot deny the excitement of witnessing Hebrew philology as a living discipline, constantly promising a better, more authentic understanding of the ancient texts. I wanted to be part of it.

I will return to Winton Thomas and his work for the Hebrew Dictionary later. A prolific scholar, he never wrote a book (apart from his *Text of the Revised Psalter* [1963], a list of emendations and philological decisions he adopted for his revision of the Psalms for the Book of Common Prayer, and his edition of Isaiah for the *Biblica hebraica stuttgartensia* [1968], the standard scholarly edition of the text of the Hebrew Bible). Few of the Hebrew scholars I looked up to, and tried to emulate, published books. They believed that scholarship was advanced by small steps, incrementally, which is to say, by articles in the learned journals. Unspoken was a sense that people who wrote books were self-advertising, perhaps somewhat shallow, certainly generalists in too much of a hurry to be deep scholars. I did not subscribe to that view, but I have found myself all my life more comfortable with writing articles rather than books. Sometimes I put this down to a low boredom threshold, but the fact is that of all the books I have published only two could be called proper monographs (I except commentaries).

Winton Thomas had an interesting habit when publishing his articles on Hebrew words. In a note for the *Journal of Theological Studies*, for example, he would suggest a new meaning for a well-known word in a particular passage, and then a couple of years later suggest the same meaning in a different verse, and repeat the process (he did this especially with his articles on the verb *yada'*, usually understood as 'know', but explained by him in the light of Arabic as a different verb, 'humiliate, chastise'). I think this habit of his arose from his modesty: he wanted to see if his original proposal gained any assent before going further with it. However, in my experience, feedback on one's publications is invariably meagre, and I wonder if he was just waiting to check that his proposal was not being shot down in flames. Today, this system of publishing is called salami publishing, slicing one idea up into many small articles so as to expand one's CV. I am sure that this would not have been Winton Thomas's motivation.

J.L. Teicher

He was an unusual scholar of rabbinics, heterodox about the Dead Sea Scrolls, which he always referred to in class as 'the Christian scrolls' (everyone else believed they were Jewish). He was about to publish an influential paper, in which he purported to show that a manuscript of prayers from the third-century CE Dura-Europos synagogue were in fact Christian prayers in Hebrew and that the Dura-Europos synagogue was not a synagogue at all but a Christian church.[1]

Teicher, who was supposed to be reading the Mishnah with us, treated us rather to weekly examples of rabbinic thinking and argumentation arising from any kind of incident in daily life, including memorably a disquisition on whether a pram being pushed across a pedestrian crossing constituted a vehicle from the point of view of the road traffic laws. It was very instructive, in its way, even if it was as unsystematic as it could possibly have been.

David Diringer

David Diringer (1900–1975), had been educated in Florence, and came to Cambridge in 1948. He was Reader in Semitic Epigraphy, and had an international reputation for his work on the alphabet, which he saw as a key to the history of humanity (the subtitle of his 1948 book *The Alphabet* was *A Key to the History of Mankind*). It was an adventure to be escorted around his Alphabet Museum, a large structure in the back garden of his house, where he displayed the various alphabets of the world. He had published in 1934 his *Le iscrizioni antico-ebraiche palestinesi*, a collection of all then known Hebrew inscriptions. We read with him all the famous Hebrew inscriptions, like that from the Siloam tunnel, but I am not sure that he kept completely up with the latest literature. I do remember that at our first class, as we sat around a large square table, I could read his lecture notes upside down (which I had a certain facility for). They had evidently been composed (with help) when he first came to Britain, for they began, 'Before I begin this lecture proper, I should like to make a few preliminary remarks …' Sebastian Brock was in this class, so I remember, along with David Marcus and Gareth Lloyd Jones and myself.

E.I.J. Rosenthal

I had two personal tutors, Rosenthal in my first year, Bullough in my second. I would visit them once a week during term time for an hour of

---

1. 'Ancient Eucharistic Prayers in Hebrew (*Dura-Europos* Parchment D. Pg. 25), Jewish Quarterly Review 54 (1963), pp. 99-109.

their time. Rosenthal (1904–1991), a graduate of Heidelberg and Berlin, had come to the UK from Nazi Germany in 1933, and was Reader in Oriental Studies. He was a prolific scholar, and a noted expert on mediaeval Jewish–Islamic relations, with his *Political Thought in Medieval Islam* (1958) and his *Judaism and Islam* (1961). He lived in a terraced house on the Chesterton Road; I would take a leisurely walk to it from St John's across Midsummer Common and over the Cam, and relish my good fortune at being able to spend an hour on a verse or two of Jeremiah.

Why he should have been tutoring me on Jeremiah 1–20 I do not know, since the Bible was a long way from his own specialisms, but I learned a lot from how he went about our sessions. I would bring him my queries about the text, and he would say, Well, let's see what Rudolph (in his 1958 commentary, the latest word in 1961, of course) has to say about it, and then, How did the Septuagint handle it?, What have BDB to say? It would be a worked example of how to go about a scholarly enquiry.

Sebastian Bullough

Fr Bullough, OP (1910–1967) was a most interesting character. His father had been professor of Italian at Cambridge, and his mother was the daughter of the famous Italian actress Eleanora Duse. He himself was a member of the Blackfriars, the Dominican Order of Preachers, who in Cambridge resided in the Bulloughs's family home which the family had left to the order. He always appeared in his white habit, but I don't remember the black cloak that was traditionally worn over it by Blackfriars. Tutorials with him did not always stick to the ostensible subject, but to be in his company was itself an educational experience. An author of many works, he was especially delighted to have been asked to write the Pelican volume on Roman Catholicism (in general!). One reviewer called it 'benign and affable', two terms that ideally characterized Sebastian Bullough himself. I was very fond of him myself, and my son Jeremy has Sebastian as a forename in tribute to him, as well as to J.S. Bach, who remains my all-time favourite composer. Sebastian Bullough sadly died at the very early age of 57.

Aramaic/Syriac

As far as I can recall, I had no formal instruction in Aramaic or Syriac in Cambridge; we were expected to handle these languages for ourselves, and so we did, though not without a little support. We must have read some Targum text; perhaps it was Proverbs 20–30, of which I remember writing out the Masoretic text, the Targum, the Septuagint and the Peshitta of each verse, to my surprise and profit. I remember also reading Targum Neofiti on Genesis, but don't know now if that was one of the set texts.

Among the Syriac texts was the somewhat hagiographic *Life of Rabbula*, the fifth-century bishop of Edessa, who had translated the Gospels into Syriac before the Peshitta version was made. There was just one copy of the text in the University Library, and before the advent of the photocopier I had to have photographic copies made in the basement of the Library in order to read the set text; nothing was made easy for the student in those days. There were also some homiletic poems, seven syllables to the line, of the fifth-century Isaac of Antioch. And we read Matthew Black's edition of *A Christian Palestinian Syriac Horologion* (1954).

The support we had for Syriac was from the Revd A.E. Goodman, a kindly man who had earlier worked on Syriac manuscripts and was now the vicar of a Cambridgeshire church. The three of us students reading the Syriac texts would foregather before our scheduled classes with him and share (and often solve) our points of difficulty with one another. Then we would take any still remaining problems to him. It was a tall order for him to be confronted only with the knottiest sentences pulled out of their contexts, and I have every sympathy with his reaction one day: Well, I used to be able to translate this; perhaps if you don't press me, I shall be able to do it again. Reading the Syriac Fathers was all a matter of translation, you will understand, and we never had to engage further with Rabbula and his peers than the words on the page.

Dr J.M. Munn-Rankin (1913–1981) was the other scholar we encountered in the Aramaic side of our curriculum. She was an archaeologist and historian of the ancient Near East, a fellow of Newnham College, and the Faculty of Oriental Studies' all-round orientalist. She did not publish much, but her chapter on 'Assyrian Military Power, 1300–1200 BCE' in the Cambridge Ancient History was praised. I know I wrote an indifferent essay on the Aramaeans for her, but I don't remember any lectures on what was not especially her subject. There was a paper in my Finals on the Aramaeans, which I probably did not excel in. Dr Munn-Rankin was the only woman scholar who ever taught me; it was still an almost exclusively male world.

J.V. Kinnier Wilson (b. 1921), the longest-lived of my Cambridge teachers, is a distinguished Assyriologist, an authority both on Mesopotamian myths and legends and on Mesopotamian diseases (his father was a noted neurologist). When I was in my first year of research (1963–1964) I took a class from him in elementary Akkadian, which I knew would be beneficial to me as a budding Hebrew Bible scholar. I gave up too soon, because he wanted us to learn the cuneiform script, which was more than

I had the energy or desire for; I would have been content with Akkadian in transliteration, and so I unfortunately missed out on adding another string to my bow.

All in all, the faculty in Cambridge were not what I had expected. Winton Thomas aside, none of the lecturers were teaching in their own fields of specialism, and I gained no sense of the onward march of scholarship, of current trends, or indeed of what might have been said to be the field, let alone the guild of practising scholars. Perhaps I expected too much, but my dream of a faculty of like-minded scholars with a common purpose was a realizable one, I later came to find. It was not to be found in Cambridge.

Tyndale House

The brightest spot in my Cambridge existence was the presence of Tyndale House, a residential library in a quiet backwater on the western edge of Cambridge, just beyond Grange Road. Tyndale House was founded in 1944 by evangelical scholars as a library for research in biblical studies, and it holds an unrivalled collection of germane books and journals. For a person like myself, both as a student and later as an academic, it was the most convenient place I have encountered to do the kind of research I want to undertake. Cambridge University Library, a couple of hundred yards away, is a much larger library, but it is the opposite of compact: its holdings are spread over many floors, and its corridors ensure that a day's research there will improve one's physical fitness as well as wasting a lot of time. At Tyndale, on the other hand, all you are likely to need will be within a few steps of your desk.

When I was in Cambridge in 1961–1964, I frequently visited Tyndale House library in my first and third years, and became a resident in my second. An evening meal was served for residents, and I would walk to the University Library or Newnham College for lunch. The arrangements for residents using the library were very informal: there was no closing time, and the last person out switched off the lights. You could keep your library books and personal materials from day to day in the workspaces beside the shelves known as carrels. Upstairs was a range of compact bedrooms. So ideal was the setting that I proposed translating John 14.2 as 'In my Father's house are many carrels' since the idea of heaven as a residential library was very appealing.

When I announced to my tutor, John Crook, that I was proposing to move to Tyndale House for my second year in Cambridge, he was not a little alarmed at the prospect of my removing myself from the hurly-burly of the College to some sectarian bolt hole. But I persevered, and I am glad I did. It was not only the perfect environment for study, there was also a lounge for coffee and tea, which served as a common room throughout the day; one could always go to relax there and find some congenial company.

Not always, though. One coffee morning I remember, though from a later time, when I was spending some sabbatical weeks at Tyndale. This was the day the USA bombed Gaddafi's Libya in April 1986. One American researcher at Tyndale (Wayne Grudem, whom I never got on with, and not just on this subject) was full of zeal in support of Reagan's action, while I was inflamed at the USA's belief that it had been appointed the world's police force.

Examinations

My two years reading for the Tripos Part II came to an end in June 1963 with the final examinations. There were eight papers, two a day from Monday to Thursday. It was a trial not only of one's acuity but also of one's stamina. In Sydney I had always had a few days between exam papers, and could devote myself to revision exclusively for the next paper on the calendar. To prepare for eight papers simultaneously was a tall order. By the Thursday morning, I had even got wrong which paper would be in the exam room waiting for me, though it didn't much matter, since I was a bit shell-shocked.

When the results were announced, I was shocked to see that our gang of three, who I thought were all much of a muchness intellectually, had come out with a II/1, a II/2 and a III. I was even more distressed for the others than I was for myself.

Some weeks later, I bumped into Winton Thomas on the street outside the Post Office. He asked if I was content with the result. I replied that I was disappointed. He said, Ah well, it was a creditable performance for someone coming from so far away. — There were so many things wrong with that remark that have only gradually surfaced in my mind over the years, but that I will leave readers to figure out for themselves.[2]

Nevertheless, whatever the result of the examinations, they were a useless indicator of the academic quality of our gang of three, and their future careers. All three became professors of Hebrew, and prolific contributors to scholarship.

2. Another example of unthinking prejudice came when Winton Thomas's successor, Professor John Emerton, remarked when the subject of Australia came up in conversion, 'Oh, but Australia is so far away!', to which DJAC went, 'Oh, but in Australia Cambridge is exactly the same distinction!'.

Chapter 6. Cambridge (1961–1964)

David Marcus (b. 1941) is Professor of Bible and Masorahat at the Jewish Theological Seminary, New York., author of *Jephthah and his Vow, From Balaam to Jonah, Scribal Wit: The Aramaic Mnemonics of the Leningrad Codex, A Manual of Akkadian, A Manual of Jewish Babylonian Aramaic*, and editor of Ezra–Nehemiah in Biblia hebraica quinta, the new edition of the Hebrew Bible.

Gareth Lloyd Jones (b. 1938) became Professor of Hebrew and Old Testament and head of the School of Theology and Religious Studies at the University of Wales, Bangor, author of the groundbreaking *The Discovery of Hebrew in Tudor England: A Third Language*, together with a slew of publications on the Hebrew Bible in Welsh, which I sadly cannot read.

Beginning research

I was determined in begin PhD research, and Winton Thomas was happy to take me on. I had a list of a dozen or so possible topics, but I kept coming back to the Image of God in Genesis 1. It seemed a very important statement, perhaps somewhat unexpected in its context, and certainly very variously interpreted, so I thought it would be a good topic to try to get to the bottom of. Winton Thomas approved, and I started in with alacrity. I knew I would have to improve my German measurably, the unwieldy term Gottebenbildlichkeit or Gottesebenbildlichkeit for 'image of God' turning up with depressing regularity in all the German resources I was locating.

I made good headway, but, looking back on it, I would have before long had to address some recalcitrant issues I hadn't thought about then. First was to settle in my mind what position I was going to take on the Pentateuchal sources: if Genesis 1 was from the priestly source P I was going to have to come to grips with that literary strand, and take myself far away from Genesis 1. Second was to locate the image of God language in a broader context of language about God, about likeness, and about humanity.

My first typed offering to Winton Thomas came back to me with more red markings than I had ever seen in my life, and I was much discouraged. But then I discovered that most of them related to his conviction that a scholar should not mention the names of other scholars in the text of one's writing, but should say, It has been suggested by…, throwing all the bibliographical material into a footnote. I had never heard of this rule, and haven't ever encountered it again. Nevertheless, I was careful to observe it in future work for my supervisor. Winton Thomas was not a theologian, but he was perfectly capable of directing my work, and I appreciated his close attention to the detail of my tyro chapters.

My Marriage to Dawn Joseph

In December 1963 I married Dawn Naomi Joseph. She was by profession a nurse, and a graduate of Melbourne Bible College. She left Sydney in 1961 on her way to Paris to perfect her French in preparation for a role as a medical missionary to Chad in Central Africa (where there had been for some time other Brethren missionaries). I had met her a week before we were both leaving on the Oriana, but she was travelling Tourist Class whereas I had my swanky First Class passage courtesy of the shipping line. Passengers in the two classes were strictly separated, but there was a room common to both classes where a daily Bible study was held, and which I sometimes attended. Having found the route to the Bible study room, I was able at other times to socialize in the evenings with Tourist Class passengers, especially on the open rear deck of the ship, rather than with the giddy students in First Class.

After her year of French at the Institut Biblique in Nogent-sur-Marne on the eastern fringe of Paris, Dawn set off for Liverpool, for a course on tropical diseases. Thereafter, it gradually became apparent that she had a health condition that would make it inadvisable (and then, impossible) for her to live in tropical Africa, and she had to abandon her plans for work in Chad. Our friendship was free to develop into a romantic relationship, which it did in the course of 1963, and we married at the end of the year.

We were married in Queen Edith Chapel, Wulfstan Way, Cambridge, the officiant being Dr Leon Morris, another Australian, a New Testament scholar who was Warden of Tyndale House. His sermon was the longest and most thorough wedding address anyone could remember, but, with the rest of our lives before us, time was not of the essence.

We settled in a flat off Cherry Hinton Road, above a kindly landlady, who was glad to have a respectable married couple in her house, and not some rowdy students. They say that everyone remembers where they were when they heard of Kennedy's assassination; we were told by our landlady who came rushing out of her house to meet us in the street. Dawn found a Cambridge nursing job, while I was getting used to being a postgraduate student with a thesis. Within a few months, however, we were planning to move to Sheffield.

Cycling

I had never had a bicycle as a child; my mother feared that I would have some dreadful accident on the hilly streets of Oatley and be permanently disfigured. You might have thought that I would make up for the deficiency of not being able to ride once I got to flat Cambridge, but I never got

Chapter 6. *Cambridge (1961–1964)*

around to it. I must have been observing my unspoken rule: When at first you don't succeed, try something else. It was shaming when Dawn and I were out, and I had to run beside her to keep up with her merrily cycling ahead of me. Eventually this disparity in locomotion got the better of me, and one very foggy night, when we had got home via our dual system of travel, I seized her cycle, and warned her she would not see me again until I could ride a bike. With no one to watch my inelegant progress round the Cambridge suburbs, and no traffic around in the fog to endanger me, I was as good as my word, and came in half an hour later announcing I was now a cyclist, and cursing myself for having left it so long to learn.

Ironically, as I said above, within a few months, however, we were planning to move to Sheffield, hillier far than Oatley, and especially than Cambridge, and only suitable for daredevils on wheels.

A publication

An early publication from this period was my translation of a work by John à Lasco (1499–1560), a sixteenth-century Polish Reformer who lived in England for a decade. The Banner of Truth Trust, whose director Iain Murray commissioned and published my translation, is a conservative evangelical publisher largely responsible for the upsurge of interest in Puritan writing and spirituality since the 1960s. I was able to track down a manuscript copy of Lasco's brief essay on vestments in Cambridge University Library, in a beautifully clear hand (not the author's, I dare say), and translate it, as THE ABOLITION OF VESTMENTS (1965).[3] I had no personal interest in the subject matter, and the translation was nothing but 'prentice work, but it was quite exciting to bring a 400-year old tractate to life again and into a contemporary debate.

Appointment to Sheffield

One day in early 1964, Winton Thomas said to me, 'Do you know, there are five academic jobs in Old Testament advertised at the moment? When they are filled, it is likely to be a long time before there is another. I would advise you to start applying.' So I did. My first application got nowhere, but my second, to Sheffield, got me called for a interview.

So I came to Sheffield, on a bitter winter's day. The professor was Aileen Guilding, of whom more anon. She had arranged for me to stay overnight before the interview at Whirlow Conference Centre, on the southwest of

---

3. I will refer to my own publications in small caps, as here, and refer the reader to the list of my writings at this end of the present work for further details.

Sheffield. However, I had been invited to dinner with David Payne and his wife Jean. He was lecturer in the Department, having been appointed by F.F. Bruce,[4] and I had met him several times through the Tyndale Fellowship. He had no voice in the appointment I was applying for (such appointments were all professors' business), so it was not improper for me to fraternize. To get to Lodge Moor, where he lived, from Whirlow was two long bus journeys, which must have taken more than an hour. As the second bus climbed ever upward (Lodge Moor, at over 1000 feet, is said to be the highest suburb in Britain), the snow became heavier and heavier. At one point, the bus simply stopped for 15 minutes. However, I got there, had a lovely dinner, and got back to Whirlow, I suppose. I should have drawn some conclusions about the wisdom of seeking a job in such a desolate place, but I was young and foolish.

The next day, I found that I was one of two candidates for the post. The other was David Hill, who had completed his PhD in New Testament at St Andrews, and had a year at Union Theological Seminary in New York. He was obviously the better candidate. It was no surprise when Professor Guilding announced at the end of the day that he was being appointed. But, she said, I should not give up hope, for she was going to see whether she could make a second appointment also. How she wangled that, I do not know, but I suppose that she liked my background in both the Classics and Semitics and fancied having two new lecturers, in New Testament and Old Testament. She later confessed that when, in negotiations with the Dean of the Faculty, all else failed she was not averse to using the tactic of tears. Whether she did so on my account, I do not know. But she was successful in getting her second post.

---

4. See his brief memoir, 'F.F. Bruce as a Teacher', *Christian Brethren Research Fellowship Journal* 22 (1971), pp. 15-16,

Chapter 7

SHEFFIELD UNIVERSITY I (1964–1975)

I will divide my account of Sheffield life into three parts, though not because of any great disjunction between the parts, but to prevent this chapter from stretching out interminably.

I came to Sheffield in September 1964, and, apart from a year in California in 1973–1974, have lived here for the rest of my life. I was appointed Assistant Lecturer in Biblical History and Literature, and gradually progressed through the ranks of Lecturer, Senior Lecturer, and Reader before being appointed Professor in 1985. By that time the Department's name had been changed (in 1968) to the more manageable Department of Biblical Studies, which included theology and various other things that were neither history nor literature. The original title had been devised in order to exclude theology, since the University is a secular foundation and could not give the appearance of promoting any particular religious opinions. The Sheffield department, as it turned out, was not in danger of doing that. And the theology of the Bible was as open to critical examination as its history and literature were, and was as likely to be called ideology as theology.

It was not that there was any animus within the Department against the Church and theology. Nevertheless, the Department has been perhaps somewhat unusual among departments in the field of theology in having as tenuous a connection with the institutional Church as it does. The Department was glad to be part of a university that numbers among its statutes a prohibition of religious tests, and it has suited it well to be located in a Faculty of Arts along with History and English and Philosophy and Archaeology and the Modern Languages.[1] Sometimes we felt it a loss

---

1. A Dutch reviewer of a later departmental production, *The Bible in Three Dimensions* (1990), was moved to an exclamation mark by this fact: 'opgenomen in Letterenfaculteit en niet in die van Theologie!' (J.T.A.G.M. van Ruiten, *Bijdragen, tijdschift voor filosofie en theologie* 54 [1993], p. 199).

not to have had adjacent departments of theology or religion, and we have regretted the absence of colleagues (and library holdings) in those cognate fields. But that has been our lot, and we do not doubt that we have benefited from having no one to talk to except literary critics and philosophers and secular historians et hoc genus omne.

I have already told the story of my appointment, and can here include some other anecdotes about my first weeks and months in the Department. Aileen Guilding (1913–2006) was a fascinating and remarkable person, and I was very glad to have been able to edit, nearly 50 years later, with my colleague J. Cheryl Exum, a volume in her honour, *The Reception of the Hebrew Bible in the Septuagint and the New Testament: Essays in Memory of Aileen Guilding* (2013).[2] She was a very hands-on Head of Department. When I moved into my office, on the sixth floor of the Hicks Building, otherwise occupied by physicists, she came along and instructed me on the art of pulling up the blinds, and decided where exactly my wastepaper bin should be positioned.

One of my teaching assignments in my first term was a course on Genesis 1–11 for the second- and third-year students. Though I had come to Sheffield in September, my appointment was from 1 October, and I would not get any salary till the end of that month. However, Aileen Guilding demanded in mid-September to see my lecture notes in preparation for the course, and was alarmed to find that I did not have a script for the whole of the course. We don't work on a hand to mouth basis here, she thundered, and said she would consider taking the course back off me. It was only a week or so before the start of term when she relented and I found I was to teach the course after all.

She had the habit of knocking on the door, popping her head in, and saying, Mr Clines, could you come and see me in … 17 minutes time? There was nothing to be done in those 17 minutes but worry about what misdemeanour I may have committed. Sometimes, however, the summons was for a word of praise: she very much approved of my pedantic proofreading of examination papers, where great chunks of Hebrew and Greek had been set up in hot metal type (no doubt at vast expense) even for the exams at the end of the first term.

Aileen Guilding had the distinction of being the first female professor in the University of Sheffield, and the first in the UK in the whole field of theology. In those pre-feminist days, such an achievement was not properly recognized. But in more recent times she has been hailed, at least

---

2. I also contributed to it a brief memoir, 'Aileen Guilding: Her Life and her Work' (2013).

in my University, as a feminist icon. Like her predecessor F.F. Bruce, she was a precise textual scholar, with an intimate knowledge of the sources, rabbinic and Septuagintal as well as the two Testaments, but with an added flair for the grand ingenious theory. She looked in others for what she called 'top spin' (was it a cricketing or a tennis metaphor?), and she had it herself (I like to think she saw a hint of it in me too[3]). She quickly gained an international reputation for her first and only book, *The Fourth Gospel and Jewish Worship* (1960), where she propounded her theory that John's Gospel had been composed according to the sequence of a Jewish lectionary of the Pentateuch. Her theory found no long-term following, but the scholarship itself was massive and impeccable.

Against a background of a remarkably enthusiastic reception of her work, the publication in 1965 of a relentless and forensic, though even-tempered, critique must have been devastating. Leon L. Morris, whom I have mentioned above, and who had become by this time Principal of Ridley College in Melbourne, published a booklet, *The New Testament and the Jewish Lectionaries* (1964), entirely devoted to exposing weaknesses both in Aileen Guilding's underlying assumptions and in her application of them to the understanding of John's Gospel. Morris's booklet does not appear to have been widely reviewed, but its implications spread rapidly by word of mouth. One reviewer, J.R. Perkin, concluded:

The critical axe, wielded more in sorrow than anger, has been laid at the root of the once-flourishing lectionary tree. The blow was delivered with finesse and half-apologetically, but all the same it seems to have severed the roots.[4]

By the autumn of 1965, however, Aileen Guilding had retired from her chair on health grounds (she was to live to the age of 93). Though I don't think it can have had anything to do with Morris's review, the effect of her retirement on the tiny Department was somewhat shocking. It left only three lecturers, Payne, Hill and myself, two of us with less than a year's service, and the University was plainly not eager to commit itself to an appointment of a new professor, which would entail the continuance of the Department for the foreseeable future.

David Payne (b. 1931), who had been F.F. Bruce's first, and most brilliant, student, and a notable linguist, was appointed acting Head of Department. The University would have done better to make him Head of

---

3. It can have been no more than a hint, for she was very clear that I would 'be of no use to her until I had served five years' (her words).
4. *Scottish Journal of Theology* 19 (1966), pp. 236-37. A balanced reassessment has been provided by John Tudno Williams, 'The Fourth Gospel and Jewish Worship: Guilding's Theory Revisited', in *The Reception of the Hebrew Bible*, pp. 126-45.

Department and given him an extra member of staff in New Testament. Before long, David left the Department (1967) after an invitation to found a new department of Semitic Studies in the Queen's University, Belfast.

As it was, after a two-year interregnum, the University made an appointment to a chair in the person of James Atkinson, who had been Reader in Theology at Hull. We in the Department were initially rather alarmed at the appointment, since James was a specialist in Luther, and not really a biblical scholar at all. He proved extremely sympathetic to the remit of the Department, nevertheless, always stressing Luther's orientation to biblical interpretation (Luther was after all a Professor of Biblical Studies, he would always say). He batted well for the Department in the Faculty and the University, got it a most positive reputation as a place of good scholarship and fair-mindedness, and became University Orator, a thankless role obliging him to concoct laudatory speeches in praise of honorary graduands in every conceivable field—much appreciated by the University.

In the Department, he focused on his own writing, his classes, and his administration, and left the development of the curriculum and the department itself to his 'young men', as he liked to call the rest of us. We had carte blanche to organize the Department as we saw fit, and so we did. An emollient man, we never saw him cross; he esteemed his staff for their biblical expertise, and his trust did not go amiss.

Such were my earliest days in the Department.

Sheffield

Sheffield is one of England's major cities, but its precise ranking depends on what criteria are used to compare city sizes. After London, if we compare 'metropolitan counties', Sheffield is fifth, after Birmingham, Manchester, Leeds–Bradford, and Liverpool, with 1,343,000 inhabitants. If it is 'cities', it is third, after Birmingham and Leeds, with 553,000. If it is 'urban areas', i.e. continuously built-up zones, it is ninth, with 706,000 (and 701st in the world). If it is primary urban areas, it is fifth, with 819,000. And if it is metropolitan areas, it is sixth, with 1,569,000. These are more data than anyone probably wants to know. But they are instructive 'facts' to make students aware of when they are struggling with the uncertainties of biblical history.

The name Sheffield means 'field by the river Sheaf', 'field' being Old English 'feld', a forest clearing, and 'sheaf' being probably connected with Old English 'shed' meaning 'division' (as in 'watershed'). The Sheaf was certainly on the boundary between the Anglo-Saxon kingdoms of Mercia and Northumbria.

Sheffield's first mention in literature and the earliest reference to its cutlery and metalwork trade comes in Chaucer's fourteenth-century *Canterbury Tales*, where it is said of the quarrelsome miller of Trumpington (in the *Reeve's Tale*) that 'a Sheffeld thwitel baar he in his hose' (as well as a cutlass and a dagger in his belt and purse). A thwitel was a small knife.

Daniel Defoe, author of *Robinson Crusoe*, wrote of Sheffield in his *Tour thro' the Whole Island of Great Britain* (1726): 'This town of Sheffield is very populous and large, the streets narrow, and the houses dark and black, occasioned by the continued smoke of the forges, which are always at work: Here they make all sorts of cutlery-ware, but especially that of edged-tools, knives, razors, axes, &. and nails; and here the only mill of the sort, which was in use in England for some time was set up, (viz.) for turning their grindstones, though now 'tis grown more common.'

Innovation in Sheffield

Sheffield has been the home of important innovations connected with metal-working. In 1742, Benjamin Huntsman's 'crucible steel process' revolutionized the production of steel, creating tougher, high-quality steel. In the next 100 years, Sheffield's steel production rose from 200 tons to 80,000 tons, almost half Europe's total production.

In 1856, Henry Bessemer's converter furnace took things further, enabling mass production of cheap refined steel for railway parts, armour plating and construction. By 1870, Sheffield was producing three-quarters of the steel for the Navy's armour-plated ships, and the USA was importing over three times as much rail track from Sheffield as it made domestically.

In 1912, the Sheffield chemist Harry Brearley invented stainless steel (100% recyclable), which is now ubiquitous, in architecture, medicine, vehicles, jewelry and watches, and in the kitchen. And at the beginning of the 20th century, Robert Hadfield discovered manganese steel, an alloy much harder than traditional steel, now widely used.

Another Sheffield specialty, though it was not invented in Sheffield, is electro-plated nickel silver (EPNS), a copper alloy with nickel and zinc used in the manufacture of cutlery, giving it a lustrous sheen. In many parts of the world, a Sheffield visitor will lift a knife or fork from a host's dinner table, and note with satisfaction the name of its manufacturer stamped beneath, with the slogan EPNS A1, Sheffield England.

Quality

Innovation is not the only mark of Sheffield products. Sheffield has been from centuries a byword for its high-quality specialist products with a cutting edge such as knives and tools; everywhere else, 'at the cutting edge' has become almost a dead metaphor for ground-breaking work in general, but in Sheffield it retains a flavour of its original sense.

'Made in Sheffield' is a protected trademark for Sheffield's specialist products. Sheffield Phoenix Press, and Sheffield Academic Press before it, like any other company wanting to use the term 'Sheffield' in its name, had to apply to the Company of Cutlers in Hallamshire for permission to use the word 'Sheffield' in its name, since they insist on assuring themselves that the name of Sheffield is not being brought into disrepute by businesses that do not uphold Sheffield standards of quality.[5]

Green Sheffield

Industrial Sheffield, twinned with Pittsburgh for obvious reasons, has long had a reputation for its blackness and unhealthiness. In Victorian times children were working in the cutlery trades from as young as six or seven years old. A grinder of knives could expect to be dead at 25.

Today Sheffield boasts in being the greenest city in Europe, with 4.5 million trees (of course, a lot depends on where the city boundaries are drawn). There are indeed 800 green spaces in the city and 80 woodlands.

Living in Sheffield: Houses

Having found a house we could buy, we lived in two flats in Sheffield while we waited for the formalities to be completed. The first was in Pitsmoor, near the Northern General Hospital, and in the same street where the Urban Theology Unit would later be established (I will write of it later). The second was above a dentist's in School Road, Crookes.

When the purchase was complete, we moved into 27 Hallamshire Road, a three-year old house on the western edge of the city. Unlike Australian cities, which straggle on interminably into their surroundings, and whose edges are rarely clearly defined, British cities often come to a sudden halt

---

5. 'Throughout its history, Sheffield and its people have been recognized as inventive, hardworking and entrepreneurial. It is a city that prides itself on getting on with things, quietly but effectively, irrespective of the challenges', says the website for Made in Sheffield (www.madeinsheffield.org). I know this is advertising, but I lend it my assent.

at their edges, and there is no mistaking the boundary between town and country. The edge of Sheffield was just 100 yards down Hallamshire Road, and the house looked up over a valley and fields to the village of Ringinglow, a gateway to the Peak District. It was a three-bedroom semi, in a development of three parallel streets of houses all built to the same design. The novelty in them was that the houses were heated by warm air heated by gas in a kitchen cupboard. Only the downstairs rooms had a grill for the warm air to come out, but, guess what, heat rises, and the bedrooms were kept reasonably warm as well. I don't think I have seen another house in the UK with such a heating system, but it seemed to me a simplified improvement on the traditional system of boiler, pipes and radiators.

We covered all the floors with linoleum since we could not afford carpets, and we bought secondhand furniture. We had to buy a lawn-mower and a washing machine on hire purchase since my lecturer's salary did not stretch to such enormous expenditures. There was a garage, but no car. The gardens both front and back were in a rough state, as if little work had been done on them since the builders moved out, and there was plenty of Saturday work for the young householders to busy themselves with.

We paid £3,400 for the house, a little more than three times my salary. It is worth £300,000 today, about 10 times a starting lecturer's salary. How does such a person get a mortgage?

Provincial Sheffield

Now I was a provincial again, in the suburbs of a provincial city. I was delighted not to be living in a metropolis, with its congestion and noise (and pollution, though we seemed not to know about that then). I was almost smug about being an outsider, of a secondary status, not responsible by way of association for the idiocies of the state and its government. In fact, a few years later I would have urged everyone to become like me: live in the provinces, visit London only when necessary. London, you see, was to me the Wen, the boil or carbuncle on the face of England, as William Cobbett had called it in his *Rural Rides* (1830). I wrote:

> Be a provincial! Breakfast on country air
> From your gracious Victorian semi before your easy drive
> Four miles in ten minutes through empty suburban streets
> For the 7.20 Master Cutler to the Wen. Admire northern
> Atmosphere, crisp Sheffield air perpetually in motion,
> Prophylactic for the lank substitute you will ingest
> Between St Pancras and the faded squares of Bloomsbury.
> Your trifling academic business done, breathe a grateful prayer,
> Settling in your homebound 125, for life beyond the Trent.

The Master Cutler is one of a select band of named trains in England. It takes its name from the annually elected head of the Company of Cutlers in Hallamshire (an old name of Sheffield), established in 1624. By custom, the Master Cutler of the year rides on one journey with the driver of the train (actually on the footplate, in the days of steam). The hourly InterCity 125 (or, High Speed Train) connecting London and Sheffield is drawn by two diesel-powered locomotives at each end of the train (the Master Cutler returns at a later time of day than I had finished my business). The Trent, at Nottingham and Derby, is historically (and for me) the divider between north and south.

Sheffield Arts Tower

A great building project was underway at the University of Sheffield during my first year there. Every lunch time, as we waited for the lift on Floor 6 in the Hicks Building, we looked out across the road to the construction site for our new Arts Tower, to see how work was getting on. It would be home to the Department for three decades. The 22-storey building would house all 18 Arts departments (except English, which had a building of its own near the Drama Studio) and Architecture, and be the tallest building in Sheffield (it is now overtopped by St Paul's Tower on Arundel Gate, 23 m higher). It was called 'the most elegant university tower block in Britain of its period' and it gave a sense of importance to the Arts subjects in Sheffield which had always had a technological emphasis.

The work was begun by digging a vast hole for the basement and sub-basement, both of which floors would be used for windowless lecture rooms (a big mistake). When those levels had been completed, the storeys of the building were laid down in concrete one of top of the other, till all 20 storeys were piled up on one another. Then hydraulic equipment was brought in to raise first the top floor above the second-top floor, and so on until all the floors were the right distance apart, the building had attained its designed 78 m (255 feet) height, and the walls and glazing could be inserted. No one to whom I have told this story of the method of its construction in subsequent years has believed me, but I and my colleagues saw it happening, every day!

The Department of Biblical History and Literature moved into Floor 6 in September 1965, and the building was formally opened by Queen Elizabeth, the Queen Mother, in June 1966. It was the nearest I have ever been to any royal personage (for the record). We shared the floor with Spanish, a department much the size of our own, and had a delightful view over Weston Park, with its art gallery and museum, and a boating pond to boot. In the far distance there were glimpses of the western edge of the city and the fields where the Peak District began. I had a corner room, with several windows, which I soon filled with bookcases—except for one that gave me my view. There was enough space on Floor 6 to give us a common room for coffee and lunch, so important for creating and sustaining our *esprit de corps*, and a lecture room of our own, where our weekly postgraduate seminar would meet. There was some open corridor space as well where students could mingle or else hang out in the expectation of seeing a faculty member for a quick word or to make an appointment. At one of our annual departmental dinners, usually in a hotel in the Peak district, I remember proposing a paper (in the days when 'reading from this place' was becoming fashionable) on 'Psalm 6.1 from the Perspective of Room 6.1'. Not as good as many of the student skits and satires for such evenings: I remember the song 'My Old Man's a Dustman' from the Cain and Abel band, and the menu in the form of the title page of a Brill book, with the motto 'Semper plus pecunia' (always more money, not proper Latin, of course).

Paternoster

The Arts Tower was (moderately) famous for one of its methods of transportation, the Paternoster lift. It was a passenger lift consisting of a chain of open compartments, each designed for two people, moving slowly in a loop up and down without stopping. Passengers could step on or off at any floor they liked. There were also some traditional lifts in the Arts Tower, but the Paternoster, at 13 seconds per floor, was faster, especially for shorter journeys. The Paternoster could move 76 people at the same time, more than a double-decker bus. The Sheffield Paternoster, still is use, with its 38 cars, is the tallest example in the world.

The professor of Spanish, Frank Pierce, explained to me one day that in Spanish a string of tramcars is called a 'rosario', and the Paternoster (the 'Our Father') was evidently so called because of the arrangement of its cars on a continuous chain.

If you got on at one of the lower floors at a busy time, you would very likely be joined by a fellow passenger, whether known or unknown:

> Carolina! What a surprise!
> Will you join me for this dance?
> One hundred and thirty-two
> Seconds precisely and we will
> Step out, slope off, each to our
> Bookish cells, Floor 10.
> Meanwhile, will you be my partner?

> Lovely. Right foot forward. Step down.
> Follow with left foot, horizontal.
> Swing about, on your spot,
> Shuffle back, lean ever so
> Delicately, hand on the
> Aluminium wall.
> Now for one hundred and
> Twenty-three seconds of
> Waltz without hesitation,
> Repetition or irrelevance.

(The Department later moved up to Floor 10.) Only a few hundred Paternosters were built, mainly in Europe. There was one in the University of Newcastle, and one appeared from time to time in the Thames Television detective series, Van der Valk, at Amsterdam police headquarters in Marnixstraat; the series, aired originally between 1972 and 1992, is currently being repeated, a nostalgia fix for me.

Writing, 1964–1975

I am quite surprised, looking at the beginning of my publications list, how little I published in my first years in Sheffield. My first paper in a mainstream Old Testament journal came in 1972, eight years after my appointment. Today I might well have been thrown out before then, for lack of productivity.

It was not that I had done nothing. In 1968, the work I had done on my PhD was published as the Tyndale Lecture on THE IMAGE OF GOD IN MAN, all 50 pages of it (when it was reprinted 30 years later in *On the Way to the Postmodern* in 1998, the title had been transformed to HUMANITY AS THE IMAGE OF GOD, since it was quite rightly no longer acceptable to use 'man' when you meant 'humanity'). And I had done two further papers for the *Tyndale Bulletin* on PSALM RESEARCH SINCE 1955: I. THE PSALMS AND THE CULT (1967), and PSALM RESEARCH SINCE 1955: II. THE LITERARY GENRES (1969). But one of my Tyndale Fellowship buddies might have slipped me the word that it was not a good idea to publish my first three scholarly papers in the same journal, one moreover that bore the name of a particular religious outlook. I had written as well two long reviews of the *New English Bible*, the publishing sensation of 1970 that had now added the Old Testament to its 1961 translation of the New.

Yet I must have known that I would have to strike out into deeper waters. 1972 saw my X, X BEN Y, BEN Y: PERSONAL NAMES IN HEBREW

NARRATIVE STYLE in *Vetus Testamentum*, long after my Sydney teacher Colin MacLaurin had advised his pupils to send their bright ideas in that direction. It was my first foray into properly literary criticism of the Hebrew Bible, merely observing how Hebrew prose writers presented the names of their heroes at varying parts of their narrative. The full form of a name, X the son of Y, was used to introduce a new character, and to mark a transition from one character to another, while calling someone simply the son of Y was derogatory. There was no source criticism or historical criticism in the paper, just an analysis of formal style.

A little paper with a literary theme, THE TREE OF KNOWLEDGE AND THE LAW OF YAHWEH (PSALM XIX), appeared in 1974. I didn't know at the time that it belonged to the genre of intertextual studies, but its aim was simply to point to the benefit of reading the well-known Psalm 19 against the background of Genesis 3: the poet might well have been meditating on the contrast between the forbidden tree in Eden and the Torah, permitted and extolled, as a means of acquiring wisdom.

My greatest inspiration for a literary approach to the Hebrew Bible had been what I regarded as a stunning article by Joseph Blenkinsopp, 'Ballad Style and Psalm Style in the Song of Deborah',[6] though Joe himself, a proper all-rounder in Hebrew Bible criticism but not especially a literary critic, was bemused to learn that he had been an inspiration for that kind of activity.

Another work of this time that I was glad to have done was my first commentary, THE SECOND LETTER TO THE CORINTHIANS (1969), for the Brethren one-volume Bible commentary, *A Bible Commentary for Today*. I came to feel that this was the most human of Paul's letters, and I was fascinated by how he presented himself to his readers in Corinth, with his rhetoric, his self-explanations, and the glimpses of his humanity behind the public persona. Though I am sore at what Paul the theologian did to the legacy of Jesus, I acquired a respect for him and a sympathy through the patient following of his text. Some decades later, I returned to Paul in PAUL, THE INVISIBLE MAN (2003), where I interrogated his masculinity.

Clearly, however, I hadn't yet found my own voice, or settled what was to be my own scholarly territory. Anyone idly thumbing through back copies of the *Journal of Biblical Literature* might be a little bemused to see an article by the embryonic literary Clines entitled THE EVIDENCE FOR AN AUTUMNAL NEW YEAR IN PRE-EXILIC ISRAEL RECONSIDERED (1974), which seems a long way from anything else I have written. Bemusement would be further compounded by discovery in an even more remote

---

6. *Bib* 42 (1961), pp. 61-76.

publication of an earlier paper REGNAL YEAR RECKONING IN THE LAST YEARS OF THE KINGDOM OF JUDAH (1972). These papers were not at all literary, but arose from misgivings about some alleged certainties of current scholarship: in this case about the New Year Festival, which my interest in the Psalms had flagged up for me, since Mowinckel and others had seen that festival as the setting of many of the Psalms. When I looked into it, I was not convinced that the Hebrews celebrated the autumn rather than the spring as the beginning of the year. My paper did not directly attack the idea of an autumn festival but pointed out how weak the evidence for it was. The paper on regnal year reckoning approached the same subject from the perspective of the data from the period 609–587/6 BCE; we have not only several precise biblical year and month dates from those years, but also, for the greater part of that period, the Babylonian Chronicle texts containing many exact datings. I concluded that the balance of the evidence pointed to a spring new year at that time at least. I don't think I changed anyone's mind, but I did at least get invited to write the article on NEW YEAR in the Supplementary Volume of the *Interpreters' Dictionary of the Bible* (1976).

New colleagues

In the 1970s, the Sheffield department was expanding. Three new appointments, which took the number of full-time teachers and researchers in Bible to six, created the critical mass that was needed and brought into the Department new intellectual interests and personalities that melded.

David Gunn

Joining us in 1970 was David Gunn (b. 1942), who had studied English and Classics in Melbourne and Theology at Knox College, Dunedin, New Zealand. Intrigued by the Parry–Lord work on oral composition in Homer, on the basis of their fieldwork among Serbo-Croat singers of tales, and hoping to apply some of their methods to the Old Testament, Gunn had come to England to study in the Religion Department at Newcastle upon Tyne with John Sawyer, one of the few people in Britain at that time who could be relied on to welcome new approaches to the Hebrew Bible. In his 14 years at Sheffield, Gunn built a international reputation for his groundbreaking work on Hebrew narrative. His first book was on the story of King David,[7] of which one chapter at least was inspired by his interest

---

7. *The Story of King David: Genre and Interpretation* (Journal for the Study of the Old Testament, 6; Sheffield: JSOT Press, 1978).

in oral composition. With his background in English, David moved into a range of literary studies, and was very soon engaged with such literary staples as irony and plot and character in Old Testament narrative. These researches soon issued in his perceptive study *The Fate of King Saul*.[8]

David Gunn and I became close friends, sharing many intellectual interests. Together we became involved in the Rhetorical Criticism Section of the Society of Biblical Literature in the USA—which was at that time the home for literary study of the Old Testament of whatever kind—and edited, along with Alan Hauser, a collection of papers, *Art and Meaning* (1982), that emanated largely from that group. David and I wrote an ambitious and rather sophisticated (I believe) joint paper, FORM, OCCASION AND REDACTION IN JEREMIAH 20 (1976), that attempted to combine the newer literary criticisms we were becoming familiar with in the 1970s with more traditional form and redaction criticism. A spin-off from that paper was our '"YOU TRIED TO PERSUADE ME" AND "VIOLENCE! OUTRAGE!" IN JEREMIAH XX 7-8' (1978), which I believe was the first application to Hebrew of the distinction worked out by the philosopher of language J.L. Austin between illocutionary and perlocutionary language. The verb *pittâ*, we argued, means '*try* to persuade' (illocutionary) in the piel but '*succeed* in persuading' (perlocutionary) in the niphal.

David Gunn was a vital force in the creation of the *Journal for the Study of the Old Testament* and of JSOT Press, of which more anon.

A new house

In 1973 I was promoted to Senior Lecturer, with an increase in salary that would justify a larger house. We found one, a Victorian semi-detached stone-built house from 1884, its price four times my new salary, and affordable only by taking in a couple of students as lodgers on the top floor.

These were the days when lecturers and professors would invite their students to Sunday lunch, and so we did. It was all a bit too formal, with the roast and all the trimmings, but the overseas students especially were glad to see inside an 'English' house (they could not know how unEnglish their Australian hosts were). I preferred the coffee-time contact with students that I had later in California.

---

8. *The Fate of King Saul: An Interpretation of a Biblical Story* (Journal for the Study of the Old Testament, 14; Sheffield: JSOT Press, 1980).

A Californian interlude

We had only had a few months in our new house on Whitworth Road when another prospect opened before us. Few people today remember the winter of 1973–1974, when from January to March 1974 the UK was subjected to a regime allowing electricity to be used commercially only on three consecutive days a week, and thus effectively closing down all business on the other days. In the University, light and lifts were shut down at 3 pm, everyone had to get out of the buildings, and for the rest of the week people shivered in their houses (unless they had gas central heating).

The cause was twofold: the oil crisis of late 1973 and the threat of industrial action by the coalminers. Virtually all of Britain's electricity came from the burning of coal, the weather was bitter, and no one could imagine how the situation could improve.

There arrived at just this time a letter inviting me to a one-year position teaching Old Testament at Fuller Theological Seminary in Pasadena in the Los Angeles area. One of their staff, Frederick Bush (1929–2017), was taking a year's sabbatical leave. How to respond was, as they say, a no-brainer. No one in the UK knew how the crisis would end, or if it would, and the thought of an escape to a warmer climate and a less harsh political environment was very attractive to us as a family.

I accepted the offer with alacrity. The three-day week restrictions were lifted at the beginning of March, as it happened, but there was a heavy toll on British life, and the Prime Minister, Edward Heath, was defeated at the general election he had called in February 1974. The three-day week was only one of Britain's troubles: the IRA had begun its bombing campaign in Northern Ireland and on the UK mainland, inflation had reached 17%, and the outlook and the public mood in the UK was far from sunny.

Philip R. Davies

My absence from the department in 1974–1975 necessitated a replacement in Old Testament for the year, and we were fortunate to be able to appoint Philip R. Davies (1945–2018). An Oxford graduate who had completed a PhD at St Andrews under William McKane and Matthew Black on the Qumran War Scroll, Davies had been teaching in Ghana. By good fortune, when I returned to Sheffield Davies's post was made permanent. So we had three in Old Testament (Clines, Gunn, Davies) and three in New Testament (Atkinson, Hill, Thiselton). Not many departments in theology could number so many biblical specialists; often there would be one Old Testament and one New Testament person, and sometimes just one person to cover the whole Bible. The concentration of focus in Sheffield was undoubtedly energizing.

Davies, with his lively and quizzical mind, was not slow in realizing that Qumran studies, to which he was already making substantial contributions, having published his thesis,[9] could not be the whole of his scholarly interests, and set about developing his interest in Israelite historiography. Caught up in the spirit that was around in the Department, he too began to worry about why we think we know what we think we know, and to offer serious and successful challenges, as he has done on numerous subsequent occasions, to many of the established so-called 'truths' of biblical scholarship. His first such assay was upon the doctrine that had grown up around the Jewish tradition of the Aqedah or Binding of Isaac, where, with Bruce Chilton, he was to study afresh the question of the relation of Christian and Jewish theology.[10] But I am rushing ahead, and should remain for the moment in that decisive year of 1974.

I will leave for later an account of Philip's work with *JSOT* and Sheffield Academic Press.

Anthony C. Thiselton

Another appointment to the Department in 1970 was also a crucial one. Anthony Thiselton (b. 1937), who had been Lecturer in New Testament at Trinity College, Bristol, came to Sheffield as Stephenson Fellow with the aim of completing his thesis on Wittgenstein's philosophy of language and its relation to the interpretation of the New Testament. The key word that Thiselton brought, and which he made sure that we all understood the ins and outs of, was hermeneutics. It was a key moment in the history of the Department, for in a very short space of time we all became more critically aware of what we had been doing as innocent readers and exegetes of texts. Tony Thiselton did not invent hermeneutics, and if he had not been in Sheffield we would somehow probably have picked up the interest sooner or later; but it was the presence in the Department of someone whose intellectual life revolved around such questions that imposed the

---

9. *1QM: The War Scroll from Qumran* (Biblica et Orientalia, 32; Rome: Biblical Institute Press, 1977).

10. P.R. Davies and B.D. Chilton, 'The Aqedah: A Revised Tradition History', *Catholic Biblical Quarterly* 40 (1978), pp. 514-46; P.R. Davies, 'Passover and the Dating of the Aqedah', *Journal of Jewish Studies* 30 (1979), pp. 59-67; 'The Sacrifice of Isaac and Passover', in Livingstone (ed.), *Studia Biblica 1978. I. Papers on Old Testament* (1979), pp. 127-32.

issue upon the Department's thinking. We do not talk these days of hermeneutics so much, but whether it is ideological criticism or postcolonial exegesis or the problems of Israelite historiography that attracts us it is at least arguable that our directions were set in those early hermeneutical days of the 1970s.

Thiselton had not completed his thesis when his Fellowship expired and we were able to offer him a post as Lecturer in New Testament. Before too long, his massive ground-breaking work, *The Two Horizons* (1980) (the term borrowed from Gadamer, who was to become his next inspiration), was published and the Department was acquiring a new reputation—for heavyweight philosophy in relation to biblical studies.[11] Among his articles of that period one much-cited one stood out: in what was coming to be recognized as the Sheffield debunking style, he effectively laid to rest the myth, to be found in many textbooks, that in the ancient world words were believed to carry a magical power.[12]

After fifteen years in Sheffield, Thiselton was to move on, to the principalship of St John's College, Nottingham, then to that of St John's College, Durham, and latterly to the Chair of Theology at Nottingham. But he had put an item on the Sheffield agenda, and although there was no one to sustain his technical expertise in philosophical hermeneutics when he had left, by the additive process that seems to have become endemic to the Department's intellectual biography, an agenda item once in place is hard to remove.

The Clines family in Los Angeles

With the children aged 8 and 5, we flew from Heathrow to Los Angeles in September 1974, and settled in to a very agreeable one-storey house in Brigden Road, Pasadena on the border of Altadena, which the Seminary had rented for us from a college lecturer away on sabbatical.

The best thing about the house was of course the swimming pool, which the children could jump into when they came home from school. We all thought that Christmas Day around the pool was the height of American luxury, and enjoyed it without guilt.

---

11. *The Two Horizons: New Testament Hermeneutics and Philosophical Description with Special Reference to Heidegger, Bultmann, Wittgenstein and Gadamer* (Exeter: Paternoster Press; and Grand Rapids: Eerdmans, 1980).

12. 'The Supposed Power of Words in the Biblical Writings', *Journal of Theological Studies* NS 25 (1974), pp. 282-99.

The car

In California, you need a car, of course, immediately. One older student knew someone with a huge white Chrysler station wagon. 18 feet long, for sale for $400. It was perfect. Jeremy, aged 6, would spend hours in it adjusting the electrically controlled seats and windows and air-conditioning (separate units for the front and the rear seats). He could sit in the boot space behind the rear seat and open the rear-facing window electrically as well. Petrol was so cheap that miles per gallon did not matter in the least.

We went camping in Yosemite, with a trailer tent (our furthest trip) and often into the hills behind Los Angeles. There were many trips across Los Angeles to the beaches, and down to San Diego hunting for odd volumes of the 20-volume *Columbia Encyclopedia*, which Pick 'n' Mix had bought up and were selling off individual volumes for 10 cents or so (we got the whole set apart from the last volume).

The children become devotees of American TV, their favourite being *I Love Lucy*. It was a good show for the children's moral education, we thought; the weekly deceptions and lies of Lucy (Lucille Ball), comically exaggerated, inevitably misfired and brought her grief.

Fuller Theological Seminary

Founded in 1947, Fuller Theological Seminary is an evangelical seminary with students from many different denominations. It was, and is, open to scholarship and to movements in biblical criticism, and it made few specific demands about one's theological beliefs on its students and teachers. For the stage of my life I was at in 1974, it was a very good fit for me, and I felt very much at home there.

When I first walked into a classroom, for an evening class since many students were taking courses part-time, I found 100 students who had signed up for my Pentateuch class, in the widest classroom I had ever been in. Their seats were raked, and there was a high swivel chair for me at the front, and I certainly needed it if I were to make eye contact with students on the left of the room and students on the right. Sitting there, I felt like a chat-show host or an impresario, and I fell without hesitation into the roles the setting seemed to ask of me.

I had done my preparation, of course, and had the stuff I wanted to get across to my students, but the setting itself encouraged me to think of myself as leading a conversation rather than as delivering material. I will have more to say later about my philosophy of teaching, but my experience in that classroom was an important factor.

I let it be known that after my Pentateuch classes Monday to Thursday, 9–10 am, I would be having coffee in the cafeteria, and would be available to all comers. There were never fewer than a dozen students around the table. At another table, George Eldon Ladd (1911–1982), the veteran New Testament professor held court in similar fashion (perhaps I copied the idea from him), and not infrequently the two groups coalesced and then continued into lunch at 12. I wish I had brought this excellent custom home to England, but perhaps it was not exportable.

In the second edition of my *The Theme of the Pentateuch* (1997; first edition, 1978), I told the story of how that book came about, and will repeat it here. In an Afterword, which the publisher proposed, and which I wrote 20 years, to the month, after the book was first conceived, I said:

I had been teaching a course on the Pentateuch at Fuller Theological Seminary in Pasadena, California, four hours a week for twelve weeks or so. I had dealt with all the conventional matters of Pentateuchal criticism, and not a few of the more unconventional. So my class had studied the source analysis of the Flood story, the kerygma of the Yahwist and the theology of Deuteronomy, form criticism, rhetorical criticism, and so on. But what I realized, on the night before my very last class, was that despite all these interesting and intensive studies, we had never tried to see the Pentateuch as a whole, or to say what we thought it was all about. Should not that be the topic of the last class? I fell asleep worrying about what I would do in the morning at 9. When I woke, early, I knew what I wanted to do, and it was really very easy. I wrote the outline for the class, which became the outline for this book. It was simply that (1) the Pentateuch was about the fulfilment—and the non-fulfilment—of the promise it contains, and it was that (2) the promise in the Pentateuch is a threefold one—of descendants, of a divine–human relationship, and of land, and it was that (3) the first of these promises is the primary theme of Genesis, the second of Exodus and Leviticus, and the third of Numbers and Deuteronomy.

So many experiences came my way in those crammed nine months in Pasadena that I remember little of my teaching at Fuller. But it was a formative time.

The students were on the whole less conservative than the faculty, I thought. Many of them were escaping from fundamentalism (to use the title of James Barr's book) and looking for a way to esteem the Bible and yet not be subject to the tyranny of sectarian churches. Their outlook was very congenial to me.

When the end of my appointment was approaching, the President of the Seminary, David Hubbard, and some senior faculty asked if I would consider staying at Fuller. I underwent their doctrinal exam that checked my theological views, and I suppose that I passed it. The family had had a very good time in California and were quite interested in staying. But I myself turned the opportunity down in the end.

There was the matter of our citizenship. We could not imagine living in the USA without being citizens, and we hesitated to give up our Australian citizenship. There had been a protracted issue with the control of schools in the area, with Fuller people much exercised about apparent attempts by Latter Day Saints to dominate the local school board. Some Fuller friends of ours were much involved in the issue, but we had no standing, not being citizens.

More important was the question whether I could expect to hold the same religious opinions for the rest of my life, and whether I might have to leave my job if I developed other ideas. This possibility came home to me when Daniel Fuller, son of the Seminary's founder and a professor at the seminary, found himself in misery because of some incautious remarks he had made on the subject of eschatology. No tenet of belief was in question, but he became aware that some supporters of the Seminary were disaffected because of his views. 'I have probably lost the Seminary thousands of dollars', he would say dejectedly for months. I didn't want to find myself in such a position.

The deciding issue, in my recollection, was whether the USA or Britain would be a better place for the children to grow up in. It was not an easy decision, but we felt that the USA was a more conformist, and not as liberal, a society as the UK. In hindsight, though both societies have their serious drawbacks, I think I am still of that opinion.

Churches

I think we found a Brethren congregation in Los Angeles, in Culver City, which we visited once (just the once), but we had many other church contacts, given the faculty and students at Fuller Theological Seminary. We probably attended Lake Avenue (Congregational) Church most often, a middle-of-the-road US church, which was a new experience to me at least. I was always amused by how ritualistic the collection was (in a very unritualized service), and the following sketch is not meant to be satirical (the identity of the church is concealed, to spare blushes):

The Collection

> Down the aisle
> burgundy-carpeted—
> while the unisex choir
> out of tone in
> pillar-box red
> exult to the king
> of all the earth—
> process the stewards
> of the last sacrament,
> bearing gifts and
> solemnly dancing
> the one ritual left
> at First Presbyterian.

My first earthquake

I happened to be sitting on the floor in Fred Bush's office, searching for some book on the bottom shelves, when it happened. I was not alarmed when the floor began shaking, but was rather intrigued, wondering how long this was going to go on, and what was happening with the family. At school, the children had been well prepared to crawl under desks, so it was an adventure for them. My son Jeremy, the other day, when I reminded him of the episode, reminded me in turn of the earthquakes he has experienced in Sheffield, not up to California standards, though.

A vegetarian holiday

Jeremy had become vegetarian at the age of 4, entirely as a matter of his own conscience. Because it was his conviction, we felt bound to honour it, despite the inconvenience to the carnivores. But California posed a challenge to vegetarians. Outside the Seminary there was a van parked that dispensed American burgers, notably one bearing the title The Works, with every conceivable addition. Jeremy was corrupted, and throughout our nine months in Pasadena, ate burgers constantly. The moment he set foot on UK soil, again, however, he reverted to his ideological position, and has not wavered since.

Pledging allegiance

Jeremy had turned 6 when the school was in touch with us, saying that he had refused to join in the pledge of allegiance to the American flag, recited each morning by the whole school with their hands over their hearts. Jeremy argued that, not being an American, he held no allegiance to the US flag, and the school principal wanted to see his parents. The outcome of the interview was satisfactory: Jeremy was in the right, and he would stick out like a sore thumb in the class every day. In fact, so I discover, the pledge of allegiance in schools is not mandatory, since enforcing it has been adjudged to breach the First Amendment (free speech). And even if you are not a US citizen, the Constitution accords you the right of free speech, as also most other rights.

Leaving for home

When our time in California was up, all our household stuff was packed up to be sent by sea to the UK, while we were to travel back via Australia, the first trip there for the children. I had been invited to do a lecture tour of Brethren churches in New Zealand, so I left the very smart Air New Zealand plane (the first long-distance flight I had taken with only three engines; the DC-10 had an engine in the tail) in Auckland and they carried on to Sydney. There they stayed with Dawn's family in the Western suburbs and in their holiday house at Pearl Beach on the Central Coast.

My New Zealand tour

It was quite a honour to receive the invitation to give Bible addresses to about a dozen New Zealand assemblies in the southern hemisphere's winter of 1974, all the more so since the last person who had done so was Professor F.F. Bruce.

The first events were in Dunedin, far to the south on the South Island (not everyone knows that Dunedin is just Edinburgh backwards, as its antipodean relative should of course be). Dunedin is home to the most southerly university in the world, the University of Otago, but I regret to say that my one memory I have of Dunedin was a visit to a department store that was still using a nineteenth-century system of pneumatic tubes to send customers' cash to a central office, and to receive back change and a receipt in less than a minute. I could have watched it all morning.

Mostly I travelled by bus, but to cross the 100 miles of the Cook Strait from Nelson, at the top of the South Island, to the capital Wellington, at the foot of the north island, I had to take a flight. It was only a half-hour flight, but it was the most terrifying I have ever taken. Especially on the descent, the plane was buffeted by the winds like a feather in a gale, and the angle of descent was so steep that I could only keep myself on my seat by leaning all my weight on the structure of the seat in front. When we arrived in Wellington, which had nothing as soft as air bridges, the passengers tumbled out of the aircraft on to the tarmac, and began walking towards the terminal. As I passed the nose of the plane, I saw the pilot leaning out of his (open, can they do that?) window having a laugh with one of the ground staff. And I suddenly said to myself, He was *enjoying* that flight, wasn't he?, the masochist! It did make me feel a little better to see that he had not been in the least alarmed, but I was still walking drunkenly.

When I got to my hosts' house, they excused themselves after lunch to go about their business, and I went to bed to recuperate. Before long, I woke with a dreadful attack of panic, which had never happened to me. It would be two hours before anyone would return to the empty house, and I watched the minutes pass on the long case clock, feeling that each minute was going to be my last. The upshot was that I was taken to hospital, and had some of my meetings cancelled. In later years, I had quite a few such panic attacks, usually without any discernible cause—that is, until one in Scotland, at our holiday house, that took me to a local doctor in Largs, whom I had not met before. He was of a dour Scottish old school, I would say. Though he listened to me, he didn't have anything very useful to say. But when I had left his office and was walking down a long corridor, I heard him call after me: Mr Clines, you're going to die. [Pause]. We all are. But you will not die from a panic attack.

I would like to be able to say that I never had another panic attack. But I believe it was never as bad again, and the canny Scot had delivered the right medicine.

Home in Sheffield

Things were improving in the UK when we returned, but we came back to winter. The first Sunday, we went to Fitzwilliam Chapel, the Brethren church to which we had belonged. Everyone was pleased to see us, and especially to see how the children had grown. But as we left the chapel, Dawn and I turned to each other and said, We won't be coming back, will we? We had seen too much of other styles of church life to settle for what we had been used to. The absence of any serious role for women in the English church was especially notable compared with our Californian experience.

But we never managed to find a congenial church home in Sheffield. We tried two Anglican churches, Christ Church, Fulwood, and St John's Church, Ranmoor, our parish church, as well as St Andrews Presbyterian (now United Reformed), and the Quakers, but I at least was ill at ease everywhere. The children continued with their youth groups at Christ Church, Dawn was more persevering than I was, and I became an early adopter of the norm for Britain, where only 5% of the population attend church. I once told my colleague Tony Thiselton that I could live with all the Apostles' Creed—apart from the belief in the 'communion of saints'. An ordained Anglican, he was appalled.

Chapter 8

SHEFFIELD UNIVERSITY II (1976–1989)

I will make 1976 begin a new chapter in my life, for that was the year of my first book, and of the creation of our Sheffield publishing enterprise. But there was no radical difference from the earlier years, and, as with a good deal of my life, change happened incrementally and (to me at least) almost imperceptibly.

It was about this time that we became more self-conscious about the Department, began to imagine that it might have a distinctive mission that marked it off from other cognate departments. Perhaps it was so soon that we began to talk also about interdisciplinarity, a very hard thing to do (as Stanley Fish reminds us). Whatever it was, nothing much would have come of it if it had not been for a certain serendipity that led to the foundation of JSOT Press (later Sheffield Academic Press, and, in its present manifestation, Sheffield Phoenix Press).

The beginnings of JSOT

The story starts with a meeting of the Society for Old Testament Study in London in December 1975. In a moment of deviation from its usual pattern of papers, the SOTS had invited the estimable Publisher of SCM Press, John Bowden, himself an Old Testament scholar and an important contributor to English-speaking biblical scholarship through his personal translation of numerous key works of continental European scholars, to talk about the future of scholarly publishing. It may not have been his main point, but what we remember him saying, as he announced the suspension of the Studies in Biblical Theology series of monographs as uneconomical (they were marvellously cheap), was that biblical scholars had better get used in future to addressing a wider audience than fellow scholars and at the very least they had to give up the luxury of expecting to have Hebrew and Greek characters printed in their books.¹ We from Sheffield were affronted, we must admit, at being robbed of cheap scholarly books, but even more by having a publisher tell us what we could and could not write as scholars.

There was a coincident factor as well. We had become very frustrated by the length of time it took for our articles to appear in the scholarly journals. When you are young, to wait two or even three years for your paper to come out is insupportable. Why did we not do it ourselves? Set up our own journal, publish our own books. Surely we could do it cheaper and faster than these wretched commercial publishers (commerce was such a swearword in academic circles in those days), and we would not have to submit to the dictates of businessmen (*sic*) about what was publishable. In the train on the way home it was decided to launch a Journal for the Study of the Old Testament, edited by Clines, Davies and Gunn (alphabetical order).

Some people have said that we founded the Journal to publish papers that no one else would. If that is intended as a slur on the quality of the journal, it is far from the truth. But there was a sense in which we believed that the already existing journals would be slow in recognizing new methods in biblical studies as appropriate (and the record has proved us right on that point). We did not particularly feel we had a mission to promote certain kinds of scholarship, though we certainly wanted a fair deal for anything we were interested in ourselves.

A perusal of the first issue of *JSOT* will show our range of interests. We asked Luis Alonso Schökel for something and he gave us permission to translate an essay of his on the poetic structure and imagery of Psalm 42–43. John Van Seters agreed to write a piece on the Court History (as it was known in those days, at least in North American parlance). And we solicited reviews of two quite recent books, Robert Boling's Anchor Bible *Judges* and John Sawyer's *Modern Introduction to Biblical Hebrew*, each book with three separate reviews and a response by the author. We thought it was a pity when scholarly books are not reviewed until three years or more have passed. We disliked it when we saw a book reviewed by just one reviewer, unsympathetic or fawning or uncomprehending perhaps. And

---

1. His paper was entitled 'Ecclesiastes 12:12 and Theological Publishing'. According to the Bulletin of the Society ('printed for private circulation', it must be acknowledged), he argued that '"Mini-publishing", as represented by Scholars Press in the USA ... [is] possible in its present form only by hidden subsidies and a narrowing of the traditional role of the publisher' (The Society for Old Testament Study, Bulletin for 1976, p. 1). For my own opinions on the subject, partly in agreement and partly still in disagreement with John Bowden, see my essay, 'Publishers: Who Needs Them?' (1998).

we believed, even then, and long before the days of the Teaching Quality Assessment that was to breathe down our necks before very long, that the teaching of the subject is an essential aspect of the discipline itself, and not a lightweight adjunct to the serious business of scholarship.

By the time of the Summer Meeting of the SOTS in 1976, our plans were far enough advanced for us to solicit subscriptions (at £4.50 or $7.00 for three issues of 80 pages). After our announcement of the Journal at the end of one session, the first to stride up to the table at the front to subscribe was John Snaith (1934–2019) in his leather motorbike kit, lecturer at Cambridge and independent thinker; we took it as a good omen for the success of the journal. By the Winter Meeting at the end of that same year the first Issue was out, and with it an announcement of the first volumes in a Supplement Series of monographs. The Journal must have met a need, for by October 1978 we were beginning a companion periodical, *Journal for the Study of the New Testament*. It was to be edited by David Hill, Ernst Bammel, Anthony Hanson and Max Wilcox, and our colleague Bruce Chilton was appointed its editorial secretary.

As always in the following decades, my projects were stimulated by the developing technology that became available. The journals became a reality because of the capability of the University's Print Unit to produce cheap offset printing, with binding and design facilities as well (their resident designer did a stunning cover, with two trumpeting angels, for Norman Whybray's *Thanksgiving for a Liberated Prophet* in 1981). In 1976, we had to use authors' typescripts since there was no means of setting up type apart from the traditional hot metal (very expensive). Other academic publishers, such as the infant SBL Scholars Press, had decided that the scholarly world would accept a diminution of print quality for the sake of easier and quicker availability of a wide range of titles.

The rest is history, as they say, even the fact that by the end of 1997 JSOT Press / Sheffield Academic Press had published over 1000 titles and had become a general university publisher not only in biblical studies, but also in the humanities, in medicine, and in science and technology. Biblical studies remained the core of its publishing activity, nonetheless.

What I would like to stress here, however, is the impact the Press had on the Department. It is not just that it became a ready vehicle for the publication of the Department's work, and it is not that new appointments to the staff of the Department were invited to carry out editorial tasks for the Press, though, as it happens, many of the teaching and research staff are doing were doing just that. It is much more that a constant stream of the latest research in biblical studies began flowing to Sheffield for evaluation and review by one of the Press's many specialist panels of international scholars. Without setting out to become a centre for current awareness in biblical scholarship, that is what Sheffield became, and not only in the fields of research for which it has become most visible. There is more: Sheffield came to be perceived as a place where things happen in biblical studies, and the Department's graduate school of 100 students, at its height, most of them working for the PhD or MPhil, and more than half of them from overseas, was evidence of that perception.

This was the era when the Department's graduate school began to develop. In the three decades up to 1975 there had been just five PhDs in the Department; now within the last five years of the 70s there were eight, and four of their theses were published: David Baker on the theological relationship of the Testaments,[2] Wesley Carr on principalities and powers in Paul,[3] John Bimson on the date of the exodus,[4] and Anthony Thiselton on New Testament hermeneutics.[5]

My books 1976-1989

I, He, We and They

As we prepared the first issue of the *Journal for the Study of the Old Testament*, I was completing a piece on Isaiah 53, too long to submit as an article in a journal, but too short for a book. We decided that my brief monograph, *I, He, We and They: A Literary Approach to Isaiah 53* (1976) would be the first in a Supplement Series to *JSOT*, which would publish works of any length. We soon learned that the economics of publishing made it difficult to sell writing of under 150 pages as independent publications, and the vast majority of the series thereafter were standard-length books. The series is still going strong under the name Library of Old

---

2. David L. Baker, now in theological education in Indonesia, published his 1975 thesis as Two Testaments, One Bible: A Study of Some Modern Solutions to the Theological Problem of the Relationship between the Old and the New Testaments (London: Inter-Varsity Press, 1976); second edition published as Two Testaments, One Bible: A Study of the Theological Relationship between the Old and New Testaments (Leicester: Apollos, 1991).

3. Wesley Carr, who was Stephenson Fellow in the Department and is now Dean of Westminster, published his 1975 thesis as Angels and Principalities: The Background, Meaning and Development of the Pauline Phrase hai archai kai hai exousiai (Society for New Testament Studies Monograph Series, 42; Cambridge: Cambridge University Press, 1981).

4. The 1977 thesis of John Bimson, now lecturer in Old Testament at Trinity College, Bristol, was published as Redating the Exodus and Conquest (Journal for the Study of the Old Testament Supplement Series, 5; Sheffield: JSOT Press, 1984).

5. The thesis of Anthony Thiselton, who presented it as a staff candidate, has already been referred to.

Testament Studies, published by T. & T. Clark (Bloomsbury), the latest volume being no. 675. In the olden days, we used to fill any blank pages at the end of a volume with a list of previous volumes in the series, but no one does that any more.

I, He, We and They was an early exercise in rhetorical criticism, which I saw as opposed to historical criticism. I laid out various features of rhetorical criticism I would undertake for Isaiah 53, such as an analysis of characters, of the visual language, of acts and agents, of speaking, of acting, and of the temporal. But I stressed that rhetorical criticism should not be a mechanical matter of identifying stylistic devices, but a movement towards the meaning and quiddity of a work from the standpoint of form rather than of content. I broadened the theme out from strictly rhetorical issues to the function of language as event (and thus not the opposite of action), taking my direction from what was being called in the 1970s the 'new hermeneutic' with its stress on language, and especially that of literary works, as the creation of a alternative world—with its own principles, values, relationships and perceptions—that confronts and potentially undermines the validity of the conventional world. I depicted Isaiah 53 as creating a topsy-turvy world, where a servant is elevated above kings, where one accomplishes what many cannot, where the innocent suffer for the guilty and where the servant's commitment to Yahweh lies in doing nothing and saying nothing but letting everything happen to one. One reviewer found the last claim in particular 'intuitively repugnant',[6] which is about as subjective a judgment as one can find in a book review. Perhaps I should not have drawn that conclusion, but at least I was developing an alternative position to mainstream historical-critical biblical scholarship, which I think I have not departed from.

The Theme of the Pentateuch

The soon to be published *The Theme of the Pentateuch* (1978), which I have already referred to, took a different tack in its literary criticism, and set itself against different targets in historical-critical research. These targets I named atomism and geneticism. Atomism is the fixation upon the accumulation of detailed results, its model being the pyramid which is constructed gradually by the superimposition of one stone upon another. I argued that

> [O]ur discipline belongs firmly in the tradition of humanistic studies, and, inasmuch as it occupies itself with the interpretation of data that are already given, has more in common with the criticism of a body of well-known

---

6. Robert M. Polzin, *CBQ* 39 (1977), pp. 354-55 (355).

literature than with the discovery, accumulation and evaluation of new data. In the sphere of literary criticism knowledge does not accumulate steadily through the industry of objectively distanced scholars, but by means of repeated personal engagement with the text. When one learns from others, it is as much from the shaft of light the critic has brought to bear on the text, a total approach to the text, a setting of the text in a new context, that one learns, as from the detail of the commentator's explications. The model is that of the guide in a darkened museum who holds up a torch to reveal an unfamiliar object, or a familiar object from a fresh angle, in a new light.[7]

We cannot do without both holistic and atomistic work, but my plea was for the former, which I thought was sadly neglected.

The other tendency, which it would be more exact to call an obsession, was toward geneticism. By that I meant

> the study of the origins and development of the extant biblical text. It is no accident that the two most significant works in Pentateuchal studies in this century, Gerhard von Rad's *The Problem of the Hexateuch* and Martin Noth's *A History of Pentateuchal Traditions* are both representative of this approach. Again a particular view of the nature of knowledge is implied by the genetic approach: it is that an object is best understood if its origins are uncovered, a text is best interpreted if its sources can be reconstructed and its pre-history determined. ... [M]any Old Testament scholars know of no other way of doing research on the Old Testament except along such lines. I do not decry such methodology; it is a scientific necessity, even if its firm results turn out to be meagre. But I do protest against the dominance of that approach, and set forth, by way of an alternative approach, the method adopted in this book as a gainful form of employment in Old Testament study.[8]

It is a matter of continuing surprise to me, not that the world has not accepted my account of the theme of the Pentateuch, but that so few have thought the attempt to say what the Pentateuch is all about, as a whole, is a matter of interest. Years later, I was still thumping the same tub, in a paper DOES THE PENTATEUCH EXIST? SEVEN QUESTIONS WE SHOULD BE ASKING IF IT DOES (2014). I was beginning to feel that perhaps there was something wrong with me in believing there was indeed such a thing as the Pentateuch. Many teachers and students, however, seemed to find the book helpful; it was just my scholarly peers I couldn't convince.[9]

---

7. *Theme of the Pentateuch*, pp. 8-9.
8. *Theme of the Pentateuch*, p. 9.
9. Walter E. Rast commented, 'Many of Clines's observations appear almost self-evident, except that they seem not to have been exploited by interpreters' (*Interpretation* 34 [1980], p. 424).

Midian, Moab and Edom

In 1983 I co-edited with John Sawyer a volume on *Midian, Moab and Edom*. These were not my subjects, but we had received for the *JSOT* Supplement Series a set of manuscripts that needed some serious copy-editing. Though I was busy at the time, there was no one else to do it except me, and I rather forwardly suggested to John that I would undertake the work if I could get a credit on the title page. He agreed.

Ezra, Nehemiah, Esther

I had been working for some years on a commentary on Ezra–Nehemiah for the Tyndale Old Testament series. I don't know when I submitted the manuscript, but two years later I had a letter from the editor, Donald Wiseman (1918–2010), Professor of Assyriology in London, and a leading evangelical scholar. It said that my manuscript was being declined because it was not theological enough; it should have included some devotional material. As far as I recollect, these elements had not been prescribed when I had been commissioned to write the commentary, and Ezra–Nehemiah was not a particularly rewarding Old Testament book to extract Christian devotional thoughts from. But I did my best, and after another long interval that version also was rejected. This was quite a blow for a fledgling scholar, and it did not boost my self-confidence.

I told my story to Ronald E. Clements (b. 1929), who was editor of the New Century Bible series. He was more than willing to have a replacement for the commentary on Ezra–Nehemiah for his series, the existing volume having been published in 1969 by L.H. Brockington. The only thing was, I would have to include also a commentary on Esther, a biblical book I had rarely opened. I gladly accepted the challenge, and found Esther so engaging that I devoted a monograph to it.

The first pages of the *Ezra, Nehemiah, Esther* commentary (1984) were written during a family holiday in the French-speaking Swiss Jura. My Cambridge friend, Timothy Stunt, had married a woman from the tiny mountain village of Vellerat (2185 ft [666 m] above sea level), with only a dozen or so houses,[10] and he had arranged for us to stay for six weeks in the house of one of his neighbours, Daniel. Daniel had a smallholding, with cows and sheep, and we helped in the fields with the harvesting. In those days, in the telephone directory, a person's occupation appeared after their name, the bachelor Daniel rejoicing in the appellation of 'inséminateur', since he also administered injections of semen to neighbourhood cows.

---

10. Improbable though it sounds, Vellerat has had an asteroid named after it in 2020 (Asteroid 212374).

I dedicated the commentary to my daughter Miriam, 'in happy memory of a long summer *en famille* in the Swiss Jura when, in between haymaking and hunting wild strawberries, the first pages were written' (a suitcase of books had travelled with me in the boot of the car).

The spin-off from the commentary on Esther was *The Esther Scroll: The Story of the Story* (1984). A complex literary and source-critical study, with much interlocking argument, I surprised myself by writing it in more or less one sweep from beginning to end. I have kept the manuscript (it was the last book I wrote before the advent of the desktop computer) as a reminder of what fluent composition can be like. There was hardly a page of my handwritten text that bears any alteration, except for occasional additions pasted in. Written at a fraught time of my life, it is a standing testimony to the mantra, Work is the best medicine.

It is a literary study through and through, but it deploys purely literary observations in order to address questions of the growth of the Esther narrative, of text criticism, of possible sources of the book, and of the relationship of the various forms of the book that are extant (i.e. of redaction criticism). In many ways, it was a conventional literary-critical study, but it would not have been possible without the undergirding of its narratological analysis. In brief, I argued that the book once ended with chap. 9 (calling this the 'proto-Masoretic' shape of the book), and that 9.1-19 and 9.20–10.3 were later additions. A yet earlier form of the book (the 'pre-Masoretic') could be reconstructed from the Alpha-text, a Greek version of the story that, while not unknown to scholars, had been misunderstood as a recension of the Septuagint and not included in standard editions of the Greek Bible. For that reason, I printed in the last 30 pages of my book the complete Alpha-text, accompanied by the first translation ever published into another language.

Whether it was anything to do with my book I do not know but there ensued in the next decade a flurry of activity on Esther and its redaction, with works by Michael V. Fox, Kristin De Troyer, Karen H. Jobes and A. Kay Fountain.[11]

---

11. Michael V. Fox, *The Redaction of the Books of Esther: On Reading Composite Texts* (Atlanta: Scholars Press, 1991); Kristin De Troyer, *The End of the Alpha Text of the Book of Esther: Translation and Narrative Technique in MT 8:1-17, LXX 8:1-17, and AT 7:14-41* (Atlanta: Scholars Press, 1996); Karen H. Jobes, *The Alpha-Text of Esther: Its Character and Relationship to the Masoretic Text* (Atlanta: Scholars Press, 1996); Charles V. Dorothy, *The Books of Esther: Structure, Genre, and Textual Integrity* (Sheffield: Sheffield Academic Press, 1997); A. Kay Fountain, *Literary and Empirical Readings of the Books of Esther* (New York: Peter Lang, 2002).

John Emerton of Cambridge, reviewing the book for *Vetus Testamentum*, remarked that '[T]his brief summary cannot do justice to the wealth of learning and cogent argumentation displayed in the book. references. All scholars working on Esther will have to come to terms with Esther will have to come to terms with this brilliant book.'

Art and Meaning

A sign that the literary turn in Hebrew Bible studies had come of age was the appearance in 1982 of a volume of essays, *Art and Meaning: Rhetoric in Biblical Literature*, edited by David M. Gunn, Alan J. Hauser and myself (there were contributions by George W. Coats, J. Cheryl Exum, John S. Kselman and others). Alan Hauser, who has spent his career at Appalachian State University, Boone, NC, was at the time the chair of the SBL section on Rhetorical Criticism, and our volume, perhaps the first book-length treatment of biblical rhetorical criticism, affirmed that the 'biblical authors were artists of language', creating their meanings through their verbal artistry. 'Meaning is ultimately inseparable from art, and those who seek to understand the Biblical must be sensitive to the writer's craft', we averred. We called our rhetorical criticism a 'approach' rather than a 'method' since there was no hard and fast way of doing rhetorical criticism and (frankly) we were still working out what exactly constituted it. But we were clear that our focus should be on the 'final form of the text', which meant that we did not share the prevailing concern with sources, redaction and editing.

My own paper in thus volume, THE ARGUMENTS OF JOB'S THREE FRIENDS (1982), affirmed, in the face of some disbelief, the coherence of the friends' speeches (which was not the same thing as persuasiveness), and more importantly that each friend had a distinctive theological position which he maintained throughout. It also introduced into the realm of the literary the criterion of tonality and the identification of 'nodal sentences' in which the essential point of each speech was encapsulated. The role of topoi, rhetorical units on general themes, was also noted. I was broadening out my own understanding of the limits of the 'literary'.

Other literary papers

I suppose my essay FALSE NAIVETY IN THE PROLOGUE TO JOB (1985) should also count as a literary study. False naivety, I said, exploits the appearance of artlessness. In reality, the naive prologue to Job is no less subtle than the complex argument of the whole book. The prologue is 'not some primitive tale that does no more than set the scene for the substantive argument of the dialogues, but a well-wrought narrative that plunges directly into issues of substance that reach as deep as the fraught dialogues themselves.'

Yet another literary study, a bit more theoretical, was THE PARALLELISM OF GREATER PRECISION. NOTES FROM ISAIAH 40 FOR A THEORY OF HEBREW POETRY (1987, 1998), which I contributed to another Sheffield volume, *New Directions in Hebrew Poetry*. I was pointing out that the second line of a parallelistic couplet is often more precise or specific than the first line, a feature of Hebrew parallelism that had not before been observed, I believe.[12] Isaiah 40.16 was a good example: Line 1 says, 'Lebanon is not enough to burn', and line 2 'And its animals not enough for a burnt offering'; line 2 specifies that it is Lebanon's animal population that is in mind in line 1 (not its trees, as one might assume, since they are what Lebanon was famous for), and that the burning referred to is of animals in sacrifice.

By the end of the paper I was drawing some conclusions about Hebrew poetry in general: the meaning of a couplet does not lie in A nor in B, nor is it in A+B, but in the whole couplet, A being affected by its juxtaposition with B, and B by its juxtaposition with A, one half of the couplet 'teaching about the other' (Menahem b. Saruq, c. 960 CE). From that it follows that the reader is more engaged in the process of interpretation of a poetic couplet than of a more linear text—the role of the reader, which was to become a focus in work of the third period of my Sheffield life, being foreshadowed for the first time in my work, I believe.

Job

This second period of my Sheffield life (1976–1989) came to an end (according to the periodization of this memoir) with the publication of the first volume of my *Job* commentary. I had been asked by the Old Testament Editor of the Word Biblical Commentary series, John D.W. Watts (1921–2013), to contribute two volumes on Job, to be published by Word Books, Waco, Texas.[13] It was a great opportunity, since Job had long been a special interest of mine (I had done courses on it in Sydney and Cambridge, and I had written a short commentary in *A Bible Commentary for Today* in 1979). I could see the need for a combination of the philological-textual

---

12. Adele Berlin anticipated me in some respects with her 'particularizing parallelism' ('Shared Rhetorical Features in Biblical and Sumerian Literature', *JANES* 10 [1978], pp. 35-42, a paper that I saw only when mine was already in proof).

13. This is well before the notorious 1993 extermination, by federal agents after a 51-day siege, of the apocalyptic cult of the Branch Davidians, who had settled just outside Waco.

and the exegetical-theological; the blending of the two especially attracted me. It was, I thought, the hardest book in the Hebrew Bible, the most theologically profound, and I couldn't resist the challenge. As it turned out, the commentary became a bit more expansive as I went along, and John Watts had no difficulty (or none that I knew of) in allowing me a third volume.

I was rather nervous, though, of suggesting that I move the position of certain chapters of the book. I had concluded that the speeches of Elihu had migrated in the course of the book's transmission to an inappropriate place. Elihu, I theorized, will have spoken after the three friends had finished their speeches (and Job 32.1-2 says explicitly that it was then that Elihu intervened). If we move Elihu's speech to follow the friends', Job's final speech (chaps. 29–31) will have been answered immediately by the divine speech from the tempest (chaps. 38–41). And the poem on wisdom (chap. 28), which apparently belongs to Job though it doesn't sound at all like him, can be better ascribed to Elihu. Again, John Watts thought I should have the courage of my convictions and rearrange the commentary chapters in accord with my reconstruction. Mind you, I did hear of a customer who returned their copy of Volume 2 because it didn't have any comments on Elihu in the place they were expecting it.

I thought the conception of the commentary series, modelled on the Biblischer Kommentar series of the Neukirchener Verlagsgesellschaft, was superb. After bibliography and an English translation of the passage (in the case of Job, of a speech of one of the characters) there followed detailed text-critical and philological notes, justifying my translation and debating other possibilities; this section was primarily for other scholars. Then came the main body of the commentary, a verse by verse exposition for the general reader. Finally, there was a page or two headed 'Explanation', in which I summarized what I thought had been going on in the passage, and where I would often step back a little from the text and make my own evaluation of it (remember, most of the time I was commenting on Job's friends, and Job himself, who were not always speaking words of wisdom, and I was very happy to tell the reader what I thought of them).

Writing a commentary on Job

What is it like to be writing a large-scale commentary?[14] In 2015, a date well beyond the confines of the present chapter of this memoir, I was

---

14. Most of what follows in the next eight pages has been copied from my essay 'Writing a Job Commentary' (2015), in *The Genre of Biblical Commentary: Essays in Honor of John E. Hartley* (ed. Timothy D. Finlay and William Yarchin; Eugene, OR: Wipf & Stock, 2015), pp. 29-39.

asked to contribute to a Festschrift with the theme, *The Genre of Biblical Commentary*. In writing that essay, I remembered a few pages I had written while I was in the middle of my Job commentary, not for publication but for the sake of capturing for myself the daily experience of commentary-writing. Here it is:

I have 55 books on Job on the shelves behind me, and about 80 volumes of dictionaries, grammars and encyclopaedias. There are 13 English versions of the Bible on the desk to my right, 27 commentaries on the mahogany dining room table that is my main desk (the solidity of that mahogany is very important to me); these are all within hands' reach, but beyond them, on another table, are photocopies of 16 older commentaries—together with all the bills and departmental files and literary magazines I am banishing to the corners of my world.

Of the English versions and 27 commentaries I read every word. Every morning I open on my Mac my two files for the day, one with *Translation and Notes* for the chapter in progress, one for the *Comment*. Before long, I will also open the Bible search program Accordance, which will display all the occurrences of a word I am considering, in Hebrew and English in parallel columns. Whenever I need to look up a verse, I will use Accordance rather than a printed Hebrew Bible, since it will show me the verse in Hebrew and English, in a dozen English versions, and with the Septuagint and Vulgate for good measure. I can ask for a wider context if I want it, or, if I have typed a row of biblical references in the *Comment*, I can copy and paste them into the search box and I can check that all my references were correct, and note all the verses where the English and the Hebrew numeration differs (since I must give the Hebrew numbering with the English in parentheses).

For the extreme right of my screen, I have a list of commentators, in chronological order, so that when I list their adherence to a particular view their names will appear in the correct date order.

When I start my commentary on a new passage of the Joban text, a strophe of four or five lines, let us say, I will begin by making my own provisional translation of the Hebrew, looking up in the dictionaries not only the words I do not know or know well but also the common words to check that I can find support for the exact rendering forming in my head. Then I will study each of my dozen English versions, and, whenever I am disposed to differ significantly from one of them, note their translation in a footnote to my translation. The differences among the translations will usually hang upon disputes over philology, text criticism or interpretation, so later, when I get into the commentaries, I will be able to discover the reasons for all the variations.

Now it is time to work on the philological notes. Typically, I begin with Driver and Gray in the ICC, incorporating in the *Notes* to the translation any points that interest me, and move on to Dhorme, Gordis, Pope, de Wilde and Fohrer, usually in just that order. When I see that an emendation was earlier proposed by Siegfried or Duhm or some other older scholar not among my desk companions, I note the fact in the appropriate place with two exclamation marks before the author's name so that I can confirm it later when I am checking their commentaries (rather than break off my routine to make an immediate check).

When I have read all the more philological commentaries, and have more or less decided my views on all the disputed issues, it is time to start writing the commentary proper. First I try to write a paragraph about the strophe as a whole, what I think it is saying in general and how it connects up with what went before. This is the most difficult part of all, and sometimes I will have to read in other commentaries before I get a sense of what I myself want to say. Fohrer is the best at giving me a kick start into this general paragraph.

And now I am ready for the verse by verse commentary (the *Comment*). I read just as much in the commentaries as I need to get me started, surveying the kinds of issues they have taken up, and then I begin to write my own commentary. Almost always, I will start by saying what I think the verse as a whole is about, as well as how it connects with what has preceded or with the general context. Then I will consider the words and phrases themselves, explaining precisely what they mean, what their resonances are and how they contribute to the sense of the present verse. When I have done writing my own commentary on the verse or the strophe, I will then read systematically through all my 27 desk companions, incorporating as I go any points or thoughts I have learned from them that I feel I should include.

When I get to the end of the chapter or the speech there is of course still a lot of busy work to be done. First I shall have to search the whole of my files for double exclamation marks, so as to find the items I still need to check. Some of those I can check now, if they are older commentators like Dillmann or Hitzig, whose books I have in my pile of photocopies; others I shall have to save up for a library visit, since they may be monographs or journal articles. But I know from experience that I shall be able to dispatch most of them pretty quickly, and I expect that on the whole they will not greatly subvert what I have already written. Sometimes, though, a little article in a journal will entirely undermine my whole train of thought, and I will have a lot of revision to do.

There is still the *Form/Content/Structure* section to write. It is a bit boring, but I have devised a set of questions to ask systematically, about strophic structure and literary forms and the like, and I think it is worth doing. The best bit is left till the very last. It is the *Explanation* section that comes at the end of each unit of text (typically a chapter), where, as I say in the Preface to Volume 1, I try hard to stand a little way off from the text to ask what has been going on and what it all means, or, as I say in the Introduction, I try to savour the essence of the speech, evaluate it as warmly and respectfully as I can, and then make no secret of what I myself think about it (I am under no obligation to agree with everything in the text, if only because we all know that the friends, and Job himself to some extent, are in the wrong on many issues). To write those concluding paragraphs, which will occupy only a page or two of the printed book, I will have to reread the whole of what I have written on the current chapter(s), put some Mahler on (it was Bach for the philological notes), go into a free associative mode—and just write (trying not to repeat what I have already said in the commentary proper).

At the end of each day, I should add, I ask my Mac to count the words in each of my current files, and I enter the new word counts and the minutes I have spent (average about 4 hours a day) into my spreadsheet called Writing Record 1996 (or whatever the year is), so that I can see how many words I have written in the day (average about 1300), what my hourly average was, what my cumulative daily average now is (c. 325), how many words of the commentary I have written so far, what proportion of the commentary is now finished, how many pages it will be when it is done, and at what date, at the present rate of progress, I may expect to have completed it. The day I have finished will not be better than the thousands of days I was just writing.

All that was written while I was in the throes of composition (about 1996). Ruminating on the whole process (about 2016), my reflections began to organize themselves into two groups: the pleasures and the perils of commentary writing.

The Pleasures of Commentary

A Defined Task

Compared to writing a monograph or a journal article, writing a commentary is a pretty clearly defined task. Especially if you are writing for a series of commentaries, the format, audience, shape and scope are predetermined. You know where to start and where to finish. The commentator can be confident about what the work is to look like in the end, not agonizing over the whole even while struggling with the particular.

It may seem very mechanical to be able to estimate every day how many words you still have to write and when you may expect to be finished, but I have found that I need rewards and incentives to keep going at a large task, and these little signs of progress gave me most of what I needed.

Avoiding Blank Page Syndrome

Because you know what lies before you in the text, you always know, in general at least, what your next move must be. It is bliss to sit down in the morning not dreading the blank page or screen, or lacking any idea of which out of hundreds of potential sentences you should begin with. With a commentary, if you are at verse 12, you can be confident that your next horizon will be verse 13. Mind you, I still have found it a good idea to attempt banishing blank page syndrome altogether by finishing work for the day in the middle of a paragraph, or even of a sentence, so that there can be no question of how the next day should begin.

In the Presence of a Great Mind

For the most part, works that call for commentary are masterworks, works that repay commentary, works that are rich, complex, profound. No doubt, not all biblical books are equally profound, but in most cases the commentator is aware of following and exploring the work of an outstanding mind. This is always a pleasurable and rewarding experience, even if the commentator is not always in total sympathy with the author. I count myself very fortunate that I was invited to comment on Job, which must be one of the most intellectually rich books of the Bible. I don't know that I ever formed much of an image of the poet as a person, but I never failed to admire the inventiveness and delicacy of his mind.

An Educational Premium

One of the greatest pleasures of commentary writing, especially as distinct from other scholarly writing, is the constant demand of the text that you should launch yourself into new fields and topics that you would otherwise probably never have touched. I recall getting into ancient metallurgy and astronomy, and, especially in commenting on the divine speeches, into the lives and habits of various living creatures (including referencing video clips of crocodiles). I suspect mine may be one of the first large-scale biblical commentaries written with constant reference to Wikipedia. I had such a sense of the immense variety of knowledges the poet draws upon that I compiled for my commentary (taking the idea from A. de

Wilde) a 'Classified Index of the Book of Job', listing, with references, the animals mentioned, the birds, aspects of the earth, the sky and the weather, language about farming, emotions, manufactures, warfare and weapons, and so on, under 42 headings altogether, over nine pages of small type. All these matters are largely incidental to the main purposes of the book, of course, but they show an artist at work who is hugely sensitive to the multiplicity of the world and of its human inhabitants.

Companionship

Most commentaries, not just commentaries on biblical books, are written on texts that have already been commented on. So today's commentator inevitably works in the presence of a commentatorial cloud of witnesses. I called my predecessor commentators my 'desk companions' because they sat at my desk with me, and I enjoyed their character and their individuality. I came over the years to feel I knew them and their minds very well, though I had never met most of them. Shut in my study, I was surrounded by human contact. They had travelled for many of the years of their lives on the same journey that would occupy me for a quarter of a century, and I came to admire their fortitude and the twists and turns of their minds as I turned to them day after day.

Efficiency

I love to be efficient. This is not a heartless quest and I hope I do not fetishize it. But I am very conscious of how much of our scholarly lives are wasted on the business of organizing ourselves to the point where we start to be productive, and I have tried to streamline the busy-work as much as I can. Early on in writing the Job commentary, I realized that accessing the relevant scholarly literature, even when one has located references to it, threatens to delay if not prevent getting on with the primary task: reading it and making good use of it. Especially because I had made it my personal goal to review the literature of the past 100 years, considering all the philological proposals and textual emendations of Job I could lay my hands on (a task that needs to be done every generation, I believe), and envisaging a very comprehensive bibliography, I saw that I needed a database to record all the items I came across. In the database I would also note what I had read and what I had still to see, and it would arrange the items in the libraries I visit (usually Sheffield and Cambridge) according to their position on the shelves.

I taught my relational database Helix the location of every volume of all the journals I use, so once I had entered JQR 21 as the reference for a journal article, for example, it would know that we did not have that volume of the *Jewish Quarterly Review* in Sheffield, and I would have to consult it in Cambridge, and at shelfmark P7.c.1 on the South Wing, Floor 3. All the other items for that location I would print out before my visit to the library, including the books, for which I had looked up the shelfmark in the electronic catalogues. Very occasionally I managed through this system to consult 100 items in a single day, but more often no more than 40.

As I entered each item in the database, I would classify it according to its destined place in the commentary, whether for the bibliography at the head of each chapter, or for a particular section of the General Bibliography at the end, so that eventually I could export the data with all the items under their appropriate heading and in alphabetical order by author. It was a pleasure to me to be able to control so much data without being overwhelmed by it. And I am happy to accept any judgment made about my character that can be inferred from that fact.

The Perils of Commentary

Mistaking the Horizon

Commentary writing is fine work, which must always be attending to particulars. But in focusing on the trees, the commentator must never lose sight of the forest. The commentator has to make a conscious effort, many times in the course of a working day, to stand back from the detailed work on the words and phrases to consider the impact of decisions about their meaning on the whole book. Balancing the needs of the micro-exegesis against those of a total perspective on the book, in a perpetual interplay between the part and the whole, is one of greatest pleasures of commentary writing, but also a realm in which it is all too easy to go astray. I think of the great commentary of Édouard Dhorme (1926; English translation, 1967), which almost never considered a wider horizon than that of the individual verse; I cannot agree with the commonly expressed opinion that it is the greatest of all biblical commentaries of our time. I came to think that Fohrer's was the most successful of Job commentaries at combining exact exegesis with the larger issues. The peril for the commentator is failing to blend the microscopic and the panoramic.

Brainwashing

If one labours for month after month at understanding a complicated text, and feels one has succeeded at last in making a tolerable sense of it, it is almost forgivable for a commentator to accept, explicitly or implicitly, the views of one's author. In fact, with the Book of Job, that is the default position of commentators. Hardly ever have I encountered a scholar saying, This is what I think the passage says (or, This is what I believe the book as a whole says), and personally I do not believe it. There is very little consensus on what the Book of Job actually says; but whatever we think the book means, that is what we ourselves tend to affirm.

The situation has only to be stated like that for us to realize its absurdity. Especially with the Book of Job, where—unlike almost every book in the Bible—contrary points of view are expounded at length, one might have thought that commentators would have felt themselves encouraged to sit loose to any or all of the ideas propounded in the book, since most of them must in some sense be 'wrong'. It could even be argued that the divine speeches themselves are not necessarily the last word on the matters that the book deals with, all the more because they systematically avoid the primary question that Job has everywhere been raising, the question whether there is justice in the divine governance of the world.

Even if one is personally disposed to accept statements in the text, it surely behooves a critical commentator to consider counter-evidence and arguments counter to what the text presents (e.g. where and how does Job or Yhwh differ from other parts of the Hebrew Bible?). I tried to do that myself in the Explanation sections of my commentary, but I am sure I did not range widely enough in my evaluations of what the speakers in the book were putting forward. The peril for the commentator is allowing oneself to be brainwashed by sustained closeness to the text and over-familiarity with it.

Hyper-professionalization

The commentator is typically a professional scholar, whose work will be read and reviewed by one's peers, who are experts in the academic study of the biblical book in question. The bibliographies with which major commentaries these days have to be festooned are the commentator's first line of defence against criticism that the work is insufficiently deep and inadequately researched. There is nothing wrong with displaying the resources for interpretation, but the peril lies in overlooking some of the crucial sources. I said in the Introduction to the first volume of my Job commentary:

I became increasingly dissatisfied with restricting my horizon to the so-called 'scholarly' works. Scholars quote scholars and create their own canon of approved literature on the Book of Job. Those writings that are not cited by previous commentators do not generally get cited by subsequent commentators ... Of course, when it comes to technical questions about philology, unscholarly remarks can be safely ignored. But when it is a matter of large-scale interpretation, of the meaning of the book as a whole and not just of a particular word or verse, one does not need to be a technically trained scholar to have valuable insights. So my 'undiscriminating' bibliography, which includes sermons and works of popular devotion alongside vast works of erudition, is meant as a kind of atonement for the principle of scholarly apartheid which reigns elsewhere in the commentary.

I call commentary-writing the quintessential form of biblical scholarship. Despite the plethora of commentaries, good, bad and indifferent, that publishers insist on setting before us, I would argue that we can never have too many commentaries. Except for commentaries that are mostly derivative, every commentary represents one person's tangling with the biblical text, and every such engagement is at the least interesting and at best profitable. I have heard commentary-writing disparaged as no more than a matter of copying from other commentaries, but I resist that blanket criticism vigorously as a simple ignorance of what goes into the creation of a commentary.

We need commentaries because we need commentary writers. The field of biblical studies needs a sizable cadre of commentators, that is, persons who have submitted themselves over a sustained period of time to the discipline of following a text, in all its windings, and grappling with questions of meaning on the large scale and the small. No other form of biblical scholarship trains the mind in the same way, or creates a sense of humility vis-à-vis the text and its author and vis-à-vis other scholars. Not all our colleagues are equally suited for commentary-writing, and it is no crime not to have written a commentary. But I must confess to asking myself about one or another esteemed colleague, who turns out not to have been perhaps of the first rank, Well, have they written a commentary?

Reflections on the Job Commentary

I found myself asking one day recently, How is my Job commentary different from other commentaries? (in the manner of the question the youngest child in the household must ask on the eve of Passover). With the hindsight of ten years on since its publication, I wondered if I yet knew what I had been doing. Here are my answers, though I fear I may be claiming rights to ideas I had picked up from other people.

1. *The Unity of the Book.* It is quite common these days to see the prose prologue and epilogue as deriving from a folktale drawn on by the author of the poem of Job but not his own creation. I took another line, believing

that the encasing of the poem inside the prose to be a masterstroke of the author, not least because of the contrast he was able to draw between the outward and the inner experiences of Job.

2. *The Profiles of the Friends*. As against a common view that the friends all present the same popular view of retribution, I felt I was able to distinguish the theological position of each of them from the others. And each of them was consistent with himself and stuck to his own position.

3. *Job's Changing Positions*. Job, by contrast, was changing all the time, always experimenting with doubts, ideas, proposals, wishes, summonses. In every speech he adopts a different intellectual position, and the crescendo of his demands is all the more insistent against the ground bass of the friends' inflexibility.

4. *Sympathies*. I believed it was possible, and desirable, to sympathize with each of the characters in the book, including Job—up to a point. But it was not difficult to see what was wrong with the views of the friends, and I made no bones about saying so. Job himself had all my sympathy, except in chaps. 29–31, his exculpation of himself, where I felt he told us at times more than we wanted to know about him.

5. *The Elihu Speeches*. I felt I restored the poet's designed shape of his book by proposing, on the basis of hints in the text, that the speeches of Elihu (chaps. 32–37) had been misplaced in the course of their transmission from their original place after the speeches of the other three friends to their present place after Job's great final speech in chaps. 29–31. In so doing, I had the divine speeches of chaps. 38-41 follow immediately upon Job's closing speech, with an evident heightening of their dramatic impact.

6. *Suffering or Justice?* It is a common view that the theme of the Book of Job is the question of innocent suffering: can there be such a thing? I denied that this is Job's question, seeing him rather as asking whether the world is governed in *justice*. He is suffering, to be sure, but the pain of it is that his suffering marks him out as a wrongdoer, and he hates the idea of a world where human behaviour is not appropriately rewarded or punished.

7. *The Purpose of the Divine Speeches*. In his responses to Job, Yhwh hardly ever refers to humans, but exhibits his delight in the rich variety of the world he has created, declaring at their climax that the crocodile is his creatorial masterpiece. In so doing, he deflects the question of justice in his dealings with the world, and effectively denies that rewarding or punishing humans is any part of his design for the universe. But this view of the deity is never stated in so many words.

8. *The Necessity of the Epilogue*. After such a masterclass in indirection, the hitherto forthright and demanding Job has quickly learned how to speak the same language. He has failed in his attempt to get the deity

to explain why he has tortured Job, but he cannot deny the divine plan for the universe. He *has* been treated unjustly, but he now knows that the world is not governed according to the principles of justice. Job has lost his case, but he has gained an understanding of the divine mind. Now that his eye has 'seen' the deity (which means, seen the universal picture from the deity's perspective), he realizes that he has uttered what he did not understand, obscuring the divine plan (42.3). So he 'melts' (if that is the meaning of *'emas* in 42.6) before the blaze of the divine vision of the totality (which means that he does not resist the new perspective), and is 'comforted' for the dust and ashes of his suffering. The epilogue has two unexpected twists in the tale: (1) Yhwh is angry with the friends because they have not spoken of him what is right, 'as my servant Job has' (42.7). The deity and Job are agreed that the world is not governed in justice: Job has said so by way of complaint, Yhwh has shown it by way of design. They are on the same side, against the friends. (2) In 42.10, in restoring Job's wealth, Yhwh gave Job twice as much as he had before. There is surely an allusion to the law of Exod. 22.4, where a thief must pay double for the theft of an animal. The universe may not be founded on a global law of retribution, but at least the deity acknowledges in the end that Job has been wronged.

I have run ahead of myself in speaking of my Job commentary, which extended over 25 years, more than half the time I was employed in Sheffield. I will return now to the period 1976–1989.

John Rogerson

James Atkinson retired as Head of Department in 1979 and his place was filled from outside the Department, by the appointment of John Rogerson (1935–2018). A graduate of Manchester and of Oxford, Rogerson had completed a book on the concept of myth in the history of biblical scholarship, a work that foreshadowed two of his overriding scholarly preoccupations: philosophy as the framework of biblical studies, and the history of Old Testament criticism, especially in Germany.[15] Before he came to Sheffield, he had been at Durham, where he had been the most junior lecturer in a Department of distinguished theologians. There he had dared to move into a new area for Old Testament scholars, social anthropology, and he published a ground-breaking survey, *Anthropology*

---

15. *Myth in Old Testament Interpretation* (Beiheft zur Zeitschrift für die alttestamentliche Wissenschaft, 134; Berlin: W. de Gruyter, 1974).

and the Old Testament.¹⁶ Two of his other key areas had been combined, theology and hermeneutics, in his *The Supernatural in the Old Testament*.¹⁷ Plainly he was an Old Testament scholar with a difference; he was not a philologian, though he was a considerable linguist with Russian and Arabic as well as the usual range of the biblical scholar's linguistic equipment, and not primarily an exegete[18] or a literary critic.[19] Without perhaps knowing it at the time, he had picked up James Atkinson's concern for the wider contexts of biblical scholarship, and broadened the horizon beyond theology to accommodate both philosophy and sociology.

There proved to be almost no area relevant to Old Testament studies in which John Rogerson did not make himself a master. Sociology? Read Rogerson on the use of sociology in Old Testament studies[20] and on the question whether ancient Israel was a segmentary society.[21] An atlas of the Bible? Rogerson could draw on his intimate acquaintance with the Middle East and his phenomenal memory to produce one of the outstanding atlases of our time, translated now into nine languages.[22]

---

16. John Rogerson, *Anthropology and the Old Testament* (Growing Points in Theology; Oxford: Blackwell, 1978; reprint edition: The Biblical Seminar, 1; Sheffield: JSOT Press, 1984). Note also his often cited essay, 'The Hebrew Conception of Corporate Personality: A Re-examination', *Journal of Theological Studies* NS 21 (1970), pp. 1-16]; reprinted in Bernhard Lang (ed.), *Anthropological Approaches to the Old Testament* (Issues in Religion and Theology, 8; Philadelphia: Fortress Press; London: SPCK, 1985), pp. 43-59.

17. John Rogerson, *The Supernatural in the Old Testament* (Guildford: Lutterworth Press, 1976). See also his 'The Old Testament View of Nature: Some Preliminary Questions', in H.A. Brongers et al. (eds.), *Instruction and Interpretation: Studies in Hebrew Language, Palestinian Archaeology and Biblical Exegesis. Papers Read at the Joint British–Dutch Old Testament Conference Held at Louvain, 1976* (Oudtestamentische Studiën, 20; Leiden: E.J. Brill, 1977), pp. 67-84.

18. He had however completed, with John McKay, for the Cambridge Bible Commentary, a textbook series designed for schools, a three-volume commentary on the Psalms: J.W. Rogerson and J.W. McKay, *Psalms 1-50, Psalms 51-100, Psalms 101-150* (The Cambridge Bible Commentary, New English Bible; Cambridge: Cambridge University Press, 1977).

19. Though he had written an important review article, 'Recent Literary Structuralist Approaches to Biblical interpretation', *Churchman* 90 (1976), pp. 165-77, which showed how well he understood what was going on in the field.

20. John W. Rogerson, 'The Use of Sociology in Old Testament Studies', in J.A. Emerton (ed.), *Congress Volume: Salamanca, 1983* (Supplements to Vetus Testamentum, 36; Leiden: E.J. Brill, 1985), pp. 245-56.

21. J.W. Rogerson, 'Was Early Israel a Segmentary Society?', *Journal for the Study of the Old Testament* 36 (1986), pp. 17-26.

22. John W. Rogerson, *The New Atlas of the Bible* (London: Macdonald, 1985).

A new textbook for introducing British university students to methods in studying the Old Testament? John Rogerson was the person to organize it.[23] A major introduction to the Old Testament for both British and American students? Ask John Rogerson.[24] His textbook on Genesis 1–11 for Sheffield's 30-volume Old Testament Guides series was arguably the best in the whole series, for it went beyond the usual questions of introduction and the conventional reviews of current resources to open the minds of students to the potential impact of sociology, feminism and the newer literary criticisms, all in a highly accessible mode.[25] And when, more recently, the Sheffield Industrial Mission, the first of its kind in Britain in its attempt to make the church relevant in the workplace, held its Jubilee conference, John Rogerson's churchmanship and his strong identification with Sheffield made him the ideal choice to edit a celebratory volume.[26]

For all that, there can be little doubt that John Rogerson's weightiest contributions to biblical studies lay in his mastery of the history of biblical scholarship, a field that he made all his own. Supported by his growing first-hand knowledge of philosophers from Kant to Habermas, his researches in German and British archives and libraries led to three penetrating studies of surprising readability: Old Testament Criticism in the Nineteenth Century: England and Germany,[27] W.M.L. de Wette, Founder of Modern Biblical Criticism: An Intellectual Biography,[28] and The Bible and Criticism in Victorian Britain: Profiles of F.D. Maurice and William Robertson Smith.[29]

---

23. John W. Rogerson (ed.), *Beginning Old Testament Study* (London: SPCK, 1983). A new edition is about to appear.

24. John Rogerson and Philip R. Davies, *The Old Testament World* (Cambridge: Cambridge University Press and Englewood Cliffs: Prentice–Hall, 1989).

25. John W. Rogerson, *Genesis 1–11* (Old Testament Guides, 1; Sheffield: JSOT Press, 1991).

26. John W. Rogerson (ed.), *Industrial Mission in a Changing World: Papers from the Jubilee Conference of the Sheffield Industrial Mission* (Sheffield: Sheffield Academic Press, 1996).

27. John W. Rogerson, *Old Testament Criticism in the Nineteenth Century: England and Germany* (London: SPCK, 1984).

28. John W. Rogerson, *W.M.L. de Wette, Founder of Modern Biblical Criticism: An Intellectual Biography* (Journal for the Study of the Old Testament Supplement Series, 126; Sheffield: JSOT Press, 1992). The present writer has adopted the subtitle of his book for the subtitle of this article.

29. John W. Rogerson, *The Bible and Criticism in Victorian Britain: Profiles of F.D. Maurice and William Robertson Smith* (Journal for the Study of the Old Testament Supplement Series, 201; Sheffield: JSOT Press, 1995).

Chapter 8. Sheffield University II (1976-1989)

This was another kind of contextualization of biblical scholarship, which relativized the present and the excitement of innovation by insisting on viewing it within a *longue durée* of historical change. If we ever were tempted to be spellbound by the latest scholarly fashion, whether structuralism or deconstruction or political exegesis, John Rogerson's historical scope had put on the Sheffield agenda the necessity for a cooler and more distanced approach.

On the New Testament side, we had made an excellent new appointment in 1976, that of Bruce D. Chilton (b. 1949). Bruce Chilton, a graduate of Bard College, a liberal arts college in Annandale-on-Hudson, New York, and of General Theological Seminary, the Episcopal Seminary in New York, now came to us from Cambridge. He had finished his PhD under Ernst Bammel and C.F.D. Moule on the concept of the kingdom of God, in the Targums and in Jesus' teaching alike, as the self-revelation of God. Not since Aileen Guilding's time had the Department benefited from the presence of a specialist in Jewish literature (Philip Davies's expertise on the Scrolls excepted), though we all acknowledged the indispensability of the field. Chilton soon published his dissertation as *God in Strength: Jesus' Announcement of the Kingdom*.[30] Together with Philip Davies, he became fascinated with the story of the Binding of Isaac (the Aqedah), tracing the forms that the legend took and engaging in polemics with a range of authors whose personal commitments seemed to have outranked their scholarly acumen.[31]

There had been another appointment of note late in the 80s, a little outside the mainstream. Ralph Martin, a graduate of Manchester and of King's College, London, where he had written his PhD thesis on the Christ hymn in Philippians in 1963 under Dennis Nineham, and lecturer in New Testament at Manchester from 1965 to 1969, had been teaching New

---

30. Bruce D. Chilton, *God in Strength: Jesus' Announcement of the Kingdom* (Studien zum Neuen Testament und seiner Umwelt, 1; Freistadt: Plöchl, 1979); reprinted as The Biblical Seminar, 8; Sheffield: JSOT Press, 1987. See also his 'Regnum Dei Deus Est', *Scottish Journal of Theology* 31 (1978), pp. 261-70.

31. P.R. Davies and B.D. Chilton, 'The Aqedah: A Revised Tradition History', *Catholic Biblical Quarterly* 40 (1978), pp. 514-46. See also Bruce D. Chilton, 'Irenaeus on Isaac (as Argued in his Adversus Haereses)', in Elizabeth A. Livingstone (ed.), *Studia Patristica. XVII, Part 2. Eighth International Conference on Patristic Studies* (Oxford: Pergamon Press, 1982), pp. 643-47. On the same broad issue, see also his article, 'Isaac and the Second Night', mentioned below, and his 'Recent Study of the Aqedah', in *Targumic Approaches to the Gospels: Essays in the Mutual Definition of Judaism and Christianity* (Studies in Judaism; London: University Press of America, 1986), pp. 39-49.

Testament at Fuller Theological Seminary in Pasadena, California since 1969. In 1988 he retired from his post there and returned to this country. Since we were about to lose David Hill, our Reader in New Testament, we came to an arrangement with Ralph Martin that he would supervise some of our graduate students each year. His title was Professor Associate, indicating that the post was part-time but the rank was that of full professor.

Martin, as an experienced and prolific New Testament scholar, was an important addition to our ranks. Following his dissertation,[32] he had written numerous commentaries on the New Testament, principally on Philippians,[33] Colossians[34] and 2 Corinthians,[35] and a number of widely used texts, on worship in the early church,[36] on Mark,[37] Paul's theology[38] and 1 Corinthians,[39] as well as a two-volume standard introduction to the New Testament.

When he came to Sheffield, his productivity did not abate. As well as continuing to serve as the New Testament editor for the highly regarded Word Biblical Commentary series, he published a second contribution to that series on James,[40] and a volume on Ephesians, Colossians and Philemon in the Interpretation commentary series.[41] There was also a

32. Ralph P. Martin, *Carmen Christi: Philippians. ii.5-11 in Recent Interpretation and in the Setting of Early Christian Worship* (Society for New Testament Studies Monograph Series, 4; Cambridge: Cambridge University Press, 1967; revised edn, Grand Rapids: Eerdmans, 1983).

33. Ralph P. Martin, *Philippians* (Tyndale New Testament Commentaries; London: Tyndale Press, 1959; revised edn, Grand Rapids: Eerdmans, 1987); *Philippians* (New Century Bible; London: Marshall, Morgan & Scott, 1976).

34. Ralph P. Martin, *Colossians and Philemon* (New Century Bible; London: Oliphants, 1974; 3rd edn, 1982).

35. Ralph P. Martin, *2 Corinthians* (Word Biblical Commentary, 40; Waco, TX: Word Books, 1986).

36. Ralph P. Martin, *Worship in the Early Church* (London: Marshall, Morgan & Scott, and Westwood, NJ: Revell, 1964; 2nd edn, 1975).

37. Ralph P. Martin, *Mark: Evangelist and Theologian* (Exeter: Paternoster; Grand Rapids: Zondervan, 1972).

38. Ralph P. Martin, *Reconciliation: A Study of Paul's Theology* (Marshalls Theological Library; London: Marshall, Morgan & Scott; and Atlanta: John Knox Press, 1981).

39. Ralph P. Martin, *The Spirit and the Congregation: Studies in 1 Corinthians 12–15* (Grand Rapids: Eerdmans, 1984).

40. Ralph P. Martin, *James* (Word Biblical Commentary, 48; Waco, TX: Word Books, 1988).

41. Ralph P. Martin, *Ephesians, Colossians and Philemon* (Interpretation: A Bible Commentary for Teaching and Preaching; Louisville, KY: Westminster/John Knox Press, 1992).

guide to the theological themes of 1 and 2 Corinthians,[42] and a contribution on the theology of Peter and Jude to a co-authored textbook,[43] to say nothing of papers on the Spirit[44] and other theological themes in 2 Corinthians,[45] and on patterns of worship in New Testament churches.[46]

Ralph Martin was presented with a Festschrift edited by former pupils in 1992.[47] He retired from the Department in 1996, by which time the New Testament side of the Department had been greatly strengthened and there were four full-time members of the teaching and research staff.

42. Ralph P. Martin, *1, 2 Corinthians* (Word Biblical Themes; Waco, TX: Word Books, 1988).

43. Andrew Chester and Ralph P. Martin, *The Theology of the Letters of James, Peter and Jude* (New Testament Theology; Cambridge: Cambridge University Press, 1994).

44. Ralph P. Martin, 'The Spirit in 2 Corinthians in Light of the "Fellowship of the Holy Spirit"', in W. Hulitt Gloer (ed.), *Eschatology and the New Testament: Essays in Honor of George Raymond Beasley-Murray* (Peabody, MA: Hendrickson, 1988), pp. 113-28.

45. Ralph P. Martin, 'Theological Perspective in 2 Corinthians: Some Notes', in David J. Lull (ed.), *Society of Biblical Literature: 1990 Seminar Papers* (Atlanta: Scholars Press, 1990), pp. 24-56.

46. Ralph P. Martin, 'Patterns of Worship in New Testament Churches' *Journal for the Study of the New Testament* 37 (1989), pp. 59-85.

47. Michael J. Wilkins and Terence Paige (eds.), *Worship, Theology and Ministry in the Early Church: Essays in Honor of Ralph P. Martin* (Journal for the Study of the New Testament Supplement Series, 87; Sheffield: JSOT Press, 1992).

Chapter 9

Sheffield University III (since 1990)

The flavour of the Sheffield department in the 1990s may be captured by a piece I wrote about it as the decade closed, THE SHEFFIELD DEPARTMENT OF BIBLICAL STUDIES: AN INTELLECTUAL BIOGRAPHY (1998),[1] from which I will quote:

> The 1990s have become, to this observer's eye at least, a time of great intellectual ferment in the academy. It is not just that we are all working a great deal harder, longer hours and at an ever faster tempo, for which our 200, 300, 350 Megahertz computers and the Internet are setting the standard, and confronted by a geometric growth in the number of books and articles that claim our attention, both from within the discipline and, increasingly, from outside. It is, rather, the re-evaluation of all values that postmodernism has brought with it that gives us furiously to think these days—think, that is, with no remission of the busyness of doing. Perhaps we should not exactly blame postmodernism, but think of postmodernism more as the name for what was happening anyway, for what we were doing to ourselves as we became more and more self-conscious about the nature of our scholarly work.[2]

---

1. Some material in this memoir has been copied from my chapter 'The Sheffield Department of Biblical Studies: An Intellectual Biography', in *Auguries: The Jubilee Volume of the Sheffield Department of Biblical Studies* (ed. David J.A. Clines and Stephen D. Moore; Journal for the Study of the Old Testament Supplement Series, 269; Sheffield: Sheffield Academic Press, 1998), pp. 14-89.

2. That is the postmodern as it has been so well characterized by Zygmunt Bauman of Leeds: 'Postmodernity is no more (but no less either) than the modern mind taking a long, attentive and sober look at itself, at its conditions and its past works, not fully liking what it sees and sensing the urge to change' (*Modernity and*

The Department ushered in the new decade with its own anniversary volume, *The Bible in Three Dimensions: Essays in Celebration of the Fortieth Anniversary of the Department of Biblical Studies in the University of Sheffield*[3]—a couple of years late for the fortieth birthday itself (on 1 October, 1987), unlike *Auguries: The Jubilee Volume of the Sheffield Department of Biblical Studies*.[4] In *The Bible in Three Dimensions* we asked all those who were teaching or had taught in the Department, together with some of its graduates, to write about their current research, and the result had a certain distinctive flavour, which some reviewers identified as a 'school'.

The concept of postmodernism was not much in evidence in *The Bible in Three Dimensions*, if at all, but it is hard to deny that it has become the key intellectual concept in the Department as the decade moved on. John Rogerson, indeed, was uncomfortable with the concept of postmodernism, taking a more Habermasian perspective and looking at our decade as more in continuity with the modernist project than the term 'postmodern' might suggest. Something new was happening, nevertheless, he agrees, and the shape his own thinking had been taking is in the form of a question, What is the human? In the 1980s he was already working on the use of the Old Testament in social and moral questions,[5] but by the 1990s the key issue had become for him, as he titled an article in the Department's anniversary volume, 'What Does It Mean to be Human? The Central Question of Old Testament Theology?'[6] In the Department's colloquium volume on the Bible and ethics, which he edited along with Margaret Davies and his former pupil Daniel Carroll, he wrote of the added dimensions the ethics

---

Ambivalence [Ithaca: Cornell University Press, 1991], p. 272). A fuller quotation from Bauman may be found in my own chapter below on 'The Postmodern Adventure in Biblical Studies'.

3. David J.A. Clines, Stephen E. Fowl and Stanley E. Porter (eds.), *The Bible in Three Dimensions: Essays in Celebration of the Fortieth Anniversary of the Department of Biblical Studies in the University of Sheffield* (Journal for the Study of the Old Testament Supplement Series, 87; Sheffield: JSOT Press, 1990).

4. *Auguries: The Jubilee Volume of the Sheffield Department of Biblical Studies* (ed. David J.A. Clines and Stephen D. Moore; Journal for the Study of the Old Testament Supplement Series, 269; Sheffield: Sheffield Academic Press, 1998).

5. John W. Rogerson, 'The Old Testament and Social and Moral Questions', *Modern Churchman* NS 25 (1982), pp. 28-35.

6. John W. Rogerson, 'What Does It Mean to be Human? The Central Question of Old Testament Theology?', in Clines, Porter and Fowl (eds.), *The Bible in Three Dimensions* (1990), pp. 285-98.

of the Old Testament brings to the Habermasian discourse ethics to which he himself was attracted.[7] Another reflection of this same project can be seen in his paper on the family and 'structures of grace', which he is distinguishing from 'structures of creation'.[8] When he reached the age of 60, we presented him with a Festschrift entitled *The Bible and Human Society*,[9] which seemed the right phrase to capture the focus of his concerns.

Departmental appointments

The most important thing that had happened intellectually to the Department in the 1990s was the four new appointments to the full-time teaching and research staff, in 1992, 1993, 1994 and 1996, together with the appointment of a full-time language tutor.

Margaret Davies came to Sheffield in 1992 after 14 years in the Department of Theology and Religious Studies at Bristol. She had graduated with the BA and PhD from Birmingham, having spent a year of her doctoral work in Oxford under the supervision of G.D. Kilpatrick. Her thesis had shown her to be an excellent text critic,[10] although almost all her subsequent work was in the theology and literature of the New Testament. As with other Sheffield colleagues in New Testament, it is hard to say whether her concentration was more on the Gospels or the Pauline and other literature. She co-authored, with E.P. Sanders, a substantial textbook, *Studying the Synoptic Gospels*,[11] and then a monograph on the rhetoric of John,[12] to which she added a literary commentary on Matthew in the Readings

---

7. John W. Rogerson, 'Discourse Ethics and Biblical Ethics', in *The Bible in Ethics: The Second Sheffield Colloquium* (ed. John W. Rogerson, Margaret Davies and M. Daniel Carroll R.; Journal for the Study of the Old Testament Supplement Series, 207; Sheffield: Sheffield Academic Press, 1995), pp. 17-26.

8. John W. Rogerson, 'The Family and Structures of Grace in the Old Testament', in Stephen C. Barton (ed.), *The Family in Theological Perspective* (Edinburgh: T. & T. Clark, 1996), pp. 25-42.

9. Mark Daniel Carroll R., David J.A. Clines and Philip R. Davies (eds.), *The Bible in Human Society: Essays in Honour of John Rogerson* (Journal for the Study of the Old Testament Supplement Series, 200; Sheffield: Sheffield Academic Press, 1995).

10. M. Davies, *The Text of the Pauline Epistles in Ms 2344 and its Relation to the Texts of Other Known Manuscripts, in particular to 330, 436 and 462* (Studies and Documents, 38; Salt Lake City: University of Utah Press, 1968).

11. E.P. Sanders and M. Davies, *Studying the Synoptic Gospels* (London: SCM Press, and New York: Trinity Press, 1989).

12. M. Davies, *Rhetoric and Reference in the Fourth Gospel* (Journal for the Study of the New Testament Supplement Series, 69; Sheffield: JSOT Press, 1992).

series from Sheffield.[13] On the Pauline side, she wrote a student guide to the Pastoral Epistles.[14]

Again like not a few of her Sheffield colleagues, she began her writing career in the 'wrong' Testament, with a paper on the succession of Solomon in reply to Edmund Leach.[15] There followed a number of papers on the Gospels, on the kingdom of heaven[16] and the son of man[17] in Matthew, on surprise and Matthew's understanding of the torah,[18] on the genre of Matthew,[19] and on the transfiguration story.[20] On John's Gospel she published papers on eschatology,[21] the question of Samaritan influence,[22] the meaning of *doxa*,[23] the son of man,[24] metaphors of going and dwelling,[25] and the concept of focus,[26] as well as special studies on John 3[27] and John

---

13. M. Davies, *Matthew* (Readings: A New Biblical Commentary; Sheffield: JSOT Press, 1993).

14. M. Davies, *The Pastoral Epistles* (New Testament Guides, 14; Sheffield: Sheffield Academic Press, 1996).

15. M. Davies, 'The Succession of Solomon: A Reply to Edmund Leach's Essay, The Legitimacy of Solomon', *Man* 7 (1972), pp. 635-43. Another later study on an Old Testament topic was her 'Canonical Criticism of the Old Testament', *Epworth Review* 12 (1985), pp. 56-64.

16. Margaret Pamment, 'The Kingdom of Heaven according to the First Gospel', *New Testament Studies* 27 (1981), pp. 211-32.

17. Margaret Pamment, 'The Son of Man in the First Gospel', *New Testament Studies* 29 (1983), pp. 116-29.

18. M. Pamment, 'Surprise and Matthew's Understanding of the Torah', *Journal for the Study of the New Testament* 17 (1983), pp. 73-86.

19. M. Davies, 'The Genre of the First Gospel', in Brian Davies (ed.), *Language, Meaning and God* (London: Chapman Cassell, 1987), pp. 162-75.

20. M. Pamment, 'Moses and Elijah in the Story of the Transfiguration', *Expository Times* 92 (1981), pp. 338-39.

21. M. Pamment, 'Eschatology and the Fourth Gospel', *Journal for the Study of the New Testament* 15 (1982), pp. 81-85.

22. Margaret Pamment, 'Is There Convincing Evidence of Samaritan Influence on the Fourth Gospel?', *Zeitschrift für die neutestamentliche Wissenschaft* 73 (1982), pp. 221-30.

23. Margaret Pamment, 'The Meaning of Doxa in the Fourth Gospel', *Zeitschrift für die neutestamentliche Wissenschaft* 74 (1983), pp. 12-16.

24. Margaret Pamment, 'The Son of Man in the Fourth Gospel', *Journal of Theological Studies* ns 36 (1985), pp. 56-66.

25. M. Pamment, 'Path and Residence Metaphors in the Fourth Gospel', *Theology* 88 (1985), pp. 118-24.

26. Margaret Pamment, 'Focus in the Fourth Gospel', *Expository Times* 97 (1985), pp. 71-75.

27. Margaret Pamment, 'John 3:5', *Novum Testamentum* 25 (1983), pp. 189-90.

17.[28] As a good Sheffielder, she worried about theory a great deal too, which led to her significant contribution to the Anchor Bible Dictionary on poststructural analysis.[29]

Her next project was on the ethics of the New Testament, for which several papers appeared, a study of homosexuality in Romans 1,[30] of the stereotyping of Pharisees in Matthew,[31] and of prostitution,[32] as well as her contribution to the present volume, 'Is There a Future for New Testament Ethics?'

Another new appointment in this decade was that of John Wade, an experienced teacher of classics, to a full-time position as Teaching Fellow. Until the beginning of the 1980s Sheffield had supported three classics departments, in Greek and Latin and Ancient History. By the end of the decade all classics teachers had either retired or taken up posts in other universities in conformity with a central decree for rationalization by the Universities Grants Committee. But, since the demand for teaching of the languages persisted, from undergraduates and graduate students alike, in 1988 the Sheffield departments of Biblical Studies and Mediaeval History began to employ John Wade on a part-time basis to teach elementary Greek and Latin, an arrangement that was so successful that from 1995 he was employed full-time in this Department to teach the Greek and Latin languages at all the undergraduate levels, to more than 100 students.

Wade's contribution to classical studies was not confined to the classroom. He was a leading member of a team engaged in constructing and furnishing a full-scale replica of a Roman villa on the site of villa buildings at Mansfield Woodhouse, about 20 miles from Sheffield. Substantial funding for the project, which cost around £2 million, was secured from

---

28. Margaret Pamment, 'John 17', *Novum Testamentum* 24 (1982), pp. 81-85.

29. Margaret Davies, 'Poststructural Analysis', in David Noel Freedman, *The Anchor Bible Dictionary* (New York: Doubleday, 1992), V, pp. 424-26.

30. M. Davies, 'New Testament Ethics and Ours: Romans 1.26-27. Homosexuality and Sexuality', *Biblical Interpretation* 3 (1995), pp. 315-31.

31. Margaret Davies, 'Stereotyping the Other: The "Pharisees" in the Gospel according to Matthew', in J. Cheryl Exum and Stephen D. Moore (eds.), *Biblical Studies/Cultural Studies: The Third Sheffield Colloquium* (Journal for the Study of the Old Testament Supplement Series; Gender, Culture, Theory; Sheffield: Sheffield Academic Press, 1998) (forthcoming).

32. M. Davies, 'On Prostitution', in Carroll, Clines and Davies (eds.), *The Bible in Human Society* (1995), pp. 225-48.

the European Regional Development Fund and English Partnerships. The villa was planned as a unique building, and a national resource.[33]

Another new appointment was that of Barry Matlock, who became Lecturer in New Testament in 1994. A graduate of Lipscomb University in Tennessee and of Westminster Theological Seminary, Philadelphia, he gained the PhD from Sheffield, where his work was supervised by Andrew Lincoln. He published his thesis as *Unveiling the Apocalyptic Paul: Paul's Interpreters and the Rhetoric of Criticism*.[34] His parallel projects in the period were on the 'new perspective' on Paul and on pragmatist hermeneutics, of which his paper on 'Biblical Criticism and the Rhetoric of Inquiry' is a sample.[35] His was no conventional approach to Pauline theology, but showed how even such a traditional subject in the biblical curriculum must be brought into relation with contemporary theory—and even cultural studies.[36]

Two following appointments to the staff of the Department resulted from the determination to invite to join us scholars of distinction who could bring with them an already established reputation. The first of these was J. Cheryl Exum, who had been teaching at Boston College since 1977. Educated at Wake Forest University, and a PhD of Columbia University in New York, she had taught at Yale University before her appointment at Boston College. By 1993, when we invited her to Sheffield, she had acquired a reputation as one of the foremost literary biblical scholars, creative, nuanced and meticulous in her scholarship. Her first three book-length publications had been volumes she conceived and edited. *Tragedy and Comedy in the Bible*[37] and *Signs and Wonders: Biblical Texts in Literary Focus*[38] were flagships of the biblical literary criticisms emerging in the 1980s, while *Reasoning with the Foxes: Female Wit in a World of Male*

---

33. D.N. Riley, P.C. Buckland and John Wade, 'Aerial Reconnaissance and Excavation at Littleborough-on-Trent, Notts', *Britannia* 26 (1995), pp. 254-84.

34. R. Barry Matlock, *Unveiling the Apocalyptic Paul: Paul's Interpreters and the Rhetoric of Criticism* (Journal for the Study of the New Testament Supplement Series, 127; Sheffield: Sheffield Academic Press, 1996).

35. R. Barry Matlock, 'Biblical Criticism and the Rhetoric of Inquiry', *Biblical Interpretation* 5 (1997), pp. 132-59.

36. Cf. his 'Almost Cultural Studies? Reflections on the "New Perspective" on Paul', in Exum and Moore (eds.), *Biblical Studies/Cultural Studies* (1998) (forthcoming).

37. J. Cheryl Exum (ed.), *Tragedy and Comedy in the Bible* (Semeia, 32; Decatur, GA: Scholars Press, 1984).

38. J. Cheryl Exum (ed.), *Signs and Wonders: Biblical Texts in Literary Focus* (Semeia Studies; Decatur, GA: Scholars Press, 1989).

Power,[39] in the same genre, took a more deliberately feminist slant on the biblical texts. And then her reflections and research on the tragic, both in biblical and in other literature, bore fruit in her impressive work, *Tragedy and Biblical Narrative: Arrows of the Almighty*.[40]

Exum's earliest publications had been in the realm of rhetorical criticism, the first of them as an undergraduate in New Testament.[41] There followed studies of structure in the Song of Songs,[42] of narrative in Judges,[43] and of poetic texts from Isaiah.[44] Broader literary issues began to emerge in studies of the theological dimension of the Samson saga,[45] and of the comic vision in the stories of Isaac, Samson and Saul,[46] and of the tragic

---

39. J. Cheryl Exum and Johanna W. H. Bos (eds.), *Reasoning with the Foxes: Female Wit in a World of Male Power* (*Semeia*, 42; Decatur, GA: Scholars Press, 1988).

40. J. Cheryl Exum, *Tragedy and Biblical Narrative: Arrows of the Almighty* (Cambridge: Cambridge University Press, 1992).

41. Cheryl Exum and Charles Talbert, 'The Structure of Paul's Speech to the Ephesian Elders (Acts 20,18-35)', *Catholic Biblical Quarterly* 29 (1967), pp. 233-36.

42. J. Cheryl Exum, 'A Literary and Structural Analysis of the Song of Songs', *Zeitschrift für die alttestamentliche Wissenschaft* 85 (1973), pp. 47-79; she later published a philological note, 'Asseverative 'al in Canticles 1:6?', *Biblica* 62 91961), pp. 416-19.

43. J. Cheryl Exum, 'Promise and Fulfillment: Narrative Art in Judges 13', *Journal of Biblical Literature* 99 (1980), pp. 43-59; 'Aspects of Symmetry and Balance in the Samson Saga', *Journal for the Study of the Old Testament* 19 (1981), pp. 3-29 (errata in *Journal for the Study of the Old Testament* 20 [1981], p. 90); most recently, 'Harvesting the Biblical Narrator's Scanty Plot of Ground: A Holistic Approach to Judges 16:4-22', in Mordechai Cogan, Barry L. Eichler and Jeffrey H. Tigay (eds.), *Tehillah le-Moshe: Biblical and Judaic Studies in Honor of Moshe Greenberg* (Winona Lake, IN: Eisenbrauns, 1997), pp. 39-46. Her article on 'The Book of Judges' in *Harper's Bible Commentary* (San Francisco: Harper & Row, 1988), pp. 245-61, though representing the practice of traditional biblical commentary, has a literary slant to it.

44. J. Cheryl Exum, 'Isaiah 28-32: A Literary Approach', in Paul J. Achtemeier (ed.), *Society of Biblical Literature 1979 Seminar Papers* (Society of Biblical Literature Seminar Papers Series, 16-17; Missoula, MT: Scholars Press, 1979), II, pp. 123-51; 'Of Broken Pots, Fluttering Birds, and Visions in the Night: Extended Simile and Poetic Technique in Isaiah', *Catholic Biblical Quarterly* 43 (1981), pp. 331-52 (reprinted in House [ed.], *Beyond Form Criticism* [1993], pp. 349-73); '"Whom will he teach knowledge?": A Literary Approach to Isaiah 28', in Clines, Gunn and Hauser (eds.), *Art and Meaning* (1982), pp. 108-39.

45. J. Cheryl Exum, 'The Theological Dimension of the Samson Saga', *Vetus Testamentum* 33 (1983), pp. 30-45.

46. J. Cheryl Exum and J. William Whedbee, 'Isaac, Samson and Saul: Reflections on the Comic and Tragic Visions', in Exum (ed.), *Tragedy and Comedy in the Bible* (1984), pp. 5-40 (reprinted in Radday and Brenner [eds]), *On Humour and the Comic*, pp. 117-59, and in House [ed.], *Beyond Form Criticism* [1993], pp. 272-309).

vision in the story of Jephthah.⁴⁷ Among her earlier feminist readings were articles the exodus story,⁴⁸ the figure of the mother in Genesis, Exodus and Judges,⁴⁹ and the matriarchs of Genesis.⁵⁰

In her feminist work, a signal of a developed attention to feminist theory in literary criticism generally was the title of a 1989 article: 'Murder They Wrote: Ideology and the Manipulation of Female Presence in Biblical Narrative'.⁵¹ And, in distinction from the earlier rhetorical criticism, a more postmodern slant was evident in her paper on thematic and textual instabilities in Judges.⁵²

Soon after her arrival in Sheffield, Exum edited, together with Clines, *The New Literary Criticism and the Hebrew Bible*,⁵³ laying down a marker of the way literary criticism in Hebrew Bible studies was developing. But her chief concentration in Sheffield has been in feminist criticism, always infused by the literary-critical perceptions she had formulated earlier. In 1993 she published *Fragmented Women: Feminist (Sub)versions of Biblical Narratives*,⁵⁴ and in 1997 asked the question, What does Judges say to

---

47. J. Cheryl Exum, 'The Tragic Vision and Biblical Narrative: The Case of Jephthah', in Exum (ed.), *Signs and Wonders* (1989), pp. 59-83.

48. J. Cheryl Exum, '"You Shall Let Every Daughter Live": A Study of Exodus 1:8–2:10', in M.A. Tolbert (ed.), *The Bible and Feminist Hermeneutics* (*Semeia*, 28; Decatur, GA: Scholars Press, 1983), pp. 63-82.

49. J. Cheryl Exum, '"A Mother in Israel": A Familiar Figure Reconsidered', in L.M. Russell (ed.), *Feminist Interpretation of the Bible* (Philadelphia: Westminster Press and Oxford: Basil Blackwell, 1985), pp. 73-85 (translated as '"Mutter in Israel": Eine vertraute Gestalt neu betrachtet', in L.M. Russell [ed.], *Befreien wir das Wort* [Munich: Chr. Kaiser, 1989], pp. 85-100).

50. J. Cheryl Exum, 'The Mothers of Israel: The Patriarchal Narratives from a Feminist Perspective', *Bible Review* 2/1 (Spring, 1986), pp. 60-66.

51. J. Cheryl Exum, 'Murder They Wrote: Ideology and the Manipulation of Female Presence in Biblical Narrative', *Union Seminary Quarterly Review* 43 (1989), pp. 19-39; reprinted in Alice Bach (ed.), *The Pleasure of Her Text* (Philadelphia: Trinity Press International, 1990), pp. 45-67, and in Clines and Eskenazi (eds.), *Telling Queen Michal's Story* (1991), pp. 176-98.

52. J. Cheryl Exum, 'The Centre Cannot Hold: Thematic and Textual Instabilities in Judges', *Catholic Biblical Quarterly* 52 (1990), pp. 410-31.

53. J. Cheryl Exum and David J.A. Clines (eds.), *The New Literary Criticism and the Hebrew Bible* (Journal for the Study of the Old Testament Supplement Series, 143; Sheffield: JSOT Press, 1993).

54. J. Cheryl Exum, *Fragmented Women: Feminist (Sub)versions of Biblical Narratives* (Journal for the Study of the Old Testament Supplement Series, 153; Sheffield: JSOT Press, and Philadelphia: Trinity Press International, 1993). One of its chapters was also published as 'Who's Afraid of "The Endangered Ancestress"?', in Exum and Clines, *The New Literary Criticism and the Hebrew Bible* (1993), pp. 91-113.

women?, in her *Was sagt das Richterbuch den Frauen?*[55] Further feminist studies were on Judges 11[56] and on the Exodus story revisited,[57] and on the Ruth and Naomi story.[58] The issue of ideology was raised again in the key question, 'Feminist Criticism: Whose Interests Are Being Served?',[59] and in her essay on prophetic texts depicting violence against women.[60] Her essay in *Auguries: The Jubilee Volume of the Sheffield Department of Biblical Studies*, 'Developing Strategies of Feminist Criticism/Developing Strategies for Commentating the Song of Songs',[61] offered her latest thinking on feminist theory as well as signalling her return to the Song of Songs, on which she completed a volume for the Old Testament Library.[62]

During these years, and in conjunction with her course on the Bible and the Arts, she developed a long-standing interest in the representation of the Bible in film, especially in classic Hollywood biblical epics, of which her 'Michal at the Movies'[63] and 'Bathsheba Plotted, Shot, and Painted' in *Biblical Glamour and Hollywood Glitz*[64] being the first samples. Her interest in cultural criticism is represented by her 1996 book, *Plotted*,

---

55. J. Cheryl Exum, *Was sagt das Richterbuch den Frauen?* (Stuttgarter Bibelstudien, 169; Stuttgart: Verlag Katholisches Bibelwerk, 1997).

56. J. Cheryl Exum, 'On Judges 11', in Athalya Brenner (ed.), *A Feminist Companion to Judges* (Sheffield: Sheffield Academic Press, 1993), pp. 131-44.

57. J. Cheryl Exum, 'Second Thoughts about Secondary Characters: Women in Exodus 1.8-2.10', in Athalya Brenner (ed.), *A Feminist Companion to Exodus to Deuteronomy* (The Feminist Companion to the Bible, 4; Sheffield: Sheffield Academic Press, 1994), pp. 75-87.

58. J. Cheryl Exum, '"Is This Naomi?": Misreading, Gender Blurring, and the Biblical Book of Ruth', in Mieke Bal (ed.), *The Practice of Cultural Analysis: Exposing Interdisciplinary Interpretation between Vision and Reflection* (Stanford: Stanford University Press, 1998) (forthcoming).

59. J. Cheryl Exum, 'Feminist Criticism: Whose Interests Are Being Served?', in Gale A. Yee (ed.), *Judges and Method* (Minneapolis: Augsburg–Fortress, 1995), pp. 65-90.

60. J. Cheryl Exum, 'The Ethics of Biblical Violence against Women', in Rogerson, Davies and Carroll, *The Bible in Ethics* (1995), pp. 246-69.

61. Clines and Moore (eds.), *Auguries*, pp. 206-49.

62. J. Cheryl Exum, *Song of Songs: A Commentary* (Old Testament Library; Louisville, KY: Westminster John Knox Press, 2005).

63. J. Cheryl Exum, 'Michal at the Movies', in Carroll, Clines and Davies (eds.), *The Bible in Human Society* (1995), pp. 273-92.

64. J. Cheryl Exum, 'Bathsheba Plotted, Shot, and Painted', in Alice Bach (ed.), *Biblical Glamour and Hollywood Glitz* (Semeia, 74; Atlanta: Scholars Press), pp. 47-73 (an expanded version appears as a chapter in *Plotted, Shot, and Painted: Cultural Representations of Biblical Women*).

Shot, and Painted: Cultural Representations of Biblical Women,[65] which showed elegantly how feminist biblical scholarship can move effectively into a whole new world. Here too belong her studies of the Bible in art, of the blinded Samson in a painting by the German impressionist Lovis Corinth[66] and (in collaboration with Fiona Black, one of her graduate students) of a stained-glass window, in a Derbyshire church some fifteen miles from Sheffield, depicting the Song of Songs by the Pre-Raphaelite painter Edward Burne-Jones.[67]

Cheryl Exum was appointed one of the two editors of the international journal *Biblical Interpretation* when it was founded in 1992 (in 1997 she became the sole editor). In addition to the regular round of editorial work, she conceived, organized and edited a special thematic issue on *The Bible and the Arts* (6/3 [1998]), representing her ongoing commitment to this area. She has also co-edited a Festschrift for her former colleague at Boston College, Philip King,[68] and in 1997 edited *The Historical Books*, one of the four Sheffield readers on the Old Testament/Hebrew Bible.[69] She additionally became the series editor of Gender, Culture, Theory, a monograph series of Sheffield Academic Press, of which four volumes had already been published by 1998.

Another appointment to our faculty came in 1996 when we were joined by Stephen Moore, a talented scholar whose innovative work in poststructuralist theory had quickly earned him an outstanding reputation in the USA. A graduate of Trinity College, Dublin, where he had also completed his PhD, he went to the United States as a postdoctoral fellow at Yale, and thereafter took up a position in New Testament at Wichita State University in Kansas. His appointment helped to fill the gap on the philosophical

---

65. J. Cheryl Exum, *Plotted, Shot, and Painted: Cultural Representations of Biblical Women* (Journal for the Study of the Old Testament Supplement Series, 215; Gender, Culture, Theory, 3; Sheffield: Sheffield Academic Press, 1996).

66. J. Cheryl Exum, 'Lovis Corinth's *Blinded Samson*', *Biblical Interpretation* 6 (1998).

67. Fiona C. Black and J. Cheryl Exum, 'Semiotics in Stained Glass: Edward Burne-Jones's Song of Songs', in J. Cheryl Exum and Stephen D. Moore (eds.), *Biblical Studies/Cultural Studies: The Third Sheffield Colloquium* (Journal for the Study of the Old Testament Supplement Series; Gender, Culture, Theory; Sheffield: Sheffield Academic Press, 1998).

68. Michael D. Coogan, J. Cheryl Exum, and Lawrence E. Stager (eds.), *Scripture and Other Artifacts: Essays on Archaeology and the Bible in Honor of Philip J. King* (Louisville: Westminster/John Knox Press, 1994) (winner of the Biblical Archaeology Society Best Book on Archaeology award, 1995).

69. J. Cheryl Exum (ed.), *The Historical Books* (The Biblical Seminar, 40; Sheffield: Sheffield Academic Press, 1997).

front that John Rogerson's departure had left, while his strong literary interests were immediately congenial to all his other colleagues here. His incursions into modern literary theory were all made in the interests of a rejuvenated and more self-aware New Testament scholarship, and he too found the mix of the theoretical and the textual the headiest brew of all.

When Stephen Moore arrived, he had already published three notable books in five years, *Literary Criticism and the Gospels: The Theoretical Challenge*,[70] *Mark and Luke in Poststructuralist Perspectives: Jesus Begins to Write*,[71] and *Poststructuralism and the New Testament: Derrida and Foucault at the Foot of the Cross*.[72] He had edited, with Janice Capel Anderson, a much used textbook, *Mark and Method: New Approaches in Biblical Studies*.[73] And he had been a member of the Bible and Culture Collective, who together had written the experimental and controversial volume, *The Postmodern Bible*.[74] He had also co-edited an issue of the journal *Semeia* on poststructuralism and exegesis.[75]

His papers were almost always theoretically inspired: his Lacanian reflections on Mark,[76] his deconstructive readings of Mark,[77] of Luke[78] and of John 4,[79] his Foucauldian 'God's Own (Pri)Son: The Disciplinary

70. Stephen D. Moore, *Literary Criticism and the Gospels: The Theoretical Challenge* (New Haven and London: Yale University Press, 1989).

71. Stephen D. Moore, *Mark and Luke in Poststructuralist Perspective: Jesus Begins to Write* (New Haven: Yale University Press, 1992).

72. Stephen D. Moore, *Poststructuralism and the New Testament: Derrida and Foucault at the Foot of the Cross* (Philadelphia: Fortress Press, 1994).

73. Janice Capel Anderson and Stephen D. Moore (eds.), *Mark and Method: New Approaches in Biblical Studies* (Minneapolis: Fortress Press, 1992).

74. Elizabeth A. Castelli, Gary A. Phillips, Stephen D. Moore and Regina Schwartz (eds.), *The Postmodern Bible* (New Haven and London: Yale University Press, 1995).

75. David Jobling and Stephen D. Moore (eds.), *Poststructuralism as Exegesis* (= *Semeia* 54 [1991]).

76. Stephen D. Moore, '"Mirror, Mirror...": Lacanian Reflections on Malbon's Mark', *Semeia* 62 (1993), pp. 165-71.

77. Stephen D. Moore, 'Deconstructive Criticism: The Gospel of the Mark', in Anderson and Moore (eds.), *Mark and Method: New Approaches in Biblical Studies* (1992) pp. 84-102 (previously published in a longer version in his *Mark and Luke in Poststructuralist Perspectives*, 1992).

78. Stephen D. Moore, 'Luke's Economy of Knowledge', in David J. Lull (ed.), *Society of Biblical Literature: 1989 Seminar Papers* (Atlanta: Scholars Press, 1989), pp. 38-56.

79. Stephen D. Moore, 'Are There Impurities in the Living Water that the Johannine Jesus Dispenses? Deconstruction, Feminism, and the Samaritan Woman', *Biblical Interpretation* 1 (1993), pp. 208-27; reprinted in John Ashton (ed.), *The Interpretation of John* (Edinburgh: T. & T. Clark, 2nd edn, 1997), pp. 279-99.

Technology of the Cross',[80] his postmodern 'Illuminating the Gospels without the Benefit of Color: A Plea for Concrete Criticism',[81] and 'The "Post-"age Stamp: Does it Stick? Biblical Studies and the Postmodernism Debate', his reader-response 'Doing Gospel Criticism as/with a "Reader"',[82] 'Rifts in (a Reading of) the Fourth Gospel',[83] and 'Negative Hermeneutics, Insubstantial Texts: Stanley Fish and the Biblical Interpreter',[84] his narratological 'Are the Gospels Unified Narratives?',[85] together with others yet more difficult to categorize: 'How Jesus' Risen Body Became a Cadaver',[86] 'The Gospel of the Look'.[87] Among these articles, there is perhaps just one without a witty or allusive title: 'Narrative Commentaries on the Bible: Context, Roots, and Prospects'.[88]

Moore had several concerns in this period. One is with the body, which leads him both into the abundant field of current cultural criticism on the body, as well as into gender studies and especially the construction of masculinity—an interest he shares with Clines. The body of God in

---

80. Stephen D. Moore, 'God's Own (Pri)Son: The Disciplinary Technology of the Cross', in *The Open Text: New Directions for Biblical Studies* (ed. Francis Watson; London: SCM Press, 1993), pp. 121-39.

81. Stephen D. Moore, 'Illuminating the Gospels without the Benefit of Color: A Plea for Concrete Criticism', *Journal of the American Academy of Religion* 60 (1992), pp. 257-79.

82. Stephen D. Moore, 'Doing Gospel Criticism as/with a "Reader"', *Biblical Theology Bulletin* 19 (1989), pp. 85-93 (previously published in David J. Lull [ed.], *Society of Biblical Literature 1988 Seminar Papers* [Atlanta: Scholars Press, 1988], pp. 141-59).

83. Stephen D. Moore, 'Rifts in (a Reading of) the Fourth Gospel, or: Does Johannine Irony Still Collapse in a Reading That Draws Attention to Itself?', *Neotestamentica* 23 (1989), pp. 5-18.

84. Stephen D. Moore, 'Negative Hermeneutics, Insubstantial Texts: Stanley Fish and the Biblical Interpreter', *Journal of the American Academy of Religion* 54 (1986), pp. 707-19.

85. Stephen D. Moore, 'Are the Gospels Unified Narratives?', in Kent Harold Richards (ed.), *Society of Biblical Literature: 1987 Seminar Papers* 26 (Society of Biblical Literature Seminar Papers Series, 26; Atlanta: Scholars Press, 1987), pp. 443-58.

86. Stephen D. Moore, 'How Jesus' Risen Body Became a Cadaver', in Elizabeth Struthers Malbon and Edgar V. McKnight (eds.), *The New Literary Criticism and the New Testament* (Journal for the Study of the New Testament Supplement Series, 109; Sheffield: Sheffield Academic Press, and Valley Forge, PA: Trinity Press International [the editors' names in the latter edition were Edgar V. McKnight and Elizabeth Struthers Malbon], 1994), pp. 269-82.

87. Stephen D. Moore, 'The Gospel of the Look', *Semeia* 54 (1991), pp. 159-96.

88. Stephen D. Moore, 'Narrative Commentaries on the Bible: Context, Roots, and Prospects', *Forum* 3 (1987), pp. 29-62.

biblical and related sources, a topic that most scholars and students did not even know was there to be researched, became one of the themes he has made his own, publishing *God's Gym: Divine Male Bodies of the Bible*,[89] as well as articles on Yahweh's body,[90] on the portrait of the deity in Revelation as hypermasculine,[91] and on the physical appearance of the historical Jesus.[92] Further ahead, studies would appear on the construction of masculinity in Matthew, of which an investigation of 4 Maccabees was a foretaste.[93]

The developing style of autobiographical criticism in biblical studies was a manifestation of the increased attention being paid to readers once the 'death' of the author had been announced[94] and meaning had come to be seen as a readerly construction. Moore was making some distinctive contributions both in form and content to the genre,[95] and an attentive reader need not to have travelled to Sheffield to get to know quite a lot about one at least of its faculty.

A third area of Stephen Moore's theoretical interests was the new historicism, on which he edited an issue of *Biblical Interpretation*,[96] contributing to it, as well as an introduction to the subject,[97] a paper, with Susan Lochrie Graham, a graduate student of the Department, 'The Quest of the New Historicist Jesus'.[98] And in addition to having become the editor of the

---

89. Stephen D. Moore, *God's Gym: Divine Male Bodies of the Bible* (New York and London: Routledge, 1996).

90. Stephen D. Moore, 'Gigantic God: Yahweh's Body', *Journal for the Study of the Old Testament* 70 (1996), pp. 87-115.

91. Stephen D. Moore, 'The Beatific Vision as a Posing Exhibition: Revelation's Hypermasculine Deity', *Journal for the Study of the New Testament* 60 (1995), pp. 27-55.

92. Stephen D. Moore, 'Ugly Thoughts: On the Face and Physique of the Historical Jesus', in Exum and Moore (eds.), *Biblical Studies/Cultural Studies* (1998).

93. Stephen D. Moore and Janice Capel Anderson, 'Taking It Like a Man: Masculinity in *4 Maccabees*', *Journal of Biblical Literature* 117 (1998), pp. 249-73.

94. Famously by Roland Barthes, 'The Death of the Author', in his *Image–Music–Text* (trans. Stephen Heath; New York: Noonday Press, 1977), pp. 142-48.

95. Stephen D. Moore, 'True Confessions and Weird Obsessions: Autobiographical Interventions in Literary and Biblical Studies', *Semeia* 72 (1995), pp. 19-50; 'Revolting Revelations', in Ingrid Rosa Kitzberger (ed.), *The Personal Voice in Biblical Scholarship* (New York and London: Routledge, 1998).

96. Stephen D. Moore (ed.), *The New Historicism and Biblical Studies* (= *Biblical Interpretation* 5/4 [1997]).

97. Stephen D. Moore, 'History after Theory? Biblical Studies and the New Historicism', *Biblical Interpretation* 5 (1997), pp. 288-98.

98. Susan Lochrie Graham and Stephen D. Moore, 'The Quest of the New Historicist Jesus', *Biblical Interpretation* 5 (1997), pp. 437-63.

Journal for the Study of the New Testament in 1997, he served as co-editor of the Third Sheffield Colloquium volume (with Cheryl Exum),[99] as well as *Auguries: The Jubilee Volume of the Sheffield Department of Biblical Studies* (with David Clines).

Sheffield's graduate students continued in this decade to make an energetic contribution to the life and research strength of the Department. Between 1990 and 1998 there were nine MPhils, and 64 PhDs; by 1998 16 of the PhDs had been or were about to be published. As the titles will show, not a few of them had been on topics traditional enough within the discipline of biblical studies, but there are few that lack any injection of the new ideas in free circulation in Sheffield. On the Old Testament there was: Paul Kissling on reliable characters in the historical books of the Old Testament,[100] Eric Christianson on Ecclesiastes,[101] Danny Carroll on Amos,[102] Yvonne Sherwood on Hosea,[103] Tony Petrotta on wordplay in Micah.[104] Among New Testament theses there was: Blaine Charette on recompense in Matthew,[105] Robert Webb on John the Baptist,[106] David

---

99. J. Cheryl Exum and Stephen D. Moore (eds.), *Biblical Studies/Cultural Studies: The Third Sheffield Colloquium* (Journal for the Study of the Old Testament Supplement Series; Gender, Culture, Theory, 6; Sheffield: Sheffield Academic Press, 1998) (forthcoming).

100. Paul J. Kissling, *Reliable Characters in the Primary History: Profiles of Moses, Joshua, Elijah and Elisha* (Journal for the Study of the Old Testament Supplement Series, 224; Sheffield: Sheffield Academic Press, 1996).

101. Eric S. Christianson, *A Time to Tell: Narrative Strategies in Ecclesiastes* (Journal for the Study of the Old Testament Supplement Series; Sheffield: Sheffield Academic Press, 1998) (forthcoming).

102. Mark Daniel Carroll R., *Contexts for Amos: Prophetic Poetics in Latin-American Perspective* (Journal for the Study of the Old Testament Supplement Series, 132; Sheffield: JSOT Press, 1992).

103. Yvonne Sherwood, *The Prostitute and the Prophet: Hosea's Marriage in Literary-Theoretical Perspective* (Journal for the Study of the Old Testament Supplement Series, 212; Gender, Culture, Theory, 2; Sheffield: Sheffield Academic Press, 1996).

104. Anthony J. Petrotta, *Lexis Ludens: Wordplay and the Book of Micah* (American University Studies, 7/105; New York and London: Peter Lang, 1991).

105. Blaine Charette, *The Theme of Recompense in Matthew's Gospel* (Journal for the Study of the New Testament Supplement Series, 79; Sheffield: JSOT Press, 1992).

106. Robert L. Webb, *John the Baptizer and Prophet: A Socio-Historical Study* (Journal for the Study of the New Testament Supplement Series, 62; Sheffield: JSOT Press, 1991).

Neale on sinners in Luke,[107] Chris Thomas on footwashing in John,[108] David Ball on the 'I Am' sayings of Jesus in John,[109] Helen Orchard on Jesus as victim in John,[110] Ray Pickett on the social significance of the death of Jesus,[111] Ian Wallis on the faith of Jesus Christ,[112] Jud Davis on Old Testament language in New Testament Christology,[113] Barry Matlock on the apocalyptic Paul,[114] Jeff Reed on a discourse analysis of Philippians.[115]

The Dictionary of Classical Hebrew

Probably my most important undertaking in these last 30 years (and certainly the most demanding) has been the creation of the *Dictionary of Classical Hebrew*, published in nine volumes between 1993 and 2016. The background to this work is the planned revision of the Hebrew lexicon Brown–Driver–Briggs, published in 1906. At the time of his unexpected death in 1970, D. Winton Thomas, my former professor of Hebrew at

---

107. David A. Neale, *None but the Sinners: Religious Categories in the Gospel of Luke* (Journal for the Study of the New Testament Supplement Series, 58; Sheffield: JSOT Press, 1991).

108. John Christopher Thomas, *Footwashing in John 13 and the Johannine Community* (Journal for the Study of the New Testament Supplement Series, 61; Sheffield: JSOT Press, 1991).

109. David Mark Ball, *'I Am' in John's Gospel: Literary Function, Background and Theological Implications* (Journal for the Study of the New Testament Supplement Series, 124; Sheffield: Sheffield Academic Press, 1996).

110. Helen C. Orchard, *Jesus as Victim: The Dynamics of Violence in the Gospel of John* (Journal for the Study of the New Testament Supplement Series, 161; Gender, Culture, Theory; Sheffield: Sheffield Academic Press, 1998) (forthcoming).

111. Raymond Pickett, *The Cross in Corinth: The Social Significance of the Death of Jesus* (Journal for the Study of the New Testament Supplement Series, 143; Sheffield: Sheffield Academic Press, 1997).

112. Ian G. Wallis, *The Faith of Jesus Christ in Early Christian Traditions* (Society for New Testament Studies Monograph Series, 84; Cambridge: Cambridge University Press, 1995).

113. Carl Judson Davis, *The Name and Way of the Lord: Old Testament Themes, New Testament Christology* (Journal for the Study of the New Testament Supplement Series, 129; Sheffield: Sheffield Academic Press, 1996).

114. R. Barry Matlock, *Unveiling the Apocalyptic Paul: Paul's Interpreters and the Rhetoric of Criticism* (Journal for the Study of the New Testament Supplement Series, 127; Sheffield: Sheffield Academic Press, 1996).

115. Jeffrey T. Reed, *A Discourse Analysis of Philippians: Method and Rhetoric in the Debate over Literary Integrity* (Journal for the Study of the New Testament Supplement Series, 136; Sheffield: Sheffield Academic Press, 1997).

Cambridge, had been working on his replacement of BDB, and had reached the letter kaph. Oxford University Press invited Professor J.B. Segal of London (1912–2003) to continue the work, but no records of such activity remain. Segal gave up the editorship in 1974 and Professor James Barr took over the editorship. He saw that a newly conceived dictionary and not a revision was called for. He wrote extensively and incisively about the principles a Hebrew dictionary should follow, but I do not know that he ever drafted a sample article for the dictionary. The Press had decided in 1980 that in view of the lack of progress since Winton Thomas's death and the assessment by Barr of what was required for the future, the project should be terminated. Barr continued to press for its survival, but by the mid-eighties it was clear there was no future for it, and we in Sheffield began to think that we could perhaps fill the gap.

As so often, our ambitions developed in tandem with technology. We had learned that one of the millstones round the neck of a revised BDB was the projected cost of typesetting it: £100 a page, so I recall (with inflation, that figure would be £300 today). But the personal computer had arrived. In 1986 I had spent some sabbatical time at Tyndale House, Cambridge, where my friend Harold Hoehner (1935–2009), from Dallas Theological Seminary, and a PhD from Cambridge, also on sabbatical, showed me his new Macintosh Plus.[116] Not only could he type beautiful Greek and Hebrew on the screen, he could enlarge or reduce the typeface with a single keystroke. Once the idea of new Dictionary formed in our heads, I knew how to solve the problem of the typesetting: the researchers who would write the drafts of the articles would do the typesetting as they went along, and the extra cost would be zero.

We began work in 1988, with a team of four in the first year, John Elwolde, Richard S. Hess (b. 1954), David Talshir and Zipora Talshir (1946–) (David and Zipora were on sabbatical leave, and sharing the job on the Dictionary). I was the editor, John Rogerson and Philip Davies served as Consulting Editors (to be joined in 1995 by Cheryl Exum). The Dictionary was intended to be the first comprehensive dictionary of the ancient Hebrew language, covering not just the biblical texts, like other Hebrew dictionaries, but all the non-biblical material down to c. 200 CE—which meant the Dead Sea Scrolls, Ben Sira and the ancient Hebrew inscriptions, but excluding the Mishnah. Its aim was to focus on the meanings of Hebrew words in their literary contexts, rather than upon the prehistory of their meanings, as many other dictionaries had done. In practice, that involved registering all the occurrences of all the words

---

116. Hoehner's magnum opus was his almost 1000-page commentary on Ephesians (Grand Rapids, MI: Baker, 2002).

(except for a few of the very commonest) and analysing them according to their syntactic role. Thus it was possible, for example, in the article on ʾāb 'father', to see all the verbs of which it is the subject or the object, and in the article ʾākal 'to eat', to see all the nouns that are its subject or its object. By the middle of 1998 the fourth volume is scheduled to be published, which will have brought the project to the half-way mark, and it has been received internationally as an indispensable work of exemplary scholarship.[117]

David Stec joined the Dictionary project in 1992. Having graduated from Leeds in Hebrew and theology, he read the Theological Tripos, Part III in Old Testament at Cambridge, and then wrote his PhD dissertation in the University of Manchester. He subsequently published his research as *The Text of the Targum of Job*,[118] and has written as well on papers on the particle *hen*[119] and the mantle of Achan.[120]

Frank Gosling, who joined the Hebrew Dictionary project in 1994, had graduated from St Andrews with the MA, MPhil and PhD. Gosling has published both on technical linguistic matters (the waw consecutive[121] and the verb *gālâ*[122]) and, more widely, on the concept of the spirit in Old

---

117. For an overview of its intentions, see David J.A. Clines, 'The Dictionary of Classical Hebrew', *Zeitschrift für Althebraistik* 3 (1990), pp. 73-80; 'The New Dictionary of Classical Hebrew', in K.-D. Schunk and M. Augustin (eds.), *Goldene Äpfel in silbernen Schalen: Collected Communications to the XIIIth Congress of the International Organization for the Study of the Old Testament, Leuven 1989* (Beiträge zur Erforschung des Alten Testaments und des antiken Judentums, 20; Frankfurt: Peter Lang, 1992), pp. 169-79.

118. David M. Stec, *The Text of the Targum of Job: An Introduction and Critical Edition* (Arbeiten zur Geschichte des antiken Judentums und des Urchristentums, 20; Leiden: E.J. Brill, 1994). Cf. also his 'The Targum Rendering of *wyg'h* in Job x 16', *Vetus Testamentum* 34 (1984), pp. 367-79.

119. David M. Stec, 'The Use of *Hen* in Conditional Sentences', *Vetus Testamentum* 37 (1987), pp. 478-86.

120. David M. Stec, 'The Mantle Hidden by Achan', *Vetus Testamentum* 41 (1991), pp. 356-59.

121. F.A. Gosling, 'An Interesting Use of the Waw Consecutive', *Zeitschrift für die alttestamentliche Wissenschaft* 110 (1998) (forthcoming).

122. F.A. Gosling, 'An Open Question Relating to the Hebrew Root hlg', *Zeitschrift für Althebraistik* 11 (1998) (forthcoming).

Testament theology,[123] on the work of W. Robertson Smith,[124] and on Judas Iscariot.[125]

Though it takes us back briefly into the previous decade, this is the place to mention some other workers on the Hebrew Dictionary. In its first year, 1998–89, we had the assistance of David and Zipora Talshir, who shared a post during their sabbatical leave from the Hebrew University in Jerusalem. David Talshir, who had written his PhD on the nomenclature of fauna in the Samaritan Targum, and published several papers arising from it,[126] had worked for some years on the Historical Dictionary of the Hebrew Language at the Academy of the Hebrew Language. While he was in Sheffield, he published his 'Reinvestigation of the Linguistic Relationship between Chronicles and Ezra–Nehemiah'.[127] Zipora Talshir, whose PhD dissertation in Jerusalem had been on 1 Esdras, was working in Sheffield on the Septuagint of 3 Kingdoms.[128] The other member of the team in that first year was Richard Hess, who after graduating from Trinity Evangelical Divinity School in Deerfield, Illinois, had gained his PhD from Hebrew Union College, Cincinnati. His speciality was in Semitic personal names, especially in the Amarna letters, and he published several articles on this[129] and other linguistic topics,[130] as well as

---

123. F.A. Gosling, 'An Unresolved Problem of Old Testament Theology', *Expository Times* 106 (1995), pp. 234-37.

124. F.A. Gosling, 'W. Robertson Smith: A Paradigm for Exegesis?', *Scandinavian Journal for the Old Testament* 11 (1997), pp. 223-31.

125. F.A. Gosling, 'Oh, Judas, What Have You Done?', *Evangelical Quarterly* 70 (1998) (forthcoming).

126. E.g. 'תתערדון in the Peshitta: The Translations and Midrashim to Deut. 14.1 and their Relation to Qorah's Affair', *Tarbiz* 49 (1980), pp. 81-101 [Hebrew]; 'אנקה—A Female Camel', in מחקרי לשון: מגשים לזאב בן־חיים (Z. Ben-Hayyim Jubilee Volume; Jerusalem: Magnes Press, 1983), pp. 219-36.

127. David Talshir, 'Reinvestigation of the Linguistic Relationship between Chronicles and Ezra–Nehemiah', *Vetus Testamentum* 38 (1988), pp. 165-93; cf. also his 'The References to Ezra and the Books of Chronicles in B. Baba Bathra 15a', *Vetus Testamentum* 38 (1988), pp. 358-60.

128. Her work was later published as *The Alternative Story of the Division of the Kingdom. 3 Kingdoms 12:24a-z* (Jerusalem Biblical Studies, 6; Jerusalem: Simor, 1993).

129. Richard S. Hess, 'Personal Names from Amarna: Alternative Readings and Interpretations', *Ugarit-Forschungen* 17 (1985), pp. 157-67; 'Divine Names in the Amarna Correspondence', *Ugarit-Forschungen* 18 (1986), pp. 149-68; 'Cultural Aspects of Onomastic Distribution in the Amarna Texts', *Ugarit-Forschungen* 21 (1989), pp. 209-16.

130. Richard S. Hess, '*'ADAM* as "Skin" and "Earth": An Examination of Some Proposed Meanings in Biblical Hebrew', *Tyndale Bulletin* 39 (1988), pp. 141-49.

a comprehensive list of the Alalakh texts,[131] a comparison of the Amarna letters with the biblical Psalms,[132] and of the genealogies of Genesis with other Semitic texts.[133]

The Distinctiveness of the Dictionary of Classical Hebrew

1. Its scope. The most important innovation of the *Dictionary of Classical Hebrew* (*DCH*), in my opinion, is that its scope was established as consisting of all evidences of the ancient Hebrew language, from its beginnings to c. 200 CE, a phase of the language generally referred to as Classical Hebrew. No previous Hebrew dictionary had as its scope the written remains of the whole of the Hebrew language of the period. Even the twentieth-century lexica remained dictionaries of Biblical Hebrew, excluding on principle and systematically (though not necessarily altogether) the Classical Hebrew texts such as Sirach that had been known since the end of the nineteenth century. It is hard to explain the omission of non-biblical Hebrew except as due to a religiously motivated (perhaps unconscious in some cases) regard for the scriptural text. It is true that the Hebrew Bible constitutes the lion's share of Classical Hebrew texts, but it is not generally recognized that the non-biblical texts are in length equivalent to about one quarter of that of the Hebrew Bible.[134] For the scholarly community to ignore for so long the extra-biblical literature in Classical Hebrew when creating dictionaries of the language constitutes something of a scandal, in my view, another instance of the continuing unacknowledged control of biblical scholarship by ecclesiastical interests.

The other major source of Classical Hebrew texts, and far outweighing Sirach in importance, has been the Dead Sea Scrolls, which are equivalent in length to 20% of the Hebrew Bible. *DCH* has been the first Hebrew dictionary to incorporate these texts, but even so, it has been possible to find fault with its achievement. One reviewer wrote (in 2017): 'The first attempt to include the Dead Sea Scrolls lexicon in a dictionary, in Clines' *Dictionary of Classical Hebrew*, failed because too much had yet

---

131. Richard S. Hess, 'A Preliminary List of the Published Alalakh Texts', *Ugarit-Forschungen* 20 (1988), pp. 69-87.

132. Richard S. Hess, 'Hebrew Psalms and Amarna Correspondence from Jerusalem: Some Comparisons and Implications', *Zeitschrift für die alttestamentliche Wissenschaft* 101 (1989), pp. 249-65.

133. Richard S. Hess, 'The Genealogies of Genesis 1–11 and Comparative Literature', *Biblica* 70 (1989), pp. 241-54.

134. The figures are shown in the Introduction to *DCH*, IX, p. 9.

not been published.'¹³⁵ It is true that there has been a flurry of Scrolls publications since 2000, but the fact remains that *DCH* contained 85,507 references to Qumran texts. How that constitutes a 'failure' is beyond me, especially since no one had even tried to bring together Qumran Hebrew with Biblical Hebrew in the half century since the first publications of the Scrolls.

2. *Its exhaustiveness*. The second feature of *DCH* is its citation of all occurrences of each word (except for some common particles like וְ *and* בְּ *in*). Inclusion of this feature was not motivated by some theoretical position (which one might say of the first distinctive mentioned above), but is there mainly because it was possible. The corpus of Classical Hebrew is small enough (c. 450,000 words, the length of a blockbuster novel) to permit such full citation, though it required an ample publication in eight volumes to present the results. Having decided on full citation, I became aware of the benefits. A lexicographer usually has the privilege of selecting typical usages for a dictionary article, and is permitted to skate over awkward, anomalous or dubious cases. Dictionaries of Biblical Hebrew have been quite good in handling difficult cases, but nevertheless the obligation on an exhaustive dictionary to deal with every single case was something of a novelty. It became necessary, for example, to decide for every occurrence of אֶרֶץ whether it meant *land* or *earth*—a decision no previous lexicographer had been compelled to make. Of course, there are instances where it is not certain which decision is the best, but the lexicographer is free to note, with an 'unless §4', for example, that a reference might be better placed under a separate sense.¹³⁶

The benefit of exhaustiveness is evident in that very article on אֶרֶץ. It becomes very plain from a quick review of the article that the sense 'land, territory', with 15 columns, is more frequently used than 'earth, world',

---

135. Eibert Tigchelaar, Review of *Hebräisches und aramäisches Wörterbuch zu den Texten vom Toten Meer einschliesslich der Manuskripte aus der Kairoer Geniza* (ed. Reinhard G. Kratz, Annette Steudel and Ingo Kottsieper), *JSJ* 48 (2017), pp. 569-72.

136. Willem K. Smelik made fun of the appearance of a reference in more than one place in *DCH* by remarking that '[A]pparently on the principle that a postmodern lexicographer will not prescribe one interpretation, D.J.A. Clines lists הזכיר under three separate entries, with the meanings 'invoke', 'display strength', and 'boast' ('The Use of הזכיר בשם in Classical Hebrew: Josh 23:7; Isa 48:1; Amos 6:10; Ps 20:8; 4Q504 III 4; 1QS 6:27', *JBL* 118 (1999), pp. 321-32 [322]). The author did not realize that the principle of *DCH* was to report the scholarly literature and that the editor of *DCH* did not personally approve of all the views he reported.

with 10 columns. That fact cannot be inferred from any previous lexicon, I believe.

3. *'New words'.* DCH was conceived more as a report of the current scholarly assessment of the Hebrew vocabulary than as a definitive statement in the name of the editor of what is actually the case. I think that the attitude of older lexicographers was the latter, and given my own formation, with its quest for 'truth', I could most naturally have been so oriented myself. But I had become very conscious of the vast variety of opinion in biblical scholarship, not just on matters of lexicography but across the board. And I knew it was impossible for me to consider every disputed issue in lexicography and come to a nuanced decision of my own. There was also the onset of the postmodern, which encouraged us—if not to celebrate—at least to live with the conflict of opinions rather than attempt to reach one superior opinion or, more improbably, to reconcile all opinions.

I must admit that I was not without opinions myself, not a few of them strong, so that I was not the best person to keep myself out of disputes and stay content with a reportage of those of others. There is therefore no doubt an unresolved tension in *DCH* and its subsequent revision, *The Dictionary of Classical Hebrew* between the stated principle of laying the choices before the reader and the foregrounding of the editor's views. It was an issue always in my mind, but I forgave myself the inconsistency by reflecting that whenever I foregrounded my own view I was doing no worse than most other lexicographers had done, and when I was leaving things open I was actually being more principled than other lexicographers had dreamed of being.

This conflict between principle and practice arose constantly in my mind over the matter of 'new words', those Hebrew words that were not in BDB. There was no problem about the words newly occurring in the extra-biblical documents that BDB had not incorporated; it was the slew of proposals that scores of scholars had been making in the last 100 years for words they claimed had not been recognized by the Masoretes or the earlier lexicography but which could now be added to the Hebrew vocabulary (as Driver and Winton Thomas had been doing). There were ample reasons for including them: their presence in the scholarly literature, their adoption in certain modern English translations such as the NEB, their attractiveness in solving long-standing problems in the biblical text. But as certain opponents of 'new words' were fond of saying, they had not in most cases yet been subjected to scholarly scrutiny, and it seemed questionable to lay them before a public (including novice Hebraists) who were not in a position to make an informed judgment about them.

If I, a professional lexicographer, was not willing and able to adjudicate these new words, how did I expect the users of my dictionary to react to them? Inasmuch as I resolved this question for myself, I decided that my chief responsibility was to reflect the level of debate and uncertainty by including all proposed new words (apart from those few that I judged to be patently wrong or that I could not understand); but I would also attempt, by way of compromise, to protect those who might be misled by their presence by affixing, as a warning sign, an asterisk before the article in which they were treated.

4. *Syntagmatic analysis*. I had always appreciated in BDB, as also in *HALOT*, the inclusion of information about the subjects and objects of verbs, though it was only ever partial information, according to the whim (or judgment) of the lexicographer, I supposed. I decided that *DCH* should present such data systematically, showing (for example) all the subjects that were used with a given verb, and all the objects—which is to say, the syntagmatic relationships each verb can have. The principle of exhaustiveness paid off, and I found one could learn a lot about the Hebrew language merely by reading through the list of subjects and objects of verbs one knows well. Who, for example, is said to רון *run*? Not only Abraham and Jeremiah, for example, but also women like Rachel and Rebekah. Yhwh runs, as do angels; and messengers and heralds, not surprisingly. A foot, a horse, and the sun also can run (but not a river or a road, as in English). What kinds of abstract things can be 'seen' (ראה)? What can be 'eaten' (אכל)? And what can 'eat' apart from living creatures? Fire and flame, it turns out, along with famine and plague, shame and curse and the new moon.

Chapter 10

WRITING AND SCHEMES
[UNFINISHED]

Methods: A Taxonomy

Methods: A Confluence

Chapter 11

TEN THINGS I HAVE BEEN SAYING
(BUT NO ONE WAS LISTENING)
[UNFINISHED]

1. The liberation of biblical scholarship from the control of religiously committed believers. I have no fault to find with religiously committed believers, or with their reading the Bible in the service of their beliefs. But using the Bible to support one's opinions is a different thing from being a scholar of the Bible.

2. I have often expressed my understanding of scholarship as a bringing to bear of a critical judgment upon the subject matter of one's discipline, whatever it is. We should hate it if all professors of politics were left wing sympathizers themselves, so why do we not hate it when the great majority of biblical scholars are adherents of a religious tradition, Christian or Jewish, and make no secret that their primary concern is to enhance the church or the religious community to which they belong?

3. I have been calling for a movement beyond interpretation to critique. I have nothing against interpretation, which is a scholarly necessity. But if all we do with our texts is interpret them, we are the prisoners of the ancient texts. It may not be the duty of every individual scholar to embark on a project of critique, but if the scholarly community as a whole does not exhibit a proper distance from its subject matter, then it has lost the right to be regarded as a scholarly community.

4. One means toward critiquing our texts is to examine their ideological

The medieval university existed for the preservation of tradition The modern university must always be on its guard against relapsing into that state

5. Teaching and learning. It is a great sadness to me to see how locked in the past the goals and processes of teaching (thing in the humans, but especially in Biblical Studies). My SBL Presidential address, designed to show a better way, apparently sank without trace.

6. The dead hand of tradition on the curriculum in Biblical Studies, and on Hebrew lexica and presumably textbooks in general.

7. Absence of recognition of the volatility of the text of the Hebrew Bible. Working with the Hebrew dictionary has shown me on every page how many variant readings and variant proposals there are for the consonantal text (which itself is far from assured).

8. Reflections on Rate my Professor. Students' uncensored remarks shows how much their teachers have failed to let them glimpse the purpose of an university education. For students (especially in the USA) it is all a matter of techniques for getting grades, and all that matters about their professors whether they are hard or easy.

holistic

being convinced is a term for a psychological state not an arguments

Masoretic fundamentlaism

A life should be a manifesto

Crclc of the blood

It took up to 30 years for William Harvey's theory of the circulation of the blood in 1648 to be accepted, but after 140 years since Wellhausen's Prolegomena the standard theory of Pentateuchal origins shows less sign of being accepted than at any point in its history.

It's not much of a counterclaim to maintain that there are still thousands of people addicted to the four-source theory and whole careers founded upon it. For it became the industry standard, and the weight of the scholarly establishment was behind it. Lord knows how hard it is to overturn the establishment. Interestingly, even after the theory of the circulation of the blood was universally accepted, people continued the practice of bloodletting for more than 200 years, until the late nineteenth century; the grounds for the efficacy of bloodletting had been entirely destroyed by the discovery of the circulation of the blood, but the practice continued because the medical establishment thought such a treatment, though unsatisfactory, was better than no treatment at all. George Washington didn't think so when he died after being relieved of nearly two litres of his blood.

Have the courage to generalize

Be perfect in spelling, but do not make perfection of spelling your goal

Conquer the peaks. I have always been returning to Genesis 1, Psalm 23, Isaiah 53. Do not sweat the small stuff.

Break fresh ground.

Be scrupulous in scholarship and rigorous with texts — and generous with ancient talent

Beware of brainwashing by the familiar

Clinesian

Publications of David J.A. Clines
(as at 1 November, 2022)

PDF versions of many of these papers and of sample pages of these books are posted at www.academia.edu; in such cases, an asterisk (*) follows the title.

In Preparation
- The Dictionary of Classical Hebrew. III. Zayin–Taw. Revised edition (Sheffield Phoenix Press, 2023).
- In Critique of the Hebrew Bible
- Byforms in Classical Hebrew
- The Text and Translation of the Hebrew Bible
- Scenes from a Provincial Life: A Memoir
- Index locorum dubiorum in Novo Testamento graeco. Index of Doubtful Passages in the Greek New Testament
- 'How to Begin a Psalm'
- 'When Does a Psalm Know It Is Finished?'
- 'Interchange and Metathesis of Consonants in Classical Hebrew'.*
- 'A Sheffield Philosopher: 1. Upsetting Executives'
- 'A Sheffield Philosopher: 2. Marriage: Yet Another Masculist Project'
- 'A Sheffield Philosopher: 3. Why Warfare?'

Forthcoming
- *Joban Papers*, forthcoming in Hebrew Bible Monographs, Sheffield Phoenix Press
- *Play the Man! The Masculine Imperative in the Bible* (2022)
- *Hebrew Philology, Hebrew Lexicography*
- 'Byforms in Classical Hebrew', forthcoming in *Journal of the Ancient Near Eastern Society (JANES)*, as a Festschrift for David Marcus.*
- 'The State of the Text of Job', for a Festschrift for Ellen van Wolde (ed. Pierre Van Hecke) [submitted for *VT* ([???], 21.4.20].*
- 'Synonym Hunting in Classical Hebrew: The How, the Why, and the Wherefore'.*
- 'Synonyms in Classical Hebrew'.*

2021
- 'Alleged Female Language about the Deity in the Hebrew Bible', *Journal of Biblical Literature* 140 (2021), pp. 229-49.*
- 'Alleged Basic Meanings of the Hebrew Verb *qdš* "Be Holy": An Exercise in Comparative Hebrew Lexicography', *Vetus Testamentum* 71 (2021), pp. 481-502.*

- 'Genesis 1: A Critique', paper to the Ehrhardt Seminar, University of Manchester, 15 April 2021, 15 pp.*
- 'A Dietary Upgrade for Eschatological Animals (Isaiah 30.24)', 6 pp.*
- 'To Mend the Infrastructure of Biblical Research', 5 pp.
- *Joban Papers*: Table of Contents, 1 p.*
- 'Byforms in Classical Hebrew, by Gloss', 259 pp.*
- 'Byforms by Hebrew Word, Alphabetically', 176 pp. •
- 'Synonym Sets in Classical Hebrew', 141 pp.*
- 'All 345 Semantic Fields in Classical Hebrew', 7 pp.*
- 'Classical Hebrew Words by Semantic Fields (Aleph–Teth)', 365 pp.*
- 'How Are the *DCH / DCHR* Dictionaries Different?', 2 pp.*
- 'The Dictionary of Classical Hebrew Revised, Volume 3. Zayin–Teth. Preface', 3 pp.*
- '*DCHR* Compared with *DCH*: A Sample of Heth'.*
- 'Publications of David J.A. Clines, as at 31 December, 2021', 33 pp.*
- 'Publications of David J.A. Clines in Alphabetical Order, as at 31 December, 2021', 12 pp.*
- 'Books by David J.A. Clines, November 2021', 3 pp.*
- 'The Dictionary of Classical Hebrew Revised: Additions and Corrections, Version 2, 8 February 2021', 57 pp.*
- 'The Dictionary of Classical Hebrew Revised: Additions and Corrections, Version 3, 31 December, 2021', 69 pp.*

2020

- 'The Ubiquitous Language of Violence in the Hebrew Bible', Viol*ence in the Hebrew Bible: Between Text and Reception. Papers Read at the Joint Meeting of the Oudtestamentisch Werkgezelschap, the Society for Old Testament Study, and the Old Testament Society of South Africa, Groningen 2018* (ed. Jacques van Ruiten and Koert van Bekkum; Oudtestamentische Studiën, 79; Leiden, Brill, 2020), pp. 23-41.*
- 'The Dictionary of Classical Hebrew Revised: Additions and Corrections, Version 1', uploaded to academia.edu, 17 February 2020.*
- 'Synonym Hunting in Classical Hebrew: The How, the Why, and the Wherefore', paper at The International Syriac Language Project session, Society of Biblical Literature Virtual Annual Meeting, Boston, November 2020, 8 pp.*
- 'New Words in Classical Hebrew', paper in the Biblical Lexicography session, Society of Biblical Literature Virtual Annual Meeting, Boston, November 2020, 7 pp. academia.edu/44571808.*
- Review, Reinhard G. Kratz, Annette Steudel and Ingo Kottsieper (eds.) *Hebräisches und aramäisches Wörterbuch zu den Texten vom Toten Meer, einschliesslich der Manuskripte aus der Kairoer Geniza*, Band I. a–b (Berlin: W. de Gruyter, 2017); Band II. g–z (Berlin: W. de Gruyter, 2018), *Journal of Semitic Studies*.*

2019

- *The Dictionary of Classical Hebrew Revised*. II. *Beth–Waw* (ed. David J.A. Clines; Sheffield: Sheffield Phoenix Press, 2019), 895 pp.
- 'The Most High Male: Divine Masculinity in the Bible', in *Hebrew Masculinities Anew* (ed. Ovidiu Creangă; Hebrew Bible Monographs, 79; Sheffield: Sheffield Phoenix Press, 2019), pp. 61-82.*

- 'What's Wrong with Genesis 1: Text and Translation', paper for Society of Biblical Literature International Meeting, Rome, July 2019, www.academia.edu/39708081.*
- 'Cattle, Flocks and Other Beasts: Why Terms for Animal Groups Matter', for the International Organization for the Study of the Old Testament Meeting, Aberdeen, 4-9 August, 2019 (www.academia.edu/39998538).*
- 'There Go the Ships (Psalm 104:26)', paper at the Biblical Hebrew Poetry session, Society of Biblical Literature Annual Meeting, San Diego, November 2019 [for an earlier version, see 2015].*

2018

- *The Dictionary of Classical Hebrew Revised*. I. *Aleph* (ed. David J.A. Clines; Sheffield: Sheffield Phoenix Press, 2018), 764 pp.
- *Biblical Reception 5: Biblical Women* (2018) (ed. J. Cheryl Exum, David J.A. Clines; Guest Editor: Diane Apostolos-Cappadona; London: Bloomsbury T. & T. Clark, 2017), xviii + 228 pp.
- 'Gendering the Magnificat', in *Let the Reader Understand: Essays in Honor of Elizabeth Struthers Malbon* (ed. Edwin Broadhead; Library of New Testament Studies, 583; London: Bloomsbury T. & T. Clark), pp. 175-82.*
- 'Job', in *New Oxford Annotated Bible: New Revised Standard Version, with the Apocrypha* (ed. Michael D. Coogan; New York: Oxford University Press, 2018), pp. 739-79.
- *The Dictionary of Classical Hebrew Revised*. I. *Aleph*, sample pages (125 pp.).*
- 'How Is This Dictionary Different? The New Dictionary of Classical Hebrew Revised' (PowerPoint). [Presentation at the Society of Biblical Literature International Meeting, Helsinki, August, 2018].*
- 'The Ubiquitous Language of Violence in the Hebrew Bible', paper for the Joint Meeting of the Het Oudtestamentisch Werkgezelschap in Nederland en België, The Society for Old Testament Study (United Kingdom) and Die Ou-Testamentische Werkgemeenskap van Suid Afrika, 22-24 August, 2018, Groningen, to be published in Oudtestamentische Studiën (Brill, 2019).*
- 'Denominative Verbs in Classical Hebrew', paper at The International Syriac Language Project session, Society of Biblical Literature Annual Meeting, Denver, November 2018.
- 'Synonyms in Classical Hebrew', paper at the Lexicography session, Society of Biblical Literature Annual Meeting, Denver, November 2018.*

2017

- 'Towards a Science of Comparative Classical Hebrew Lexicography', in *From Ancient Manuscripts to Modern Dictionaries: Select Studies in Aramaic, Hebrew, and Greek* (Perspectives on Linguistics and Ancient Languages; ed. Tarsee Li and Keith Dyer; Piscataway, NJ: Gorgias Press, 2017), pp. 227-46.*
- 'Made in Sheffield: The First Dictionary of the Ancient Hebrew Language', in *History, Politics and the Bible: From the Iron Age to the Media Age* (Festschrift for Keith W. Whitelam; LHB/OTS, 651; London: Bloomsbury T. & T. Clark, 2016), pp. 136-45.*
- 'A Voyage round my Library', *Biblical Interpretation* 25 (2017), pp. 440-77 [paper read at the Conference on The Futures of Biblical Studies, at University of Kent, Canterbury, 1-2 June 2016].*

- 'Alleged Female Language about the Deity in the Hebrew Bible', paper read to the Society for Old Testament Study, 100th Anniversary Meeting, King's College, London, July 2017.*
- 'Byforms in Classical Hebrew', paper read in the International Syriac Language Project, Society of Biblical Literature International Meeting, Berlin, 9 August, 2017 [academia.edu/34122192].*
- 'The Vocabulary of Classical Hebrew: New Facts and Figures', paper read to the Biblical Lexicography session, Society of Biblical Literature Annual Meeting, Boston, 20 November 2017, 12 pp.*
- 'Classical Hebrew: All 3,308 Byforms, Alphabetically'.*
- 'Classical Hebrew: All 3,308 Byforms, by Gloss' [academia.edu/34122191].*
- 'Classical Hebrew: Interchange of Consonants Table' [academia.edu/34122193].*
- 'Classical Hebrew: All 330 Denominative Verbs', 12 pp.*
- 'Classical Hebrew: All 660 Verbal Nouns', www.academia.edu.*
- 'How Is the Dictionary of Classical Hebrew (*DCH*) Different from All Other Hebrew Dictionaries? and How Will the Dictionary of Classical Hebrew Revised (*DCHR*) Be Different from *DCH*?', 2 pp., www.academia.edu.*

2016

- *The Dictionary of Classical Hebrew. IX. English–Hebrew Index; Word Frequency Tables* (Sheffield: Sheffield Phoenix Press, 2016), 834 pp.* [sample pages]
- *Biblical Reception 4: A New Hollywood Moses: On the Spectacle and Reception of Exodus: Gods and Kings* (2016) (ed. J. Cheryl Exum, David J.A. Clines and David Tollerton; *Bloomsbury T. & T. Clark, 2016*), ix + 329 pp.
- 'The Wisdom of Job's Conclusion (Job 42:1-6)', in *Goochem in Mokum / Wisdom in Amsterdam: Papers on Biblical and Related Wisdom Read at the Fifteenth Joint Meeting of the Society for Old Testament Study and the Oudtestamentisch Werkgezelschap, Amsterdam, July 2012* (ed. George J. Brooke and Pierre van Hecke, with Bob Becking and Eibert Tigchelaar; Oudtestamentische Studiën, 68; Leiden: Brill, 2016), pp. 34-42.*
- 'A Century of SOTS Papers', for *SOTS at 100: Centennial Essays of the Society for Old Testament Study* (ed. John Jarick; London: Bloomsbury T. & T. Clark, 2016), pp. 89-105.*
- 'A Voyage Round my Library', paper read at the Conference on The Futures of Biblical Studies, at University of Kent, Canterbury, 1-2 June 2016. Forthcoming in *Biblical Interpretation*.*
- 'Alleged Female Language about the Deity in the Hebrew Bible', paper read at the section Feminist Interpretations at the SBL International Meeting, Seoul, July 2016.*
- 'Revising the Hebrew Dictionary (*DCH*). 6. Reaping, Threshing and Winnowing: Twenty-Four Agricultural Terms Defined', www.academia.edu/27218562.*
- 'Alleged Basic Meanings of the Hebrew Verb *qdš* 'be holy': An Exercise in Comparative Hebrew Lexicography', paper read at the International Organization for the Study of the Old Testament, Stellenbosch, September 2016.*
- 'How Many Israelites Do We Know by Name? With a Plan for a Hebrew Prosopography', paper read at the Hebrew Bible, History, and Archaeology section of the SBL Annual Meeting, San Antonio, TX, November 2016.*

- 'The New Hezekiah Seal: Outstanding Questions', paper read at the Archaeology of the Biblical World section, SBL Annual Meeting, San Antonio, TX, November 2016.*

2015
- *Biblical Reception* 3 (2014) (ed. J. Cheryl Exum and David J.A. Clines; Sheffield: Sheffield Phoenix Press, 2015), xi + 330 pp.
- 'Contemporary Methods in Hebrew Bible Criticism', for *Hebrew Bible / Old Testament: The History of its Interpretation. III. From Modernism to Post-Modernism.* Part II. *The Twentieth Century—From Modernism to Post-Modernism* (ed. Magne Sæbø; Vandenhoeck & Ruprecht, 2015), pp. 148-69.*
- 'The Recovery of the Ancient Hebrew Language: The Astonishing Wealth of its Unrecognized Vocabulary', in *Biblical Lexicology: Hebrew and Greek. Semantics—Exegesis—Translation* (ed. Eberhard Bons, Jan Joosten and Regine Hunziker-Rodewald; Beihefte zur *Zeitschrift für die alttestamentliche Wissenschaft*, 443; Berlin: Walter de Gruyter, 2015), pp. 71-82.*
- 'Misapprehensions, Ancient and Modern, about Lions (Nahum 2.13)', for *Poets, Prophets, and Texts in Play: Studies in Biblical Poetry and Prophecy in Honour of Francis Landy* (ed. Ehud Ben Zvi, Claudia V. Camp, David M. Gunn, and Aaron W. Hughes; London: Bloomsbury T. & T. Clark, 2015), pp. 58-76.*
- 'The Decalogue as the Avoidance of Theft', in *New Perspectives on Old Testament Prophecy and History: Essays in Honour of Hans M. Barstad* (ed. Rannfrid I. Thelle, Terje Stordalen and Mervyn E.J. Richardson; VTSup, 168; Leiden: Brill, 2015), pp. 293-305.*
- 'One or Two Things You May Not Know about the Universe: The Cosmology of the Divine Speeches in Job 38', in *Perspectives on Israelite Wisdom: Proceedings of the Oxford Old Testament Seminar* (ed. John Jarick; Library of Hebrew Bible / Old Testament Studies, 616; Bloomsbury T. & T. Clark, 2015), pp. 170-84.
- 'Writing a *Job* Commentary', in *The Genre of Biblical Commentary: Essays in Honor of John E. Hartley* (ed. Timothy D. Finlay and William Yarchin; Eugene, OR: Wipf & Stock, 2015), pp. 29-39.*
- 'The Scandal of a Male Bible' (The Ethel M. Wood lecture, King's College London, 24 February 2015) (video: *www.youtube.com/watch?v=sfXfeaC7WTE*).*
- 'The Holy and the Clean: An Excursion in Comparative Lexicography'. Paper read at the session of the International Syriac Language Project, Society of Biblical Literature Annual Meeting, Atlanta, 23 November, 2015.*
- 'Introducing the Dictionary of Classical Hebrew.' Presentation to the Ancient History Research Seminar, Macquarie University, Sydney, 27 March, 2015.*
- 'How Corrupt is the Text of the Hebrew Bible? An Empirical Approach from Ezra 2 || Nehemiah 7'. Paper in the Working with Biblical Manuscripts (Textual Criticism) Section of the Society of Biblical Literature International Meeting, Buenos Aires, 21 July 2015.*
- 'The Most High Male: Divine Masculinity in the Bible.' Paper in the Feminist Interpretations Section of the Society of Biblical Literature International Meeting, Buenos Aires, 22 July 2015.*
- 'A Very Short Commentary on the Book of Job'.*
- 'Revising the Hebrew Dictionary (*DCH*). 1. Hezekiah'.*
- 'Revising the Hebrew Dictionary (*DCH*). 2. The Goliath Family'.*
- 'Revising the Hebrew Dictionary (*DCH*). 3. There go the ships (Psa. 104.26)'.*

- 'Revising the Hebrew Dictionary (*DCH*). 4. New Definitions for Aleph Words.*
- 'Revising the Hebrew Dictionary (*DCH*). 5. Seals of Hezekiah: A New Addition.*

2014

- 'Does the Pentateuch Exist? Seven Questions We Should Be Asking if It Does', in *A Pillar of Cloud to Guide: Text-Critical, Redactional, and Linguistic Perspectives on the Old Testament in Honour of Marc Vervenne* (ed. Hans Ausloos and Benedicte Lemmelijn; Bibliotheca ephemeridum theologicarum lovaniensium, 269; Leuven: Peeters, 2014), pp. 31-41.*
- 'How my (Lexicographical) Mind Has Changed, or Else Remained the Same', for *Reflections on Lexicography: Explorations in Ancient Syriac, Hebrew, and Greek Sources* (ed. Richard A. Taylor and Craig E. Morrison; Perspectives on Linguistics and Ancient Languages, 4; Piscataway, NJ: Gorgias Press, 2014), pp. 233-40.*
- 'A Martian Reads the Psalms, in Particular Psalm 19', in *Intellect Encounters Faith: A Synthesis. A Festschrift in Honor of Jay Harold Ellens* (ed. John T. Greene; Newcastle-upon-Tyne: Cambridge Scholars Publishing, 2014), pp. 121-31.*
- 'The Future of the Dictionary of Classical Hebrew Project.' Paper to the Biblical Lexicography section, Society of Biblical Literature Annual Meeting, San Diego, November 2014.*
- 'Towards a Science of Comparative Classical Hebrew Lexicography'. Paper read on 2 July 2014 at the 14th International Conference of the International Syriac Language Project, held in St Petersburg under the auspices of the Institute of Oriental Manuscripts, Russian Academy of Sciences, 29 June–4 July 2014. To be published in *From Ancient Manuscripts to Modern Dictionaries: Select Studies in Aramaic, Hebrew, and Greek* (Perspectives on Linguistics and Ancient Languages; ed. Tarsee Li, Keith Dyer and Alexey Muraviev; Piscataway, NJ: Gorgias Press).

2013

- *The Reception of the Hebrew Bible in the Septuagint and the New Testament: Essays in Memory of Aileen Guilding* (ed. David J.A. Clines and J. Cheryl Exum; Hebrew Bible Monographs, 55; Sheffield: Sheffield Phoenix Press, 2013).
- *Biblical Reception* 2 (2013) (ed. J. Cheryl Exum and David J.A. Clines; Sheffield: Sheffield Phoenix Press, 2013), x + 267 pp.
- 'Aileen Guilding: Her Life and her Work', in *The Reception of the Hebrew Bible in the Septuagint and the New Testament: Essays in Memory of Aileen Guilding* (ed. David J.A. Clines and J. Cheryl Exum; Hebrew Bible Monographs, 55; Sheffield: Sheffield Phoenix Press, 2013), pp. 1-8.*
- 'Source Criticism: Putting Source Criticism in its Place: The Flood Story as a Test Case', in *Biblical Interpretation and Method: Essays in Honour of John Barton* (ed. Katharine J. Dell and Paul M. Joyce; Oxford: Oxford University Press, 2013), pp. 3-14.*
- 'The Flood Story in Middle English: The Fourteenth-Century Alliterative Poem, *Cleanness*', *Biblical Reception* 2 (2013), pp. 254-69.*
- 'The Decalogue: The Scholarly Tradition Critiqued', in *The Decalogue and its Cultural Influence* (ed. Dominik Markl; Hebrew Bible Monographs, 58; Sheffield: Sheffield Phoenix Press, 2013), pp. 330-39.*
- 'The Worth of Animals in the Divine Speeches of the Book of Job', in *Where the Wild Ox Roams: Biblical Essays in Honour of Norman C. Habel* (ed. Alan

- Cadwallader with Peter Trudinger; Hebrew Bible Monographs, 59; Sheffield: Sheffield Phoenix Press, 2013), pp. 101-13.*
- 'The KJV Translation of the Old Testament: The Case of Job', in *The King James Version at 400: Assessing its Genius as Bible Translation and its Literary Influence* (ed. David G. Burke, John F. Kutsko and Philip H. Towner; Society of Biblical Literature Biblical Scholarship in North America; Atlanta: Society of Biblical Literature, 2013), pp. 235-52.
- 'Seven Interesting Things about the Epilogue to Job', *Biblica et patristica thoruniensia* (Toruń, Poland) 6 (2013), pp. 11-21.*
- 'Varieties of Creation in the Bible'. Paper for the conference on New Directions in Cosmology, St John's College, Durham University, 10–11 January 2013. A handout with the biblical texts discussed is at the end of the paper. Posted 9 January, 2013. Video of the lecture and discussion at https://biblicalstudiesonline.wordpress.com/2015/02/22/david-clines-varieties-of-creation-in-the-bible/.*
- 'Classical Hebrew: All 2114 Personal Names'.*
- 'Classical Hebrew: All 2634 Verbs'.*
- 'Classical Hebrew: 837 Qumran Words with More Occurrences than in Biblical Hebrew'.*
- 'Classical Hebrew: 2225 Qumran Words More Frequent than in Biblical Hebrew'.*
- 'Classical Hebrew: 2225 Qumran Words More Frequent than in Biblical Hebrew, Arranged by Order of Frequency'.*
- 'Classical Hebrew: 580 Qumran Words More Frequent than in Biblical Hebrew, Arranged by Order of Frequency (Excluding Fewer than 10 Qumran Occurrences)'.*
- 'Characteristic Qumran Vocabulary: Empirical Data'.*

2012

- *Making a Difference: Essays on the Hebrew Bible and Judaism in Honor of Tamara Cohn Eskenazi* (ed. David J.A. Clines, Kent Harold Richards and Jacob L. Wright; Hebrew Bible Monographs, 49; Sheffield: Sheffield Phoenix Press, 2012), xxiv + 367 pp.*
- *Biblical Reception* 1 (2012) (ed. J. Cheryl Exum and David J.A. Clines; Sheffield: Sheffield Phoenix Press, 2012), xiv + 423 pp.*
- 'The Failure of the Flood', in *Making a Difference: Essays on the Hebrew Bible and Judaism in Honor of Tamara Cohn Eskenazi* (ed. David J.A. Clines, Kent Harold Richards and Jacob L. Wright), pp. 74-84.*
- 'Preface' (with Kent Harold Richards and Jacob L. Wright), in *Making a Difference: Essays on the Hebrew Bible and Judaism in Honor of Tamara Cohn Eskenazi*, pp. ix-xi.
- 'Editorial Preface' (with J. Cheryl Exum), in *Biblical Reception* 1 (2012), p. ix.
- 'The Many Voices of Isaiah 40', in *Let Us Go up to Zion: Essays in Honour of H.G.M. Williamson on the Occasion of his Sixty-Fifth Birthday* (ed. Iain Provan and Mark J. Boda; Leiden: Brill, 2012), pp. 113-26.*

2011

- *Job 38–42* (Word Biblical Commentary, 18B; Nashville: Thomas Nelson, 2011), xxxv + 501 pp. ISBN 9780785252672.
- *The Dictionary of Classical Hebrew*. VIII. *Sin–Taw* (Sheffield: Sheffield Phoenix Press, 2011), 817 pp.

- *A Critical Engagement: Essays on the Hebrew Bible in Honour of J. Cheryl Exum* (ed. David J.A. Clines and H.G.M. Williamson; Hebrew Bible Monographs, 38; Sheffield: Sheffield Phoenix Press, 2011), xvi + 428 pp.
- *Pour lire le Pentateuque* (traduit de l'anglais par Michael Clifton sous la direction de J.M. Poirier; Perpignan: Artège spiritualité, 2011), 221 pp.
- 'Reading the Song of Songs as a Classic', in *A Critical Engagement: Essays on the Hebrew Bible in Honour of J. Cheryl Exum* (ed. David J.A. Clines and Ellen van Wolde; Hebrew Bible Monographs, 38; Sheffield: Sheffield Phoenix Press, 2011), pp. 116-31.*
- 'What Remains of the Hebrew Bible: The Accuracy of the Text of the Hebrew Bible in the Light of the Qumran Samuel (4QSam^a)', in *Studies on the Text and Versions of the Hebrew Bible in Honour of Robert Gordon* (ed. Geoffrey Khan and Diana Lipton; Leiden: Brill, 2011), pp. 211-20.*
- 'Translating Psalm 23 Today', *RE Today* 28/2 (2011), pp. 40-41.
- 'The Magnificat: A Disenchantment'. Paper at the Society of Biblical Literature Annual Meeting, San Francisco, November 2011.*

2010

- *The Dictionary of Classical Hebrew*. VII. *Ṣade–Qoph* (Sheffield: Sheffield Phoenix Press, 2010), 679 pp. ISBN 9781906055523.
- *The Centre and the Periphery: A European Tribute to Walter Brueggemann* (ed. Jill Middlemas, David J.A. Clines and Else Holt; Hebrew Bible Monographs, 27; Sheffield: Sheffield Phoenix Press, 2010), x + 239 pp.
- *The Book of Job* by John Gray (ed. David J.A. Clines; The Text of the Hebrew Bible, 1; Sheffield: Sheffield Phoenix Press, 2010), x + 518 pp.
- 'Psalm 23 and Method: Reading a David Psalm', in *The Fate of King David: The Past and Present of a Biblical Icon. Essays in Honor of David M. Gunn* (ed. Tod Linafelt, Claudia V. Camp and Timothy Beal; Library of Hebrew Bible/Old Testament Studies, 500; London: T. & T. Clark International, 2010), pp. 175-84 .*
- 'Learning, Teaching, and Researching Biblical Studies, Today and Tomorrow', *Journal of Biblical Literature* 129 (2010), pp. 5-29.* [Chinese version: *Biblical Literature Studies* (圣经文学研究所. Sheng jing wen xue yan jiǔ) 7 (2013), pp. 1-33 (trans. M.A. Lemei)]
- 'Coming to a Theological Conclusion: The Case of the Book of Job', in *The Centre and the Periphery: A European Tribute to Walter Brueggemann* (ed. Jill Middlemas, David J.A. Clines and Else Holt; Hebrew Bible Monographs, 27; Sheffield: Sheffield Phoenix Press, 2010), pp. 199-213. *
- 'Dancing and Shining at Sinai: Playing the Man in Exodus 32–34', in *Men and Masculinity in the Hebrew Bible and Beyond* (ed. Ovidiu Creangă; Bible in the Modern World, 33; Sheffield: Sheffield Phoenix Press, 2010), pp. 54-63.*
- 'Final Reflections on Men and Masculinity', in *Men and Masculinity in the Hebrew Bible and Beyond* (ed. Ovidiu Creangă; Bible in the Modern World, 33; Sheffield: Sheffield Phoenix Press, 2010), pp. 234-39.*
- 'Teaching the Biblical Languages: Time for a Rethink?', in *Foster Biblical Scholarship: Essays in Honor of Kent Harold Richards* (ed. Frank Ritchel Ames and Charles William Miller; Society of Biblical Literature Biblical Scholarship in North America, 24; Atlanta, GA: Society of Biblical Literature, 2010), pp. 161-68.*
- Review of Ellen van Wolde, *Reframing Biblical Studies: When Language and Text Meet Culture, Cognition, and Context* (2009). Response read to the Joint Meeting

of the Cognitive Linguistics in Biblical Interpretation Section and the Linguistics and Biblical Hebrew Section at the Society of Biblical Literature Annual Meeting, Atlanta, 22 November, 2010.*

2009

- *The Concise Dictionary of Classical Hebrew* (Sheffield: Sheffield Phoenix Press, 2009), xii + 496 pp. ISBN 9781906055783, paperback 9781906055790.
- 'The Challenge of Hebrew Lexicography Today', in *Congress Volume, Ljubljana 2007* (ed. André Lemaire; Vetus Testamentum Supplements, 133; Leiden: Brill, 2009), pp. 87-98 .*
- 'Historical Criticism: Are its Days Numbered?', *Teologinen aikakauskirja* 6 (2009), pp. 542-58.*
- 'Introduction to Jonathan Z. Smith', *Journal of Biblical Literature* 128 (2009), pp. 4-5.
- 'The Book of Job: A Short Explanation', 53 pp.
- 'Response to Rolf Rendtorff's "What Happened to the Yahwist? Reflections after Thirty Years"', in *Probing the Frontiers of Biblical Study* (ed. J. Harold Ellens; Eugene, OR: Pickwick Publications, 2009), pp. 49-53.

2008

- *On Psalms* (克萊斯論詩篇 *Kelaisi lun shi pian: Fan yi liao zuo zhe zai Zhong yuan da xue de yan jiang he bu fen lun wen*) (Chung Yuan Christian University Masterpieces Series, 2 [Zhong yuan da xue, da shi xi lie, 2]; trans. Zhiying Wu, Yongcai Chen and Lezhi Xie; Kong: Logos, and Xianggang: Ji dao chu ban she, 2008), xv + 146 pp.
- 'Lesen, Unlesbarkeit und Dekonstruktion', in *Bibel als Literatur* (ed. Hans-Peter Schmidt and Daniel Weidner; Trajekte; Munich: Wilhelm Fink, 2008), pp. 189-203.
- 'The Many Voices of Isaiah 40', *Biblical Literature Studies* (Republic of China).
- 'Psalm 23 and Method', paper to the International Meeting of the Society of Biblical Literature, Auckland, 7 July, 2008 [www.shef.ac.uk/bibs/DJACcurrres/ps23method]
- 'Job's Crafty Conclusion', paper to Wisdom in Israelite and Cognate Traditions Section, Annual Meeting, Society of Biblical Literature, Boston, 22-25 November 2008

2007

- *The Dictionary of Classical Hebrew*. VI. *Samekh–Pe* (Sheffield: Sheffield Phoenix Press, 2007), 999 pp.
- *The Ideology of the Psalms* (International Conference on Hermeneutics and the Reading the Bible; Hong Kong, 2007), 13 pp. [English and Chinese].
- 'Being a Man in the Book of the Covenant', In *Reading the Law: Studies in Honour of Gordon J. Wenham* (ed. J.G. McConville and Karl Möller; London: T. & T. Clark International, 2007), pp. 3-9.*
- 'Was There a jrb II "vex" or jrb III "wound, bruise, pierce" or jrb IV "bar" in Classical Hebrew?', in *Shai le-Sara Japhet: Studies in the Bible, its Exegesis, and its Language* (ed. Moshe Bar-Asher, Dalit Rom-Shiloni, Emanuel Tov and Nili Wazana; Jerusalem: The Bialik Institute, 2007), pp. 285-304.*

- 'A Hebraist Reads the Chicago Assyrian Dictionary' (paper to the Assyriology and the Bible Section of the Society of Biblical Literature, Annual Meeting, San Diego, 18 November 2007).*
- 'Psalm 23 and a Confluence of Methods' (詩篇二十三篇與詮釋方法的匯聚), *Sino-Christian Studies* 4 (2007), pp. 7-37 (previously entitled 'The Confluence of Hermeneutical Methodologies for the Book of Psalms (Psalm 23 in Particular)', paper to International Conference on Hermeneutics and the Reading of the Bible, Chung Yuan Christian University, Taiwan, 23 March, 2007).
- 'The Bible and the Emotions', paper to Fu Jen Catholic University, Taipei, Taiwan, March 2007, 29 pp.*
- 'What Do We Really Want to Know about the Pentateuch?', Response to the Session, Sources of the Pentateuch: Ancient Writings, Modern Constructs, SBL International Meeting, Vienna, 24 July 2007.*

2006

- *Job 21–37* (Word Biblical Commentary, 18A; Nashville: Thomas Nelson, 2006), xxiv + 536 pp.
- 'Ezra–Nehemiah', in *The HarperCollins Study Bible, Fully Revised and Updated: New Revised Standard Version including the Apocryphal/Deuterocanonical Books* (ed. Harold W. Attridge; San Francisco: HarperSanFrancisco), pp. 646-79.
- '1 Esdras', in *The HarperCollins Study Bible, Fully Revised and Updated: New Revised Standard Version including the Apocryphal/Deuterocanonical Books* (ed. Harold W. Attridge; San Francisco: HarperSanFrancisco), pp. 1548-67.
- 'Translating Psalm 23', in *Reflection and Refraction: Studies in Biblical Historiography in Honour of A. Graeme Auld* (ed. Robert Rezetko, Timothy H. Lim and W. Brian Aucker; Vetus Testamentum Supplements, 113; Leiden: Brill, 2006), pp. 67-80.*
- 'The Lord is my Shepherd in East and South East Asia', *Journal of Sino-Christian Studies* 1 (2006), pp. 37-54.*
- 'Response to Rolf Rendtorff's "What Happened to the Yahwist? Reflections after Thirty Years", *SBL Forum* [www.sbl-site.org/Article.aspx?ArticleId=551].*
- 'The PhD in Theory and Practice: Personal Reflections' (panel paper to the Graduate Biblical Studies; Ethos and Discipline', Society of Biblical Literature International Meeting, Edinburgh, 5 July 2006).*
- 'The Practical and the Political in Hebrew Lexicography' (Panel Paper for session on The Politics of Language and the Language of Politics: Practical Issues in Dictionary Production, Biblical Lexicography Section, Society of Biblical Literature, Washington, DC, 18 November 2006).*
- 'One or Two Things You May Not Know about the Universe: The Cosmology of the Divine Speeches in Job' (paper to the Biblical Criticism and Literary Criticism Section, Society of Biblical Literature, Washington, 19 November 2006).
- 'How Many Voices Does It Take to Perform Isaiah 40?' (paper to the Biblical Hebrew Poetry Section, Society of Biblical Literature, Washington, 20 November, 2006).

2005

- *The Sheffield Manual for Authors and Editors in Biblical Studies* (Sheffield: Sheffield Phoenix Press, 2nd edn, 2005), 130 pp.
- *The Bible and the Modern World* (Sheffield: Sheffield Phoenix Press, revised edn, 2005), 116 pp.

- 'Jobs God," in *De God van Job* (ed. Ellen van Wolde; Zoetermeer: Uitgeverij Meinema, 2005), pp. 74-92.
- '*Job's* God: A Surfeit of Theologies?' (Plenary Paper to the SBL International Meeting, Singapore, 27 June 2005).
- '*Job's* God: A Surfeit of Theologies?' (Plenary Paper to the ANZATS/ANZSTS Annual Conference with the Society of Biblical Literature, Perth, Australia, 6 July 2005).*
- 'Jacques Berlinerblau, *The Secular Bible: Why Nonbelievers Must Take Religion Seriously* (Cambridge, 2005)' (Panel contribution, Social Sciences and the Interpretation of the Hebrew Scriptures Section, Society of Biblical Literature, Philadelphia, 19 November 2005).

2004

- '725 New Words Beginning with Mem or Nun', in *"Basel und Bibel": Collected Communications to the XVIIth Congress of the International Organization for the Study of the Old Testament (IOSOT), Basel 2001* (ed. Matthias Augustin and Hermann Michael Niemann; Beiträge zur Erforschung des Alten Testaments und des antiken Judentums, 51; Frankfurt a.M.: Peter Lang, 2004), pp. 281-96.
- 'Lamentations', in *Eerdmans Commentary on the Bible* (ed. James D.G. Dunn and John W. Rogerson; Grand Rapids: Eerdmans, 2004), pp. 617-22.
- 'Putting Elihu in his Place: A Proposal for the Relocation of Job 32–37', paper for the SBL Annual Meeting, Toronto, November 2002; submitted toqjsot qq *Journal for the Study of the Old Testament* 29 (2004), pp. 115-25.*
- 'Job's Fifth Friend: An Ethical Critique of the Book of Job', *Biblical Interpretation* 12 (2004), pp. 233-50.*
- 'Job's God', in *Job's God* (ed. Ellen van Wolde; Concilium 2004/4; London: SCM Press, 2004), pp. 39-51 [German translation, 'Ijobs Gott', *Concilium: Internationale Zeitschrift für Theologie* 40/4 [2004], pp. 403-15].
- 'Making Waves Gently: The Contribution of Norman Whybray to British Old Testament Study', in *Wisdom: The Collected Articles of Norman Whybray* (ed. Katharine Dell and Margaret Barker; Society for Old Testament Study Monograph Series; Aldershot, Hants.: Ashgate Publishing, 2004), pp. ix-xxvi.*
- 'The Recovery of the Ancient Hebrew Language: The Astonishing Wealth of its Unrecognized Vocabulary' (Paper to the Language and Linguistics Section of the SBL International Meeting, Groningen, The Netherlands, 28 July 2004).
- 'Legally Male: Being a Man in the Laws of the Hebrew Bible' (paper to the Biblical Law and Feminist Hermeneutics of the Bible Sections, Society of Biblical Literature, San Antonio, Texas, 22 November 2004).

2003

- *Weisheit in Israel: Beiträge des Symposiums »Das Alte Testament und die Kultur der Moderne« anlässlich des 100. Geburtstags Gerhard von Rads (1901–1971), Heidelberg, 18.-21. Oktober 2001* (ed. David J.A. Clines, Hermann Lichtenberger and Hans-Peter Müller; Altes Testament und Moderne, 12; Münster: Lit Verlag, 2003), 205 pp. ISBN 9783825854591.
- 'The Fear of the Lord is Wisdom' (Job 28:28): A Semantic and Contextual Study', in *Job 28: Cognition in Context* (ed. Ellen van Wolde; Biblical Interpretation Series, 64; Leiden: Brill, 2003), pp. 57-92. *

- 'Does the Book of Job Suggest that Suffering is Not a Problem?', in *Weisheit in Israel: Beiträge des Symposiums 'Das Alte Testament und die Kultur der Moderne' anlässlich des 100. Geburtstags Gerhard von Rads (1901–1971), Heidelberg, 18.-21. Oktober 2001* (ed. David J.A. Clines, Hermann Lichtenberger and Hans-Peter Müller; Altes Testament und Moderne, 12; Münster: Lit Verlag, 2003), pp. 93-110.*
- אדם, the Hebrew for "Human, Humanity": A Response to James Barr', *Vetus Testamentum* 53/3 (2003), pp. 297-310. *
- 'Esther and the Future of the Commentary', in *The Book of Esther in Modern Research* (ed. Sidnie White Crawford and Leonard J. Greenspoon; JSOTSup, 380; London: T. & T. Clark, 2003), pp. 17-30. *
- 'On the Poetic Achievement of the Book of Job', in *Palabra, prodigio, poesía: in memoriam P. Luis Alonso Schökel, S.J.* (ed. Vicente Collado Bertomeu; Analecta biblica, 151; Rome: Editrice Pontificio Istituto Biblico and Jávea (Alicante): Huerto de Enseñanzas (ALAS), 2003), pp. 243-53.*
- 'Paul, the Invisible Man', in *New Testament Masculinities* (ed. Janice Capel Anderson and Stephen D. Moore; Semeia Studies, 45; Atlanta: Society of Biblical Literature, 2003), pp. 157-68.*

2002

- 'What Remains of the Hebrew Bible? Its Text and Language in a Postmodern Age', *Studia theologica* 56 (2002), pp. 76-95.*
- 'He-Prophets: Masculinity as a Problem for the Hebrew Prophets and their Interpreters', in *Sense and Sensitivity: Essays on Reading the Bible in Memory of Robert Carroll* (ed. Alastair G. Hunter and Philip R. Davies; JSOTSup, 348; Sheffield: Sheffield Academic Press, 2002), pp. 311-28.*
- 'The fear of the Lord is wisdom' (Job 28.28): A Semantic and Contextual Study', 16 pp. (see under 2003).*
- 'Putting Elihu in his Place: A Proposal for the Relocation of Job 32–37', 8 pp. (see under 2004).*
- 'Accordance: A Basic Guide for Students of the English Bible', 4 pp.
- 'Accordance: A Basic Guide for Students of Greek', 6 pp.
- 'Accordance: A Basic Guide for Students of Hebrew', 6 pp.
- 'Dictionary of Classical Hebrew: Addenda and Corrigenda, Version 1, December 2002', 27 pp.

2001

- *The Dictionary of Classical Hebrew. V. Mem–Nun* (Sheffield: Sheffield Academic Press, 2001), 957 pp.
- 'The Disjoined Body: The Body and the Self in Hebrew Rhetoric', in *Biblical Interpretation* (ed. G.A. van der Heever and S.W. van Heerden; University of South Africa, Pretoria, 2001), pp. 148-57.*
- 'Editor's Foreword', *Journal for the Study of the Old* Testament 92 (2001), p. 3.
- 'Foreword', in C.-S. Abraham Cheong, *A Dialogic Reading of the Steward Parable (Luke 16:1-9)* (Studies in Biblical Literature, 28; New York: Peter Lang, 2001), pp. xiii-xv.
- 'The Dictionary of Classical Hebrew, Vol. 5 Mem-Nun: Bibliography to Mem'.
- 'The Dictionary of Classical Hebrew, Vol. 5 Mem-Nun: Bibliography to Nun'.
- '725 New Words Beginning with Mem or Nun', 16 pp.
- '725 New Words Beginning with Mem or Nun: Handout with List of Words', 16 pp.

- 'What Remains of the Old Testament? Its Text and Language in a Postmodern Age', 26 pp.*
- 'Does the Book of Job Suggest that Suffering is Not a Problem?', 15 pp.*
- 'Writing a Program for Alphabetizing Hebrew', 9 pp.*
- 'The Poetic Achievement of the Book of Job', 7 pp.*
- 'Guide for (Somewhat) Advanced Users of Office 2001, Especially Word 2001', 11 pp.
- 'All 2194 Words Beginning Mem and Nun', 63 pp.
- 'All 2194 Words Beginning Mem and Nun, by Frequency', 62 pp.
- 'All 2052 Qumran Words Beginning Aleph to Nun', 53 pp.
- 'All 1343 Common Nouns Beginning Mem and Nun', 37 pp.
- 'All 1343 Common Nouns Beginning Mem and Nun, by Gender', 39 pp.
- 'All 1451 Words Beginning Mem and Nun, in BDB', 42 pp.
- 'All 1985 Words Beginning Mem and Nun in Biblical Hebrew', 54 pp.
- 'All 725 New Words Beginning with Mem or Nun, by Corpus', 15 pp.
- 'All 725 New Words in Classical Hebrew Beginning Mem and Nun by their First Proposer', 22 pp.
- 'All 534 New Words in Biblical Hebrew Beginning Mem and Nun, with their First Proposer', 13 pp.
- 'All 534 New Words in Biblical Hebrew Beginning Mem and Nun, with the Cognate Language They Depend On', 13 pp.
- 'All 534 New Words in Biblical Hebrew Beginning Mem and Nun, with the Date They Were First Proposed', 18 pp.
- 'All 534 New Words in Biblical Hebrew Beginning Mem and Nun, with the Place of Publication and School of the Author', 21 pp.
- 'All 51 New Words in Classical Hebrew Inscriptions Beginning Mem and Nun', 2 pp.
- 'All 56 New Words in Classical Hebrew Beginning Mem and Nun Noted by Koehler–Baumgartner', 2 pp.
- 'All 91 New Words in Classical Hebrew Beginning Mem and Nun Noted by D. Winton Thomas', 3 pp.

2000

- *Postmodernism and Ideology: Biblical Criticism* (Korean New Society, 2000), 374 pp.
- 'Job's Fifth Friend: An Ethical Critique of the Book of Job', 14 pp.
- 'He-Prophets: Masculinity as a Problem for the Hebrew Prophets and their Interpreters', 23 pp. (see under 2002).
- 'μda, the Hebrew for "Human, Humanity": A Response to James Barr', 11 pp. (see under 2003).
- 'Esther and the Future of the Commentary', 13 pp. (see under 2003).
- 'Esther: A PolyCommentary Sample' (website).
- 'Notes on the Preliminary Edition of the Biblia Hebraica Quinta (Fasciculus extra seriem: Librum Ruth praeparavit Jan de Waard [Stuttgart: Deutsche Bibelgesellschaft, 1998])', 4 pp.
- 'Lamentations', 29 pp. (see under 2004).
- 'Before We All Get Too Excited about Electronic Publishing …', 10 pp.
- 'The Disjoined Body: The Body and the Self in Hebrew Rhetoric', 10 pp (see under 2001).

- 'Job: A Workshop', 5 pp.
- 'Masculinity's Debt to Feminist Biblical Criticism' (PowerPoint presentation).
- 'Paul, the Invisible Man', 11 pp. (see under 2003).
- 'Psalms, The: A Module in Biblical Studies' (website for a course).
- 'Reading the Song of Songs as a Classic', 14 pp.
- 'Teaching and Learning the Psalms, Inductively, or, Keeping Gunkel and Friends out of the Classroom', 9 pp.
- 'The Prophetic Assessment Exercise (PAE)', 4 pp.
- 'Of Viking and Parking', 2 pp.

1999

- 'The Postmodern Adventure in Biblical Studies', in *Interpretation of the Bible. International Symposium on the Interpretation of the Bible on the Occasion of the Publication of the New Slovenian Translation of the Bible* (ed. Jože Krašovec; Ljubljana: The Slovenian Academy of Sciences and Arts, 1998; JSOTSup, 289; Sheffield: Sheffield Academic Press, 1999), pp. 1603-18.*
- 'The Future of Biblical Studies', *Religious Studies News* (November 1999).
- 'Introduction to the Biblical Story: Genesis–Esther', in *Harper's Bible Commentary* (ed. James L. Mays; San Francisco: Harper & Row, 1988; 2nd edition, 1999), pp. 74-84; a revised and expanded version was published in *What Does Eve Do to Help?* (1990), pp. 85-105.
- 'Esther', in *Harper's Bible Commentary* (ed. James L. Mays; San Francisco: Harper & Row, 1988; 2nd edition, 1999), pp. 387-94.
- 'The Additions to Esther', in *Harper's Bible Commentary* (ed. James L. Mays; San Francisco: Harper & Row, 1988; 2nd edition, 1999), pp. 815-19.

1998

- *The Dictionary of Classical Hebrew. IV. Yodh–Lamedh* (Sheffield: Sheffield Academic Press, 1998), 642 pp.
- *On the Way to the Postmodern: Old Testament Essays, 1967–1998*, 2 vols. (Journal for the Study of the Old Testament Supplement Series, 292-293; Sheffield: Sheffield Academic Press, 1998), xx, xiv, 897 pp.
- *The World of Genesis: Persons, Places, Perspectives* (ed. Philip R. Davies and David J.A. Clines; Journal for the Study of the Old Testament Supplement Series, 257; Sheffield: Sheffield Academic Press, 1998), 179 pp.
- *Auguries: The Jubilee Volume of the Sheffield Department of Biblical Studies* (ed. David J.A. Clines and Stephen D. Moore; Journal for the Study of the Old Testament Supplement Series, 269; Sheffield: Sheffield Academic Press, 1998), 332 pp.
- 'Methods in Old Testament Study' [revision of 1982 chapter], in *Beginning Old Testament Study* (ed. J.W. Rogerson, London: SPCK, and St Louis: Chalice Press, new, revised edition, 1998), pp. 25-48; reprinted in *On the Way to the Postmodern: Old Testament Essays, 1967–1998*, vol. 1 (Journal for the Study of the Old Testament Supplement Series, 292; Sheffield: Sheffield Academic Press, 1998), pp. 23-45.*
- 'The Sheffield Department of Biblical Studies: An Intellectual Biography', in *Auguries: The Jubilee Volume of the Sheffield Department of Biblical Studies* (ed. David J.A. Clines and Stephen D. Moore; Journal for the Study of the Old

- Testament Supplement Series, 269; Sheffield: Sheffield Academic Press, 1998), pp. 14-89.*
- 'The Postmodern Adventure in Biblical Studies', in *Auguries: The Jubilee Volume of the Sheffield Department of Biblical Studies* (ed. David J.A. Clines and Stephen D. Moore; Journal for the Study of the Old Testament Supplement Series, 269; Sheffield: Sheffield Academic Press, 1998), pp. 276-91; a revised and expanded version is reprinted as 'The Pyramid and the Net: The Postmodern Adventure in Biblical Studies' in *On the Way to the Postmodern: Old Testament Essays, 1967–1998*, vol. 1 (Journal for the Study of the Old Testament Supplement Series, 292; Sheffield: Sheffield Academic Press, 1998), pp. 138-57.*
- 'Research, Teaching and Learning in Sheffield: The Material Conditions of their Production', in *Auguries: The Jubilee Volume of the Sheffield Department of Biblical Studies*, (ed. David J.A. Clines and Stephen D. Moore; Journal for the Study of the Old Testament Supplement Series, 269; Sheffield: Sheffield Academic Press, 1998), pp. 294-302.*
- 'The Postmodern Adventure in Biblical Studies', *Australasian Pentecostal Studies*, 1 (March 1998), pp. 41-54.
- '"Ecce vir", or, Gendering the Son of Man', in J. Cheryl Exum and Stephen D. Moore (eds.), *Biblical Studies/Cultural Studies: The Third Sheffield Colloquium* (Journal for the Study of the Old Testament Supplement Series, 266; Gender. Culture, Theory, 7; Sheffield: Sheffield Academic Press, 1998), pp. 352-75.*
- 'Quarter Days Gone: Job 24 and the Absence of God', in *God in the Fray: A Tribute to Walter Brueggemann*, (ed. Tod Linafelt and Timothy Beal; Minneapolis: Augsburg Fortress, 1998), pp. 242-58; reprinted in *On the Way to the Postmodern: Old Testament Essays, 1967–1998*, vol. 2 (Journal for the Study of the Old Testament Supplement Series, 293; Sheffield: Sheffield Academic Press, 1998), pp. 801-19.*
- 'The Pyramid and the Net: The Postmodern Adventure in Biblical Studies', in *On the Way to the Postmodern: Old Testament Essays, 1967–1998*, vol. 1 (Journal for the Study of the Old Testament Supplement Series, 292; Sheffield: Sheffield Academic Press, 1998), pp. 138-57.*
- 'From Salamanca to Cracow: What Has (And Has Not) Happened at SBL International Meetings', in *On the Way to the Postmodern: Old Testament Essays, 1967–1998*, vol. 1 (Journal for the Study of the Old Testament Supplement Series, 292; Sheffield: Sheffield Academic Press, 1998), pp. 158-93.
- 'From Copenhagen to Oslo: What Has (And Has Not) Happened at Congresses of the IOSOT', in *On the Way to the Postmodern: Old Testament Essays, 1967–1998*, vol. 1 (Journal for the Study of the Old Testament Supplement Series, 292; Sheffield: Sheffield Academic Press, 1998), pp. 194-221.
- 'Philology and Power', in *On the Way to the Postmodern: Old Testament Essays, 1967–1998*, vol. 2 (Journal for the Study of the Old Testament Supplement Series, 293; Sheffield: Sheffield Academic Press, 1998), pp. 613-30.*
- 'Squares and Streets: The Distinction of בוחר "Square" and תובוחר "Streets"', in *On the Way to the Postmodern: Old Testament Essays, 1967–1998*, vol. 2 (Journal for the Study of the Old Testament Supplement Series, 293; Sheffield: Sheffield Academic Press, 1998), pp. 631-36.*
- 'Universal Dominion in Psalm 2?' in *On the Way to the Postmodern: Old Testament Essays, 1967–1998*, vol. 2 (Journal for the Study of the Old Testament Supplement Series, 293; Sheffield: Sheffield Academic Press, 1998), pp. 701-707.*

- 'Those Golden Days: Job and the Perils of Nostalgia', in *On the Way to the Postmodern: Old Testament Essays, 1967–1998*, vol. 2 (Journal for the Study of the Old Testament Supplement Series, 293; Sheffield: Sheffield Academic Press, 1998), pp. 792-800.*
- 'The History of Bo Peep: An Agricultural Employee's Tragedy in Contemporary Literary Perspective', in *On the Way to the Postmodern: Old Testament Essays, 1967–1998*, vol. 2 (Journal for the Study of the Old Testament Supplement Series, 293; Sheffield: Sheffield Academic Press, 1998), pp. 823-29.*
- 'New Directions in Pooh Studies: Überlieferungs- und religionsgeschichtliche Studien zum Pu-Buch', in *On the Way to the Postmodern: Old Testament Essays, 1967–1998*, vol. 2 (Journal for the Study of the Old Testament Supplement Series, 293; Sheffield: Sheffield Academic Press, 1998), pp. 830-39.*
- 'Making Waves Gently: The Contribution of Norman Whybray to British Old Testament Study'.
- 'Paul, the Invisible Man; or, The Full Apostolic Monty'.

1997

- *The Poetical Books A Sheffield Reader* (ed. David J.A. Clines; The Biblical Seminar; Sheffield: Sheffield Academic Press, 1997), 370 pp.
- *The Theme of the Pentateuch* (Journal for the Study of the Old Testament Supplement Series, 10; Sheffield: Sheffield Academic Press, 2nd edn, 1997), 175 pp.
- *The Sheffield Manual for Authors and Editors in Biblical Studies* (Manuals, 12; Sheffield: Sheffield Academic Press, 1997), 200 pp.
- *The Bible and the Modern World* (The Biblical Seminar, 59; Sheffield: Sheffield Academic Press, 1997), 116 pp.
- 'Selections from *I, He, We, They: A Literary Approach to Isaiah 53*', in *The Theological Interpretation of Scripture: Classic and Contemporary Readings* (ed. Stephen E. Fowl; Blackwell Readings in Modern Theology; Blackwell: Cambridge, MA, 1996 Oxford: Blackwell, 1997), pp. 210-18.
- 'Haggajs tempel: konstrueret, dekonstrueret og rekonstrueret', in Pernille Carstens and Hans J. Lundager Jensen (eds.), *Tekst og teologi 1. Læsninger og tolkninger af Det Gamle Testamente* (Frederiksberg: Forlaget Anis, 1997), pp. 153-79 (translated from the 1993 article).
- Selections from *I, He, We and They: A Literary Approach to Isaiah 53*, in *The Theological Interpretation of Scripture: Classic and Contemporary Readings* (ed. Stephen E. Fowl; Malden, MA: Blackwell, 1997).
- 'Publishers: Who Needs Them?', *invited paper for the Constructs of the Social and Cultural Worlds of Antiquity Group of the Society of Biblical Literature, Annual Meeting, San Francisco, 22 November 1998.*
- 'Dancing and Shining at Sinai: Playing the Man in Exodus 32–34', paper to the Biblical Law Section of the Society of Biblical Literature, Annual Meeting, San Francisco, 22 November 1997 .*

1996

- *The Dictionary of Classical Hebrew*. III. *Zayin–Teth* (Sheffield: Sheffield Academic Press, 1996), 424 pp.
- 'The God of the Pentateuch' (shortened version of The Peake Memorial Lecture, June 1994), *Epworth Review* 23/1 (1996), pp. 55-64.

- 'Varieties of Indeterminacy', in *Textual Indeterminacy, Part Two* (ed. Robert C. Culley and Robert B. Robinson) = *Semeia* 63 (1995), pp. 17-27 [published 1996]; reprinted in *On the Way to the Postmodern: Old Testament Essays, 1967–1998*, vol. 1 (Journal for the Study of the Old Testament Supplement Series, 292; Sheffield: Sheffield Academic Press, 1998), pp. 126-37.*
- Response to review by F.I. Andersen of *The Dictionary of Classical Hebrew*, in *Australian Biblical Review* 43 (1995), pp. 72-75.
- 'Bible Bashers' [letter], *Times Higher Educational Supplement*, January 1996
- Review of Ludwig Koehler, Walter Baumgartner, Johann Jakob Stamm, *The Hebrew and Aramaic Lexicon of the Old Testament*, vol. 1: *Aleph–Heth* (ed. and tr. M.E.J. Richardson, *Journal of Semitic Studies* 41 (1996), pp. 137-42.
- 'Loin-girding and Other Male Activities in the Book of Job'.
- 'Confessions of an Autodidact: Response to Carol Newsom's Review of Exum and Clines, *The New Literary Criticism and the Hebrew Bible*'.*
- 'Books on the Net: A Publisher's View'.
- 'Does Hebrew אדם Mean "Humanity"? A Response to James Barr, "Words and Meanings, This Century and Next"'.*
- 'Gender and Hermeneutics: A Response to Hanna Stenström, "Revelation 14:1-5 and the Necessity and Limitations of Feminist Interpretation of the Bible"'.*

1995

- *The Dictionary of Classical Hebrew*. II. *Beth–Waw* (Sheffield: Sheffield Academic Press, 1995), 660 pp.
- *Interested Parties: The Ideology of Writers and Readers of the Hebrew Bible* (Journal for the Study of the Old Testament Supplement Series, 205; Gender, Culture, Theory, 1; Sheffield: Sheffield Academic Press, 1995), 296 pp.; Korean edition, *Postú Motunnisem kwa ideologu Súngsú Pipyúng* (trans. Byung Ha Kim, Sang Lae Kim, Jong Yun Kim and Sung Woo Chung; Seoul: Handl Publishing House, 2000), 373 pp.
- *The Bible in Human Society: Essays in Honour of John Rogerson* (ed. R. Daniel Carroll R., David J.A. Clines and Philip R. Davies; Journal for the Study of the Old Testament Supplement Series, 200; Sheffield: Sheffield Academic Press, 1995), 479 pp.
- 'Job and the Spirituality of the Reformation', in *The Bible, the Reformation and the Church: Essays in Honour of James Atkinson* (ed. W.P. Stephens; Journal for the Study of the New Testament Supplement Series, 105; Sheffield: Sheffield Academic Press, 1995), pp. 49-72; reprinted in *Interested Parties: The Ideology of Writers and Readers of the Hebrew Bible* (1995), pp. 145-71.*
- 'Deconstructing the Book of Job', *Bible Review* 11/2 (April, 1995), pp. 30-35, 43-44 (an abbreviation of the 1990 article) (responses in *Bible Review* 11/4 (1995).*
- 'The Ten Commandments, Reading from Left to Right', in *Words Remembered, Texts Renewed: Essays in Honour of John F.A. Sawyer* (ed. Jon Davies, Graham Harvey and Wilfred G.E. Watson; Journal for the Study of the Old Testament Supplement Series, 195; Sheffield: Sheffield Academic Press, 1995), pp. 97-112 (abstract in Society for Old Testament Study Bulletin, 1993); a revised version was published in *Interested Parties: The Ideology of Writers and Readers of the Hebrew Bible* (1995), pp. 26-45.*
- 'Beyond Synchronic/Diachronic', in *Synchronic or Diachronic? A Debate on Method in Old Testament Exegesis* (ed. Johannes C. de Moor; Oudtestamentische

studiën, 34; Leiden: E.J. Brill, 1995), pp. 52-71; reprinted in *On the Way to the Postmodern: Old Testament Essays, 1967–1998*, vol. 1 (Journal for the Study of the Old Testament Supplement Series, 292; Sheffield: Sheffield Academic Press, 1998), pp. 68-87.*

- 'Psalm 2 and the MLF (Moabite Liberation Front)', in *The Bible in Human Society: Essays in Honour of John Rogerson* (ed. M. Daniel Carroll R., David J.A. Clines and Philip R. Davies; Journal for the Study of the Old Testament Supplement Series, 200; Sheffield: Sheffield Academic Press, 1995), pp. 158-85; a revised version was published in *Interested Parties: The Ideology of Writers and Readers of the Hebrew Bible* (1995), pp. 244-75.*
- 'Ethics as Deconstruction, and, The Ethics of Deconstruction', in *The Bible in Ethics: The Second Sheffield Colloquium* (ed. John W. Rogerson, Margaret Davies and M. Daniel Carroll R.; Journal for the Study of the Old Testament Supplement Series, 207; Sheffield: Sheffield Academic Press, 1995), pp. 77-106; reprinted in *On the Way to the Postmodern: Old Testament Essays, 1967–1998*, vol. 1 (Journal for the Study of the Old Testament Supplement Series, 292; Sheffield: Sheffield Academic Press, 1998), pp. 95-125.*
- '[Reply to F.I. Andersen]', *Australian Biblical Review* 43 (1995), pp. 72-74 (Andersen's review of *The Dictionary of Classical Hebrew*, vol. 1, in pp. 51-71; Andersen's rejoinder, pp. 74-75.
- 'Language as Event', in *'The place is too small for us': The Israelite Prophets in Recent Scholarship* (ed. Robert P. Gordon; Sources for Biblical and Theological Study, 5; Winona Lake, IN: Eisenbrauns, 1995), pp. 166-75 (reprint of *I, He, We, and They* [1976], pp. 53-56).
- 'The Book of Psalms, Where Men Are Men…: On the Gender of Hebrew Piety'

1994

- 'Job', in *New Bible Commentary Revised* (ed. D.A. Carson, R.T. France, J.A. Motyer and G.J. Wenham; Leicester: Inter-Varsity Press; Downers Grove, IL: Intervarsity Press, 21st Century Edition, 1994), pp. 459-84.*
- 'Why is There a Song of Songs, and What Does It Do to You If You Read It?', *Jian Dao: A Journal of Bible and Theology* 1 (1994), pp. 3-27; a revised version was published in *Interested Parties: The Ideology of Writers and Readers of the Hebrew Bible* (1995), pp. 94-121.*
- 'Why Is There a Book of Job, and What Does It Do to You If You Read It?', in *The Book of Job* (ed. W.A.M. Beuken; Bibliotheca ephemeridum theologicarum lovaniensium, 114; Leuven: Leuven University Press and Peeters, 1994), pp. 1-20; a revised version was published in *Interested Parties: The Ideology of Writers and Readers of the Hebrew Bible* (1995), pp. 122-44.*
- 'Church Times' [letter], *Times Higher Educational Supplement*
- 'The Message of Proverbs', in *The Bible for Everyday Life* (ed. Robin Keeley and George Carey; Oxford: Lion Publishing), pp. 102-104 [=*The Message of the Bible* (ed. R. Keeley; Tring, Herts.: Lion, 1988), pp. 86-88].
- 'The Message of Ecclesiastes', in *The Bible for Everyday Life* (ed. Robin Keeley and George Carey; Oxford: Lion Publishing), pp. 105-106 [=*The Message of the Bible* (ed. R. Keeley; Tring, Herts.: Lion, 1988), pp. 89-90].
- 'Theme in Genesis 1–11', in *'I Studied Inscriptions before the Flood': Ancient Near Eastern, Literary, and Linguistic Approaches to Genesis 1–11* (ed. Richard S. Hess and David Toshio Tsumura; Sources for Biblical and Theological Study,

4; Eisenbrauns: Winona Lake, IN, 1994), pp. 285-309 (reprinted from *Catholic Biblical Quarterly* 38 [1976], pp. 483-507).

1993

- *The Dictionary of Classical Hebrew*. I. *Aleph* (Sheffield: Sheffield Academic Press, 1993), 475 pp.
- *Among the Prophets: Imagery, Language and Structure in the Prophetic Writings* (ed. Philip R. Davies and David J.A. Clines; Journal for the Study of the Old Testament Supplement Series, 144; Sheffield: JSOT Press, 1993), 212 pp.
- *Of Prophets' Visions and the Wisdom of Sages: Essays in Honour of R. Norman Whybray on his Seventieth Birthday* (ed. Heather A. McKay and David J.A. Clines; Journal for the Study of the Old Testament Supplement Series, 162; Sheffield: JSOT Press, 1993), 335 pp.
- *The New Literary Criticism and the Hebrew Bible* (ed. J. Cheryl Exum and David J.A. Clines; Journal for the Study of the Old Testament Supplement Series, 143; Sheffield: JSOT Press, 1993, 276 pp.
- 'Metacommentating Amos', in *Of Prophets' Visions and the Wisdom of Sages: Essays in Honour of R. Norman Whybray on his Seventieth Birthday* (ed. Heather A. McKay and David J.A. Clines; Journal for the Study of the Old Testament Supplement Series, 162; Sheffield: JSOT Press, 1993), pp. 142-60; reprinted in *Interested Parties: The Ideology of Writers and Readers of the Hebrew Bible* (1995), pp. 76-93.*
- (with J. Cheryl Exum) 'What Is the New Literary Criticism?', in *The New Literary Criticism and the Hebrew Bible* (ed. J. Cheryl Exum and David J.A. Clines; Journal for the Study of the Old Testament Supplement Series; Sheffield: JSOT Press, 1993), pp. 11-25.
- 'A World Founded on Water (Psalm 24): Reader Response, Deconstruction and Bespoke Interpretation', in *The New Literary Criticism and the Hebrew Bible* (ed. J. Cheryl Exum and David J.A. Clines; Journal for the Study of the Old Testament Supplement Series; Sheffield: JSOT Press, 1993), pp. 79-90; a revised version was published in *Interested Parties: The Ideology of Writers and Readers of the Hebrew Bible* (1995), pp. 172-86.*
- 'Ezra–Nehemiah', in *The HarperCollins Study Bible: New Revised Standard Version with the Apocryphal/Deuterocanonical Books* (ed. Wayne A. Meeks *et al.*; London: HarperCollins), pp. 699-735.
- '1 Esdras', in *The HarperCollins Study Bible: New Revised Standard Version with the Apocryphal/Deuterocanonical Books*, ed. Wayne A. Meeks *et al.*; London: HarperCollins), pp. 1723-45.
- 'Possibilities and Priorities of Biblical Interpretation in an International Perspective', *Biblical Interpretation. A Journal of Contemporary Approaches* 1 (1993), pp. 67-87; reprinted in *On the Way to the Postmodern: Old Testament Essays, 1967–1998*, vol. 1 (Journal for the Study of the Old Testament Supplement Series, 292; Sheffield: Sheffield Academic Press, 1998), pp. 46-67 (responses by Pheme Perkins, 'Canon, Paradigms and Progress? Reflections on the Essays by Rendtorff, Sugirtharajah and Clines', *Biblical Interpretation. A Journal of Contemporary Approaches* 1 (1993), pp. 88-95, and by David Jobling, 'Globalization in Biblical Studies / Biblical Studies in Globalization', *Biblical Interpretation. A Journal of Contemporary Approaches* 1 (1993), pp. 96-110).*

- 'Haggai's Temple, Constructed, Deconstructed and Reconstructed', in *Second Temple Studies* (ed. Tamara C. Eskenazi and Kent H. Richards; Journal for the Study of the Old Testament Supplement Series, 175; Sheffield: JSOT Press, 1993), pp. 51-78.*
- 'Haggai's Temple, Constructed, Deconstructed and Reconstructed', *Scandinavian Journal of the Old Testament* 7 (1993), pp. 19-30; a revised version was published in *Interested Parties: The Ideology of Writers and Readers of the Hebrew Bible* (1995), pp. 46-75.
- 'Pentateuch', in *The Oxford Companion to the Bible* (ed. Bruce M. Metzger and Michael D. Coogan; New York: Oxford University Press, 1993), pp. 579-82.
- 'Job', in *The Oxford Companion to the Bible* (ed. Bruce M. Metzger and Michael D. Coogan (New York: Oxford University Press, 1993), pp. 368-70.
- 'Image of God', in *Dictionary of Paul and his Letters* (ed. Gerald F. Hawthorne and Ralph P. Martin; Downers Grove, IL and Leicester: InterVarsity Press, 1993), pp. 426-28.
- 'Sacred Space, Holy Places and Suchlike', in *Trinity Occasional Papers: Essays Presented in Honour of Revd Professors Han Spykeboer and Bruce Upham* 12/2 (November, 1993), pp. 19-30; reprinted in *On the Way to the Postmodern: Old Testament Essays, 1967–1998*, vol. 2 (Journal for the Study of the Old Testament Supplement Series, 293; Sheffield: Sheffield Academic Press, 1998), pp. 542-54.

1992

- 'Was There an *'bl* II "be dry" in Classical Hebrew?', *Vetus Testamentum* 42 (1992), pp. 1-10; reprinted in *On the Way to the Postmodern: Old Testament Essays, 1967–1998*, vol. 2 (Journal for the Study of the Old Testament Supplement Series, 293; Sheffield: Sheffield Academic Press, 1998), pp. 585-94.*
- 'The Shape and Argument of the Book of Job', in *Sitting with Job: Selected Studies on the Book of Job* (ed. Roy B. Zuck; Baker Book House, Grand Rapids, 1992), pp. 125-40 [reprinted from *Job 1–20*, pp. xxxiv-xlvii].
- 'A Brief Explanation of Job 1–3', in *Sitting with Job: Selected Studies on the Book of Job* (ed. Roy B. Zuck; Grand Rapids: Baker Book House, 1992), pp. 249-52; reprinted from *Job 1–20*, pp. 65-66.
- 'A Brief Explanation of Job 12–14', in *Sitting with Job: Selected Studies on the Book of Job* (ed. Roy B. Zuck; Grand Rapids: Baker Book House, 1992),pp. 261-64; reprinted from *Job 1–20*, pp. 337-39.
- 'The Arguments of Job's Three Friends', in *Sitting with Job: Selected Studies on the Book of Job* (ed. Roy B. Zuck; Grand Rapids: Baker Book House, 1992), pp. 265-78; reprinted from *Art and Meaning: Rhetoric in Biblical Literature*, pp. 199-214.
- 'Mordecai', in *The Anchor Bible Dictionary* (ed. D.N. Freedman; New York: Doubleday, 1992), vol. 4, pp. 902-904
- 'The New Dictionary of Classical Hebrew', *Goldene Äpfel in silbernen Schalen. Collected Communications to the XIIIth Congress of the International Organization for the Study of the Old Testament, Leuven 1989* (ed. K.-D. Schunk and M. Augustin; Beiträge zur Erforschung des Alten Testaments und des antiken Judentums, 20; Frankfurt: Peter Lang, 1992), pp. 169-79 .
- 'God in the Pentateuch', in *Studies in Old Testament Theology: Historical and Contemporary Images of God and God's People* (Festschrift for David L. Hubbard; ed. Robert L. Hubbard, Jr, Robert K. Johnston and Robert P. Meye; Dallas: Word Books), pp. 79-98; a revised version was published as 'God in the Pentateuch:

- Reading against the Grain', in *Interested Parties: The Ideology of Writers and Readers of the Hebrew Bible* (1995), pp. 186-211.
- 'Story and Poem: The Old Testament as Literature and as Scripture', in *Beyond Form Criticism: Essays in Old Testament Literary Criticism* (ed. Paul R. House; Winona Lake, IN: Eisenbrauns, 1992), pp. 25-38; reprinted from *Interpretation* 34 (1980), pp. 115-27; reprinted in *On the Way to the Postmodern: Old Testament Essays, 1967–1998* vol. 1 (Journal for the Study of the Old Testament Supplement Series, 292; Sheffield: Sheffield Academic Press, 1998), pp. 225-39.
- 'Reconceptualizing Old Testament Theology'. Unpublished.*

1991

- *Telling Queen Michal's Story. An Experiment in Comparative Interpretation* (ed. David J.A. Clines and Tamara C. Eskenazi; Journal for the Study of the Old Testament Supplement Series, 119; Sheffield: JSOT Press, 1991), 301 pp.
- 'Michal Observed: An Introduction to Reading her Story', in *Telling Queen Michal's Story: An Experiment in Comparative Interpretation* (ed. David J.A. Clines and Tamara C. Eskenazi; Journal for the Study of the Old Testament Supplement Series, 119; Sheffield: JSOT Press, 1991), pp. 24-63.
- 'X, X *ben* Y, *ben* Y: Personal Names in Hebrew Narrative Style', in *Telling Queen Michal's Story: An Experiment in Comparative Interpretation* (ed. David J.A. Clines and Tamara C. Eskenazi; Journal for the Study of the Old Testament Supplement Series, 119; Sheffield: JSOT Press, 1991), pp. 124-28; an excerpt reprinted from 1972 article; the whole article is reprinted in *On the Way to the Postmodern: Old Testament Essays, 1967–1998*, vol. 1 (Journal for the Study of the Old Testament Supplement Series, 292; Sheffield: Sheffield Academic Press, 1998), pp. 240-62.
- 'The Story of Michal, Wife of David, in its Sequential Unfolding', in *Telling Queen Michal's Story: An Experiment in Comparative Interpretation* (ed. David J.A. Clines and Tamara C. Eskenazi; Journal for the Study of the Old Testament Supplement Series, 119; Sheffield: JSOT Press, 1991), pp. 129-40.
- 'The Quest for the Historical Mordecai', *Vetus Testamentum* 41 (1991), pp. 129-36; reprinted in *On the Way to the Postmodern: Old Testament Essays, 1967–1998*, vol. 1 (Journal for the Study of the Old Testament Supplement Series, 292; Sheffield: Sheffield Academic Press, 1998), pp. 436-43.
- 'Frederick Fyvie Bruce 1910–1990. In Memoriam', *Journal. Christian Brethren Research Fellowship* no. 123 (August 1991), pp. 53-54.
- 'Lamentations', in *Guidelines* 8/1 (January-April 1992), pp. 90-96 (reprint of 1988 article).

1990

- *What Does Eve Do to Help? and Other Readerly Questions to the Old Testament* (Journal for the Study of the Old Testament Supplement Series, 94; Sheffield: JSOT Press, 1990)
- *The Bible in Three Dimensions. Essays in Celebration of the Fortieth Anniversary of the Department of Biblical Studies in the University of Sheffield* (ed. David J.A. Clines, Stephen E. Fowl and Stanley E. Porter; Journal for the Study of the Old Testament Supplement Series, 87; Sheffield: JSOT Press, 1990), 408 pp.
- 'Deconstructing the Book of Job', in *The Bible as Rhetoric: Studies in Biblical Persuasion and Credibility* (ed. Martin Warner; Warwick Studies in Philosophy

- and Literature; London: Routledge, 1990), pp. 65-80; reprinted in *What Does Eve Do to Help?* (1990), pp. 106-23.*
- 'Reading Esther from Left to Right: Contemporary Strategies for Reading a Biblical Text', in *The Bible in Three Dimensions: Essays in Celebration of Forty Years of Biblical Studies in the University of Sheffield* (ed. David J.A. Clines, Stephen E. Fowl and Stanley E. Porter; Journal for the Study of the Old Testament Supplement Series, 87; Sheffield: JSOT Press, 1990), pp. 22-42; reprinted in *On the Way to the Postmodern: Old Testament Essays, 1967–1998*, vol. 1 (Journal for the Study of the Old Testament Supplement Series, 292; Sheffield: Sheffield Academic Press, 1998), pp. 3-22.*
- 'The Dictionary of Classical Hebrew', *Zeitschrift für Althebraistik* 3 (1990), pp. 73-80; reprinted in *On the Way to the Postmodern: Old Testament Essays, 1967–1998*, vol. 2 (Journal for the Study of the Old Testament Supplement Series, 293; Sheffield: Sheffield Academic Press, 1998), pp. 602-12.
- 'Holistic Interpretation', in *A Dictionary of Biblical Interpretation* (ed. R.J. Coggins and J.L. Houlden; London: SCM Press, and Philadelphia: Trinity Press International, 1990), pp. 292-95.

1989

- *Job 1–20* (Word Biblical Commentary, 17; Waco, Texas: Word Books, 1989), cviii + 501 pp. Korean translation by Yong Song Han, 데이빗 J.A. 클라인스 지음; 한영성 옮김. 한영성, *Yogpi* (Sŏul-si: Sollomon, 2006).
- 'The Force of the Text: A Response to Tamara C. Eskenazi's "Ezra-Nehemiah: From Text to Actuality"', in *Signs and Wonders: Biblical Texts in Literary Focus* (ed. J. Cheryl Exum; Semeia Studies; Atlanta: Scholars Press, 1989), pp. 199-215; reprinted in *On the Way to the Postmodern: Old Testament Essays, 1967–1998*, vol. 1 (Journal for the Study of the Old Testament Supplement Series, 292; Sheffield: Sheffield Academic Press, 1998), pp. 351-67.*
- 'The Wisdom Books', in *Creating the Old Testament: The Emergence of the Hebrew Bible* (ed. Stephen Bigger; Oxford: Basil Blackwell, 1989), pp. 269-91.
- 'Job', in *The Books of the Bible. I. The Old Testament/The Hebrew Bible* (ed. Bernhard W. Anderson; New York: Charles Scribner's Sons, 1989), pp. 181-201.
- 'Lamentations: Proposal for the Handling of Grief', *The Harvester* 68/3 (1989), pp. 6-7; 68/4 (1989), pp. 6-7.
- 'Job. I. Acceptance and Denial', *The Harvester* 68/6 (1989), pp. 6-7.
- 'Job. II. Beyond all Proportion', *The Harvester* 68/7 (1989), pp. 6-7.
- 'Job. III. Suffering is a Hippopotamus', *The Harvester* 68/8, pp. 6-7.
- 'Job. IV. Happily Ever After?', *The Harvester* 68/9 (1989), pp. 6-7.
- Abstracts of articles on the Old Testament, for *Zeitschrift für die alttestamentliche Wissenschaft* 101/1 (1989), p. 125; 101/2 (1989), pp. 295, 302.
- Translation (from French), Pierre Auffret, 'Note on the Literary Structure of Psalm 134', *Journal for the Study of the Old Testament* 45 (1989), pp. 87-89.

1988

- 'Belief, Desire and Wish in Job 19:23-27. Clues for the Identity of Job's "Redeemer"', in *«Wünschet Jerusalem Frieden.» Collected Communications to the XIIth Congress of the International Organization for the Study of the Old Testament, Jerusalem 1986* (ed. M. Augustin and K.-D. Schunk; Beiträge zur Erforschung des Alten Testaments und des antiken Judentums, 13; Frankfurt: Peter Lang, 1988), pp.

- 363-70; reprinted in *On the Way to the Postmodern: Old Testament Essays, 1967–1998*, vol. 2 (Journal for the Study of the Old Testament Supplement Series, 293; Sheffield: Sheffield Academic Press, 1998), pp. 762-69.
- 'Introduction to the Biblical Story: Genesis–Esther', in *Harper's Bible Commentary* (ed. James L. Mays; San Francisco: Harper & Row, 1988; 2nd edition, 1999), pp. 74-84; a revised and expanded version was published in *What Does Eve Do to Help?* (1990), pp. 85-105.
- 'Esther', in *Harper's Bible Commentary* (ed. James L. Mays; San Francisco: Harper & Row, 1988; 2nd edition, 1999), pp. 387-94.
- 'The Additions to Esther', in *Harper's Bible Commentary* (ed. James L. Mays; San Francisco: Harper & Row, 1988; 2nd edition, 1999), pp. 815-19.
- 'Ruth', 'Lamentations', in *Guidelines* 4/1 (January-April 1988), pp. 3-5, 42-47.
- 'The Message of Proverbs', 'The Message of Ecclesiastes', in *The Message of the Bible* (ed. R. Keeley; Tring, Herts.: Lion, 1988), pp. 86-90.
- Abstracts of articles on the Old Testament, for *Zeitschrift für die alttestamentliche Wissenschaft* 100/1 (1988), pp. 122, 124, 125, 128; 100/2 (1988), pp. 281, 286.

1987

- 'The Parallelism of Greater Precision. Notes from Isaiah 40 for a Theory of Hebrew Poetry', in *New Directions in Hebrew Poetry* (ed. Elaine R. Follis; Journal for the Study of the Old Testament Supplement Series, 40; Sheffield: JSOT Press, 1987), pp. 77-100; reprinted in *On the Way to the Postmodern: Old Testament Essays, 1967–1998*, vol. 1 (Journal for the Study of the Old Testament Supplement Series, 292; Sheffield: Sheffield Academic Press, 1998), pp. 314-36.*
- Paragraphs on Abraham and Job in *The Good Book. An Introduction to the Bible*, ed. B. Redhead and F. Gumley, London: Duckworth, 1987, pp. 31, 33, 116-18.

1986

- 'Biblical Thoughts on the Religious Professional', *Christian Brethren Review* 37 (1986), pp. 57-64.

1985

- 'False Naivety in the Prologue to Job', *Hebrew Annual Review* 9 (1985), pp. 127-36 (=*Biblical and Other Studies in Memory of Shelmo Dov Goitein* [ed. Reuben Ahroni]); reprinted in *On the Way to the Postmodern: Old Testament Essays, 1967–1998*, vol. 2 (Journal for the Study of the Old Testament Supplement Series, 293; Sheffield: Sheffield Academic Press, 1998), pp. 735-44.*

1984

- *Ezra, Nehemiah, Esther* (New Century Bible; London: Marshall, Morgan & Scott, and Grand Rapids: Eerdmans, 1984), 384 pp.
- *The Esther Scroll: The Story of the Story* (JSOTSup, 30; Sheffield: JSOT Press, 1984), 260 pp.

1983

- *Midian, Moab and Edom: The History and Archaeology of Late Bronze and Iron Age Jordan and North-West Arabia* (ed. John F.A. Sawyer and David J.A. Clines;

- Journal for the Study of the Old Testament Supplement Series, 24; Sheffield: JSOT Press, 1983), 172 pp.
- 'In Search of the Indian Job', *Vetus Testamentum* 33 (1983), pp. 398-418; reprinted in *On the Way to the Postmodern: Old Testament Essays, 1967–1998*, vol. 2 (Journal for the Study of the Old Testament Supplement Series, 293; Sheffield: Sheffield Academic Press, 1998), pp. 770-91.*
- Translation (from French) (with J.L Michaud and M. Bert), Pierre Auffret, 'The Literary Structure of Exodus 6.2-8', *Journal for the Study of the Old Testament* 27 (1983), pp. 46-54.

1982

- *Art and Meaning: Rhetoric in Biblical Literature* (ed. David J.A. Clines, David M. Gunn and Alan J. Hauser; Journal for the Study of the Old Testament Supplement Series, 19; Sheffield: JSOT Press, 1982), 274 pp.
- 'The Arguments of Job's Three Friends', in *Art and Meaning: Rhetoric in Biblical Literature* (ed. David J.A. Clines, David M. Gunn and Alan J. Hauser; Journal for the Study of the Old Testament Supplement Series, 19; Sheffield: JSOT Press, 1982), pp. 199-214; reprinted in *On the Way to the Postmodern: Old Testament Essays, 1967–1998*, vol. 2 (Journal for the Study of the Old Testament Supplement Series, 293; Sheffield: Sheffield Academic Press, 1998), pp. 719-34.
- 'Methods in Old Testament Study', in *Beginning Old Testament Study* (ed. J.W. Rogerson; Philadelphia: Westminster, 1982, and London: SPCK, 1983), pp. 26-43.
- 'Biblical Hermeneutics in Theory and Practice', *Christian Brethren Review* nos. 30/31 (1982), pp. 65-77 [www.biblicalstudies.org.uk/pdf/cbr/hermeneutics_clines.pdf].

1981

- 'Job 5,1-8: A New Exegesis', *Biblica* 62 (1981), pp. 185-94; reprinted in *On the Way to the Postmodern: Old Testament Essays, 1967–1998*, vol. 2 (Journal for the Study of the Old Testament Supplement Series, 293; Sheffield: Sheffield Academic Press, 1998), pp. 752-61.*
- 'Nehemiah 10 as an Example of Early Jewish Biblical Exegesis', *Journal for the Study of the Old Testament* 21 (1981), pp. 111-17; reprinted in *On the Way to the Postmodern: Old Testament Essays, 1967–1998*, vol. 1 (Journal for the Study of the Old Testament Supplement Series, 292; Sheffield: Sheffield Academic Press, 1998), pp. 88-94.*
- 'Hermeneutics', *Journal. Christian Brethren Research Fellowship (New Zealand)* no. 88 (1981), pp. 3-11.

1980

- 'Story and Poem: The Old Testament as Literature and as Scripture', *Interpretation* 34 (1980), pp. 115-27; reprinted in *On the Way to the Postmodern: Old Testament Essays, 1967–1998*, vol. 1 (Journal for the Study of the Old Testament Supplement Series, 292; Sheffield: Sheffield Academic Press, 1998), pp. 225-39.*
- 'Verb Modality and the Interpretation of Job iv 20-21', *Vetus Testamentum* 30 (1980), pp. 354-57; reprinted in *On the Way to the Postmodern: Old Testament Essays, 1967–1998*, vol. 2 (Journal for the Study of the Old Testament Supplement Series, 293; Sheffield: Sheffield Academic Press, 1998), pp. 748-51.

- 'Yahweh and the God of Christian Theology', *Theology* 83 (1980), pp. 323-30 (reprinted in *On the Way to the Postmodern: Old Testament Essays, 1967–1998*, vol. 2 [Journal for the Study of the Old Testament Supplement Series, 293; Sheffield: Sheffield Academic Press, 1998], pp. 498-507; see also Irene Mary, 'Yahweh and the God of Christian Theology' [reply to D.J.A. Clines], *Theology* 84 (1981), pp. 42-43; and Francis Landy, 'The Name of God and the Image of God and Man: A Response to David Clines', *Theology* 84 (1981), pp. 164-70).

1980

- 'Job 4.13: A Byronic Suggestion', *Zeitschrift für die alttestamentliche Wissenschaft* 92 (1980), pp. 289-91; reprinted in *On the Way to the Postmodern: Old Testament Essays, 1967–1998*, vol. 2 (Journal for the Study of the Old Testament Supplement Series, 293; Sheffield: Sheffield Academic Press, 1998), pp. 745-47.*
- 'Limited Paradise', *Third Way* 4/5 (May 1980), p. 21.
- 'Ahava', 'Ecbatana', 'Image', 'Magbish', 'Nehemiah, Book of', 'Tobiah', in *The Illustrated Bible Dictionary* (ed. J.D. Douglas *et al.*; Leicester: IVP, 1980), vol. 1, pp. 25, 407; vol. 2, pp. 683-84, 930, 1070-74; vol. 3, p. 1574.
- Translation (from French), H. Cazelles, 'The Canonical Approach to Torah and Prophets', *Journal for the Study of the Old Testament* 16 (1980), pp. 28-31.

1979

- 'Hosea 2: Structure and Interpretation', in *Studia Biblica 1978. I. Old Testament and Related Themes. Sixth International Congress on Biblical Studies, Oxford, 3-7 April, 1978* (ed. E.A. Livingstone; JSOT Supplement Series, 11; Sheffield: JSOT Press, 1979), pp. 83-103; reprinted in *On the Way to the Postmodern: Old Testament Essays, 1967–1998*, vol. 1 (Journal for the Study of the Old Testament Supplement Series, 292; Sheffield: Sheffield Academic Press, 1998), pp. 293-313.*
- 'The Significance of the "Sons of God" Episode (Genesis 6:1-4) in the Context of the "Primeval History" (Genesis 1–11)', *Journal for the Study of the Old Testament* 13 (1979), pp. 33-46; reprinted in *On the Way to the Postmodern: Old Testament Essays, 1967–1998*, vol. 1 (Journal for the Study of the Old Testament Supplement Series, 292; Sheffield: Sheffield Academic Press, 1998), pp. 337-50.*
- 'Introduction to the Pentateuch', in *A Bible Commentary for Today* (ed. G.C.D. Howley; London and Glasgow: Pickering & Inglis, 1979), pp. 97-103; a reworked version conforming to the New International Version English text in *The International Bible Commentary* (ed. F.F. Bruce; Basingstoke, Hants.: Marshall Pickering, and Grand Rapids: Zondervan, 1986), pp. 78-83.
- 'Job' [a commentary], in *A Bible Commentary for Today* (ed. G.C.D. Howley; London and Glasgow: Pickering & Inglis, 1979), pp. 559-592; a reworked version conforming to the New International Version English text in *The International Bible Commentary* (ed. F.F. Bruce; Basingstoke, Hants.: Marshall Pickering, and Grand Rapids: Zondervan, 1986), pp. 520-51.
- 'Belshazzar', 'Cyrus', 'Darius', in *The International Standard Bible Encyclopedia*, vol. 1 (ed. G.W. Bromiley; Grand Rapids: Eerdmans, 1979), pp. 455-56, 845-49, 867-68.

1978

- *The Theme of the Pentateuch* (Journal for the Study of the Old Testament Supplement Series, 10; Sheffield: JSOT Press, 1978), 152 pp.

- (joint authorship with D.M. Gunn) '"You tried to persuade me" and "Violence! Outrage!" in Jeremiah xx 7-8', *Vetus Testamentum* 28 (1978), pp. 20-27; reprinted in *On the Way to the Postmodern: Old Testament Essays, 1967–1998*, vol. 1 (Journal for the Study of the Old Testament Supplement Series, 292; Sheffield: Sheffield Academic Press, 1998), pp. 285-92.
- 'Isaiah 52.13–53.12', in *Readings in Biblical Hebrew* (ed. J.H. Eaton, Birmingham: Dept of Theology, University of Birmingham, 1978), pp. 105-12.
- 'Religion and Worship in the Bible', in *The Lion Encyclopedia of the Bible*, ed. P. Alexander, Berkhamsted: Lion, 1978, pp. 130-51; reprinted separately as *Religion and Worship in the Bible* (*The Lion Encyclopedia of the Bible*, Part 5), Berkhamsted: Lion, 1980, 32 pp.; reprinted in *The Lion Concise Bible Encyclopedia*, Tring, Herts.: Lion Publishing, 1980, pp. 29, 57-58, 82-83, 95-97, 122, 142-44, 155-57, 159, 192, 198-99, 199-202, 206-209, 214-15, 218, 228-29, 229-33, 236, 253 [Lithuanian: *Biblijos enciklopedija* (Vilnius: Alna litera, 1993), pp. 346-52].
- 'The Books of the Old Testament', in *Introduction to the Bible*, by J.I. Packer, L.C. Allen, D.[J.A.] Clines, A.E. Cundall, F.F. Bruce and D. Guthrie (London: Scripture Union, 1978), pp. 17-27.
- 'Work: A Biblical and Theological Perspective', *Shaftesbury Project Study Group on Work and Unemployment. Occasional Paper* (October, 1978).

1977

- 'Jonah: An Interpretation', *Journal of the Christian Brethren Research Fellowship (New Zealand)* no. 74 (1977), pp. 1-10.
- Translation (from German), H.H. Schmid, 'In Search of New Approaches in Pentateuchal Research', *Journal for the Study of the Old Testament* 3 (1977), pp. 33-42.
- Translation (from German), Rolf Rendtorff, 'Pentateuchal Studies on the Move', *Journal for the Study of the Old Testament* 3 (1977), pp. 43-45.
- Translation (from French), Pierre Auffret, *The Literary Structure of Psalm 2* (Journal for the Study of the Old Testament Supplement Series, 2; Sheffield: JSOT Press, 1977), 41 pp.

1976

- *I, He, We and They: A Literary Approach to Isaiah 53* (Journal for the Study of the Old Testament Supplement Series, 1; Sheffield: JSOT Press, 1976), 65 pp.
- 'Theme in Genesis 1–11', *Catholic Biblical Quarterly* 38 (1976), pp. 483-507.
- (joint authorship with D.M. Gunn) 'Form, Occasion and Redaction in Jeremiah 20', *Zeitschrift für die alttestamentliche Wissenschaft* 88 (1976), pp. 390-409; reprinted in *On the Way to the Postmodern: Old Testament Essays, 1967–1998*, vol. 1 (Journal for the Study of the Old Testament Supplement Series, 292; Sheffield: Sheffield Academic Press, 1998), pp. 363-84.*
- 'Krt 111-114 (I iii 7-10): Gatherers of Wood and Drawers of Water', *Ugarit-Forschungen* 8 (1976), pp. 23-26; reprinted in *On the Way to the Postmodern: Old Testament Essays, 1967–1998*, vol. 2 (Journal for the Study of the Old Testament Supplement Series, 293; Sheffield: Sheffield Academic Press, 1998), pp. 595-601.*
- 'Styles of Leadership in Ancient Israel', *Evangelical Fellowship for Missionary Studies Bulletin* 6 (1976), pp. 1-15.
- 'On Being the Servant of the Lord', *The Harvester* 55 (1976), pp. 194-97.

- 'Social Responsibility in the Old Testament', *Christian Brethren Research Fellowship (N.Z.)* no. 72 (Sept. 1976), pp. 1-15; reprinted in *Interchange* 20 (1976), pp. 194-207; published separately as *Shaftesbury Project Papers*, No. C.7 (1980); Sound Recording: Brisbane: University of Queensland, 1975.
- 'New Year', in *The Interpreter's Dictionary of the Bible. Supplementary Volume*, ed. K. Crim *et al.*, Nashville: Abingdon, 1976, pp. 625-29; reprinted in *On the Way to the Postmodern: Old Testament Essays, 1967–1998*, vol. 1 (Journal for the Study of the Old Testament Supplement Series, 292; Sheffield: Sheffield Academic Press, 1998), pp. 426-35.
- 'The Christian Use of the Old Testament: A Study in Attitude and Style', *Journal of the Christian Brethren Research Fellowship (New Zealand)* no. 71 (1976), pp. 1-15.
- 'Sin and Maturity', *Care and Counsel Symposium* (June, 1976), pp. 15-32; a revision published in *Journal of Psychology and Theology* 5 (1977), pp. 183-96; reprinted in *Third Way* 4/10 (Nov. 1980), pp. 8-10; 4/11 (Dec.-Jan. 1980–81), pp. 11-14; reprinted in *Psychology and Christianity: Integrative Readings*, ed. J.R. Fleck and J.D. Carter, Nashville: Abingdon, 1981, pp. 124-39; reprinted in *On the Way to the Postmodern: Old Testament Essays, 1967–1998*, vol. 2 (Journal for the Study of the Old Testament Supplement Series, 293; Sheffield: Sheffield Academic Press, 1998), pp. 555-73.
- 'New Directions in Pooh Studies: Überlieferungs- und traditionsgeschichtliche Studien zum Pu-Buch', *Theolog Review* 12 (1976), pp. 2-10; reprinted in *On the Way to the Postmodern: Old Testament Essays, 1967–1998*, vol. 2 (Journal for the Study of the Old Testament Supplement Series, 293; Sheffield: Sheffield Academic Press, 1998), pp. 830-39.
- Translation (from Spanish) (with P.R. Davies), L. Alonso Schökel, 'A Response to Ridderbos and Kessler', *Journal for the Study of the Old Testament* 1 (1976), pp. 61-65.

1975

- 'The Psalms and the King', *Theological Students' Fellowship Bulletin* no. 71 (1975), pp. 1-6; reprinted in *On the Way to the Postmodern: Old Testament Essays, 1967–1998*, vol. 2 (Journal for the Study of the Old Testament Supplement Series, 293; Sheffield: Sheffield Academic Press, 1998), pp. 687-700.*
- 'Predestination in the Old Testament', in *Grace Unlimited*, ed. C.H. Pinnock, Minneapolis: Bethany, 1975, pp. 110-26; reprinted in *On the Way to the Postmodern: Old Testament Essays, 1967–1998*, vol. 2 (Journal for the Study of the Old Testament Supplement Series, 293; Sheffield: Sheffield Academic Press, 1998), pp. 524-41; reprinted in *Grace for All: The Arminian Dynamics of Salvation* (ed. Clark H. Pinnock and John D. Wagner; Eugene, OR: Wipf & Stock, 2015).
- 'The Psalm of a Man Who Listens (Psalm 19)', in *The Witness* 105 (1975), pp. 245-47, 251; reprinted in *The Indian Christian* 67 (1976), pp. 15-19.
- 'Notes for an Old Testament Hermeneutic', *Theology News and Notes* [Fuller Theological Seminary] 21 (1975), pp. 8-10.
- 'The Kingdom of God' [in the teaching of Jesus], *The Witness* 105 (1975), pp. 43-45.
- 'Biblical Criticism and Christian Faith: The Patriarchal Narratives as a Test Case', sound recording, University of Queensland, Department of Religious Studies, 1975.

1974

- 'The Evidence for an Autumnal New Year in Pre-Exilic Israel Reconsidered', *Journal of Biblical Literature* 93 (1974), pp. 22-40; reprinted in *On the Way to the Postmodern: Old Testament Essays, 1967–1998*, vol. 1 (Journal for the Study of the Old Testament Supplement Series, 292; Sheffield: Sheffield Academic Press, 1998), pp. 371-94.*
- 'The Tree of Knowledge and the Law of Yahweh (Psalm xix)', *Vetus Testamentum* 24 (1974), pp. 8-14; reprinted in *On the Way to the Postmodern: Old Testament Essays, 1967–1998*, vol. 2 (Journal for the Study of the Old Testament Supplement Series, 293; Sheffield: Sheffield Academic Press, 1998), pp. 708-15.*
- 'The Etymology of Hebrew ṣelem', *Journal of Northwest Semitic Languages* 3 (1974), pp. 19-25; reprinted in *On the Way to the Postmodern: Old Testament Essays, 1967–1998*, vol. 2 (Journal for the Study of the Old Testament Supplement Series, 293; Sheffield: Sheffield Academic Press, 1998), pp. 577-84.*
- 'The Oracles of Malachi', *The Witness* 104 (1974), pp. 93-96.

1973

- 'The Theology of the Flood Narrative', *Faith and Thought. Journal of the Transactions of the Victoria Institute* 100 (1973), pp. 128-42; reprinted in *On the Way to the Postmodern: Old Testament Essays, 1967–1998*, vol. 2 (Journal for the Study of the Old Testament Supplement Series, 293; Sheffield: Sheffield Academic Press, 1998), pp. 508-23.
- 'God in Human Form: A Theme in Biblical Theology', *Christian Brethren Research Fellowship Journal* no. 24 (1973), pp. 24-40.
- 'Predestination in Biblical Thought', *Theological Students' Fellowship Bulletin* no. 66 (1973), pp. 1-5.
- 'The Apocrypha', in *The Lion Handbook to the Bible* (ed. D.S. and P. Alexander; Berkhamstead: Lion, 1973), pp. 461-463 (2nd revised edition, 1983); reprinted in *The Lion Concise Bible Handbook* (Tring, Herts.: Lion, 1980), pp. 251-54.

1972

- 'X, X ben Y, ben Y: Personal Names in Hebrew Narrative Style', *Vetus Testamentum* 22 (1972), pp. 266-87; reprinted in *On the Way to the Postmodern: Old Testament Essays, 1967–1998*, vol. 1 (Journal for the Study of the Old Testament Supplement Series, 292; Sheffield: Sheffield Academic Press, 1998), pp. 240-62.
- 'Regnal Year Reckoning in the Last Years of the Kingdom of Judah', in *Essays in Honour of E.C.B. MacLaurin on his Sixtieth Birthday* (= *The Australian Journal of Biblical Archaeology* 2 [1972]), pp. 9-34; reprinted in *On the Way to the Postmodern: Old Testament Essays, 1967–1998*, vol. 1 (Journal for the Study of the Old Testament Supplement Series, 292; Sheffield: Sheffield Academic Press, 1998), pp. 395-425.
- 'A Biblical Doctrine of Man', *Social Workers' Christian Fellowship Occasional Papers* (1972), 31 pp.; reprinted in *Christian Brethren Research Fellowship Journal* no. 28 (1978), pp. 9-28.

1970

- 'The New English Bible: Old Testament', *Theological Students' Fellowship Bulletin* no. 58 (1970), pp. 6-9.

- 'The New English Bible', *Evangelical Quarterly* 42 (1970), pp. 168-75.
- 'Psalm Research since 1955: II. The Literary Genres', *Tyndale Bulletin* 20 (1969), pp. 105-125; reprinted in *On the Way to the Postmodern: Old Testament Essays, 1967–1998*, vol. 2 (Journal for the Study of the Old Testament Supplement Series, 293; Sheffield: Sheffield Academic Press, 1998), pp. 665-86.*

1969

- 'The Language of the New Testament', in *A New Testament Commentary* (ed. G.C.D. Howley, F.F. Bruce and H.L. Ellison; London: Pickering & Inglis, 1969), pp. 30-36; reprinted in *A Bible Commentary for Today* (ed. G.C.D. Howley; London and Glasgow: Pickering & Inglis, 1979), pp. 1076-82; a reworked version conforming to the New International Version English text in *The International Bible Commentary* (ed. F.F. Bruce; Basingstoke, Hants.: Marshall Pickering, and Grand Rapids: Zondervan, 1986), pp. 1012-18.
- 'The Second Letter to the Corinthians' [a commentary], in *A New Testament Commentary* (ed. G.C.D. Howley, F.F. Bruce and H.L. Ellison; London: Pickering & Inglis, 1969), pp. 416-42; reprinted in *A Bible Commentary for Today* (ed. G.C.D. Howley; London and Glasgow: Pickering & Inglis, 1979), pp. 1462-88; a reworked version conforming to the New International Version English text in *The International Bible Commentary* (ed. F.F. Bruce; Basingstoke, Hants.: Marshall Pickering, and Grand Rapids: Zondervan, 1986), pp. 1389-1414.
- 'Predestination and Responsibility: A Biblical Perspective', *Social Workers' Christian Fellowship Occasional Papers* (1969), 10 pp.

1968

- 'Reply on Liturgy', *Christian Brethren Research Fellowship Journal* no. 18 (May 1968), pp. 49-53.
- 'The Image of God in Man [in the Old Testament]', *Tyndale Bulletin* 19 (1968), pp. 53-103; reprinted as 'Humanity as the Image of God', in *On the Way to the Postmodern: Old Testament Essays, 1967–1998*, vol. 2 (Journal for the Study of the Old Testament Supplement Series, 293; Sheffield: Sheffield Academic Press, 1998), pp. 447-97.
- 'Do We Need Another Translation of the Bible?', *Christian Graduate* 21 (1968), pp. 23-24.

1967

- 'Psalm Research since 1955: I. The Psalms and the Cult', *Tyndale Bulletin* 18 (1967), pp. 103-26; reprinted in *On the Way to the Postmodern: Old Testament Essays, 1967–1998*, vol. 2 (Journal for the Study of the Old Testament Supplement Series, 293; Sheffield: Sheffield Academic Press, 1998), pp. 639-64.*
- 'The Churches Next Door', *Christian Brethren Research Fellowship Papers* (October 1967), pp. 4-14.
- 'The Christian and Class', *Christian Graduate* 20 (1967), pp. 9-13.
- 'The Biblical Idea of the Trinity', *Inter-Varsity* 36 (1967), pp. 4-7.
- 'Liturgy without Prayerbook', *Christian Brethren Research Fellowship Journal* no. 15 (1967), pp. 6-18; reprinted in *Journal. Christian Brethren Research Fellowship (New Zealand)* (October 1977), pp. 11-22.

1965

- 'Women in the [New Testament] Church—A Survey of Recent Opinion', *Christian Brethren Research Fellowship Journal* no. 10 (1965), pp. 33-40.
- Translation (from Latin), John à Lasco, 'The Abolition of Vestments', in *The Reformation of the Church* (ed. I. Murray; London: Banner of Truth Trust, 1965), pp. 63-69.

1960

- Translation (from Latin), Titus Maccius Plautus, *Rudens* ('The Rope') (Sydney: Sydney University Classical Society, 1960), 43 pp.

1959

- 'John and Ezekiel', *Study* (Emmaus Bible School, Sydney) 1 (1959), pp. 6-8.

———-

Dedicated to David J.A. Clines
- *Reading from Right to Left: Essays on the Hebrew Bible in Honour of David J.A. Clines* (ed. J. Cheryl Exum and H.G.M. Williamson)
- *Interested Readers: Essays on the Hebrew Bible in Honour of David J.A. Clines* (ed. James K. Aitken, Jeremy M.S. Clines and Christl M. Maier)
- *Probing the Frontiers of Biblical Studies* (ed. J. Harold Ellens; Princeton Theological Monographs, 111; Eugene, OR: Pickwick Publications, 2009)

Other studies
- Engin Obucic, *An Intertextual Reading of the Concept of the Other in David Clines' Study* I, He, We and They *and Emmanuel Levinas's work* Totality and Infinity
- Stewart Goodall Weaver, *Empathy, Metaphor and Symbol: A Rhetorical Study of the Servant Songs in their Deutero-Isaianic Context, Based on the Work of D.J.A. Clines*, PhD Edinburgh, 2000

Appendix One: Author's Notes

[Unfinished]

1st electric train service in Sydney ran between Central station & Oatley station on 9 December 1926.
Provincialize Europe
I love a sunburnt country
Henry and Ruth Backhouse
Miriam
Jeremy
Empson
Net et clair (though clair et net in more common); English clean and clear is even more striking as advice for writing
Moberly rhetoric
Bach, Mahler, Stravinsky
Youth concerts
FFB
Greek, Latin, Ancient History
Emmaus: Don Fleming and Thai biblical teaching
New Guinea missionaries
Travels fastest who travels alone
Dad and Lithgow
Haggai: Joachim Schaper: "Treasury and foundry were at the core of the temple administration in its function as a fiscal instrument". er, "The Jerusalem Temple as an Instrument of the Achaemenid Fiscal Administration," *VT* 45 (1995) 528-39, here 5

Themes
Department
feminism
disce doce
RAE, teaching assessment

new courses
teaching students
supervising PhDs, including Urban Theology Unit

SAP/SPP
pricing
limits
P.O.D.
editors
blurbs
housestyle
embrace new technology, typesetting

research
StarPlus
KVK vs. COPAC

Index of Names

Allen, L.C. 21
Anderson, J.C. 118, 120
Atkinson, J. 62, 102

Baker, D.L. 85
Ball, D.M. 122
Bammel, E. 84
Barr, J. 123
Basser, L. 24
Beck, F. 23
Bembrick, E. 23
Berlin, A. 91
Bessemer, H. 63
Bimson, J. 85
Black, F. 117
Black, M. 52, 72
Blenkinsopp, J. 69
Boling, R. 83
Bos, J.W.H. 114
Bowden, J. 82
Brearley, H. 63
Brock, S. 50
Brockington, L.H. 88
Bruce, F.F. 21, 39, 58, 61
Buckland, P.C. 113
Bullough, S. 51
Bush, F. 72, 78

Carr, W. 85
Carroll R., M.D. 110, 121
Castelli, E.A. 118
Charette, B. 121
Chilton, B.D. 73, 105
Christianson, E. 121
Clements, R.E. 88
Clines, A.W. 9, 10
Clines, J. 51, 75, 78, 79
Clines, M. 11, 89
Clines, P. 1, 6, 42
Coats, G.W. 90

Cobbett, W. 65
Cohen, H. 23
Coogan, M.D. 117
Crook, J. 53
Croucher, R. 27, 31, 38
Cullis, S. 1

Darby, J.N. 15, 21
Davies, M. 110-12
Davies, P.R. 72, 73, 83, 104, 105, 110, 123
Davis, C.J. 122
Davis, J. 7
De Troyer, K. 89
Defoe, D. 63
Dhorme, E. 98
Diringer, D. 50
Dorothy, C.V. 89
Driver, G. 48
Dunston, A.J. 33
Duse, E. 51

Edmonds, H. 23
Eichrodt, W. 39
Einfeld, M. 23
Elwolde, J. 123
Emerton, J. 54, 90
Evans, G. 37
Exum, J.C. 60, 90, 113-17, 121, 123

Fish, S. 82
Flynn, C. 41
Fountain, A.K. 89
Fowl, S.E. 109
Fox, M.V. 89

Gesenius, W. 21
Gooding, D. 21
Goodman, A.E. 52
Gordon, R.P. 21

Index of Names

Gosling, F. 124, 125
Graham, S.L. 120
Grudem, W. 54
Guilding, A. 57, 58, 60, 61
Gunn, D. 70, 71, 83, 90

Hadfield, R. 63
Hanson, A. 84
Harnack, A. von 17
Harvey, W. 132
Hauser, A.J. 90
Heard, (teacher) 5
Heath, E. 72
Hess, R.S. 123, 125, 126
Hill, D. 58, 84, 106
Hoehner, H. 123
Hubbard, D. 77
Hughes, R. 37
Huntsman, B. 63

James, C. 7
Jobes, K.H. 89
Jobling, D. 118
Jones, G.L. 50, 55
Joseph, D.N. 56, 57

King, P. 117
Kissling, P. 121
Knight, G.A.F. 39
Kselman, J.S. 90

Ladd, G.E. 76
à Lasco, J. 57
Leach, E. 111

MacLaurin, E.C.B. 35, 36, 69
Macquarie, L. 4
Maddox, R. 23
Marcus, D. 50, 55
Martin, R.P. 106, 107
Matlock, M. 113, 122
McGuiness, P. 35
McKane, W. 72
McKay, J. 103
Moore, S.D. 108, 117-21
Morris, L.L. 61
Munn-Rankin, J.M. 52

Neale, D. 122

Oatley, F. 4
Oatley, J. 4
Orchard, H. 122

Paige, T. 107
Pamment, M. 111, 112
Payne, D. 58, 61
Payne, J. 58
Perkin, J.R. 61
Petrotta, T. 121
Phiilips, G.A. 118
Pickett, R. 122
Pierce, F. 67
Polzin, R.M. 86
Porter, S.E. 109
Porush, I. 36
Predelles, S.P. 21

Quincey, J.H. 35

Rad, G. von 39
Rast, W.E. 87
Reed, J.T. 122
Riley, D.N. 113
Ritchie, B. 34
Rogerson, J. 102-104, 109, 110, 118, 123
Rosenthal, E.I.J. 50, 51
Ruiten, J.T.A.G.M. van 59

Sanders, E.P. 110
Sawyer, J. 70, 83, 88
Schökel, L.A. 83
Schwartz, R. 118
Segal, J.B. 123
Seters, J. van 83
Sheldon, J. 41, 43
Sherwood, Y. 121
Shipp, G.P. 33, 34
Smelik, W.K. 127
Smith, J.M. 18
Smith, W.R. 125
Snaith, J. 84
Snaith, N. 39
Sobers, G. 22
Stager, L.E. 117
Stec, D. 124
Stockton, E. 36
Stunt, T. 88

Talbert, C. 114
Talshir, D. 123, 125
Talshir, Z. 123, 125
Teicher, J.L. 50
Thiselton, A.C. 73, 74, 85
Thomas, J.C. 122
Tigchelaar, E. 127

Wade, J. 112, 113
Wallis, I.G. 122
Watts, J.D.W. 91
Webb, R. 121
Wellhausen, J. 132
Wellings, P. 6
Wells, F. 12

Wells, M. 12
Wells, R.C. 11-13
Wells, T. 12
Wells, V. 12
Whedbee, J.W. 114
Whybray, N. 84
Wilcox, M. 84
Wilde, A. de 97
Wilenksi, P. 23
Wilkins, M.J. 107
Williams, J.T. 61
Wilson, J.V. 52
Winton Thomas, D. 48, 49, 53-55, 57, 122, 123
Wiseman, D. 88

www.ingramcontent.com/pod-product-compliance
Lightning Source LLC
Chambersburg PA
CBHW070332230426
43663CB00011B/2289